PMP® Examination Practice Questions

400 Practice Questions and Answers to help you Pass

Third Edition

Sean Whitaker

Apress®

PMP®Examination Practice Questions: 400 Practice Questions and Answers to help you Pass, Third Edition

Sean Whitaker
ChristChurch, Canterbury, New Zealand

ISBN-13 (pbk): 978-1-4842-1882-2   ISBN-13 (electronic): 978-1-4842-1883-9
DOI 10.1007/978-1-4842-1883-9

Library of Congress Control Number: 2016940412

Managing Director: Welmoed Spahr
Lead Editor: Steve Anglin
Technical Reviewer: Mike Roberts
Editorial Board: Steve Anglin, Pramila Balan, Louise Corrigan, Jonathan Gennick,
    Robert Hutchinson, Celestin Suresh John, Michelle Lowman, James Markham,
    Susan McDermott, Matthew Moodie, Jeffrey Pepper, Douglas Pundick,
    Ben Renow-Clarke, Gwenan Spearing
Coordinating Editor: Mark Powers
Copy Editor: Mary Behr
Compositor: SPi Global
Indexer: SPi Global
Artist: SPi Global

Distributed to the book trade worldwide by Springer Science+Business Media New York, 233 Spring Street, 6th Floor, New York, NY 10013. Phone 1-800-SPRINGER, fax (201) 348-4505, e-mail orders-ny@springer-sbm.com, or visit www.springeronline.com. Apress Media, LLC is a California LLC and the sole member (owner) is Springer Science + Business Media Finance Inc (SSBM Finance Inc). SSBM Finance Inc is a **Delaware** corporation.

For information on translations, please e-mail rights@apress.com, or visit www.apress.com.

Apress and friends of ED books may be purchased in bulk for academic, corporate, or promotional use. eBook versions and licenses are also available for most titles. For more information, reference our Special Bulk Sales–eBook Licensing web page at www.apress.com/bulk-sales.

Any source code or other supplementary materials referenced by the author in this text are available to readers at www.apress.com/9781484218822. For detailed information about how to locate your book's source code, go to www.apress.com/source-code/. Readers can also access source code at SpringerLink in the Supplementary Material section for each chapter.

Contents at a Glance

Contents

About the Author

Sean Whitaker, BA, MSc, MBA, PMP, has a diverse project management background, having successfully managed complex projects in the construction, telecommunications, and IT industries. He brings this diversity of experience into sharp focus with his emphasis on professional project management.

In addition to this book, Sean is the author of many books on project management including *PMP® Training Kit* (Microsoft Press/O'Reilly Publishing, 2013), *PMP® Rapid Review* (Microsoft Press/O'Reilly Publishing, 2013), *The Professional Project Manager* (CreateSpace Independent Publishing Platform, 2014), and *The Practically Perfect Project Manager* (CreateSpace Independent Publishing Platform, 2012).

Sean regularly trains, coaches, teaches, and speaks about professional project management around the globe. He has been a volunteer with the Project Management Institute since 2005. When not teaching, speaking, or writing about project management, Sean is a keen and accomplished musician.

Please visit his web site at www.seanwhitaker.com.

About the Technical Reviewer

Mike Roberts is a New Zealand-based project management professional and trainer. Mike offers project management services across the IT sector and has experience delivering projects through both traditional and Agile techniques.

Mike is the Principal Trainer and Partner of Falcon Training. He has been facilitating project management training for a number of years. He has a reputation for his ability to connect with his students and for his commitment to learning. He is always happy to discuss the application of the wide variety of approaches available across all industries—IT, construction, health, retail, government, and more!

Mike is also an active volunteer with the New Zealand Chapter of the Project Management Institute. He was recently awarded the PMINZ Volunteer of the Year award to recognize and honor his significant contribution to the Project Management Institute and the project management profession.

Foreword

Sean Whitaker has a real passion for project management, like no one I have met before.

Sean is not only a recognized Fellow and a former President of the New Zealand Chapter of the Project Management Institute, but he is also a passionate practitioner, consultant, speaker, teacher, and mentor in the global project management community. He has dedicated a great deal of time to the profession of project management and to anyone who shows an interest in it.

This book offers a fantastic aid for those preparing to sit their PMP examination, the world's leading project management certification. The PMP exam is hard; there is no doubt about it. The theory is extensive, and the examination questions are challenging.

Having the opportunity to apply your knowledge of the theory to 400+ practice questions, well in advance of the exam, is incredibly valuable. It's a good way to indicate your readiness for the real thing.

I operate a New Zealand-based project management training company called Falcon Training. We offer both public and tailored training services throughout the country and across Asia-Pacific. We use a number of Sean's materials in our PMP Examination Preparation courses because I see the value they add to our students' learning. Sean has the unique ability of being able to rephrase complex theory into meaningful words, drastically improving the rate at which our students learn.

Speaking from personal experience, by incorporating Sean's work into your study program, I know you'll appreciate the value gained just as much as I did.

I wish you the best of luck with your upcoming exam and your ongoing career as a professional project manager.

—Mike Roberts, PMP, PMI-ACP, BICT, GDipPM
Principal Trainer and Partner, Falcon Training
www.falcontraining.com

Introduction

Welcome, and congratulations!

You have either committed to taking the globe's leading project management credential or are seriously considering it. The Project Management Institute (PMI®) Certification Program is recognized worldwide, and PMI is the world's leading association relating to the profession of project management. Gaining the Project Management Professional (PMP®) certification is a great way to prove your existing experience, gain insight into best practices, and advance your career prospects.

This book contains over 400 practice questions for the PMP® examination, based on the contents of the PMBOK® Guide, 5th edition. They are created to provide revision and preparation for when you decide to sit the exam. It is a difficult exam, and you will need to make a significant investment in study time to ensure that you will pass.

You can use this book in a way that suits your study style. You can work through each of the questions in sequence, randomly pick ones from different sections, or assign yourself a time limit to answer a particular set of questions.

No collection of practice questions can fully replicate the questions found in the real exam, although I have aimed to get them as close as possible. Examination preparation questions, like these, are focused on a single knowledge area, while many of the exam questions draw scenarios from several different process groups and knowledge areas. Be prepared for this: study the inputs into each process and identify where they originate as outputs. Additionally, study the outputs from each process and where they are used as inputs. You will find that outputs from processes in one knowledge area become inputs in an entirely separate knowledge area.

Here are some other study tips to increase your chance of passing the exam:

1. Start by finding out how you best learn. Some people can only learn by taking notes, or by reading and rereading. You may learn better by drawing diagrams or by teaching to others. Visit a web site like `www.vark-learn.com` to figure out how you learn best.

2. Use mnemonics to help you remember things. Mnemonics are phrases or acronyms that can jog your memory, like "In Summer The Cruel Queen Has Cold Runny Porridge Snacks." The first letter of each word represents the ten knowledge areas in the PMBOK® Guide: Integration, Scope, Time, Cost, Quality, Human Resource, Communications, Risk, Procurement, and Stakeholder Management. You can use this one if it helps, but they are usually more memorable if you make up your own.

3. Plan your study well in advance and set aside time just for study. Stick to it. Life and work can get in the way of your best-laid plans, so if you miss a scheduled study time, be sure to make it up.

4. Teach the topic to someone, anyone! Teach it to your wife, husband, children, work colleagues, family pet, or stuffed toy. Simply verbalizing and trying to explain things in your own words to someone (or something else) will expose holes in your knowledge pretty fast.

5. Make games and puzzles of information that you have to learn. Write out processes on pieces of card and throw them on the floor and try to reassemble them in the correct order. There is a great game waiting for you as a free download on my web site.

6. Draw mind maps that link important concepts in a logical fashion. There is a set of blank ones as a free download on my web site.

7. Put together a study group with others aiming to sit the exam as well. Share ideas, experience, and knowledge.

8. Use a commercial training provider that offers courses specifically designed to help you pass the exam. I strongly recommend that you look for a PMI Registered Education Provider® (R.E.P.) to ensure you are getting a quality trainer.

9. Remember that although the PMBOK® Guide contains a lot of the theory found in the exam, the exam itself is not based on the PMBOK® Guide but on the PMP Examination Content Outline. A study guide that covers all the material is much better than relying solely on the PMBOK® Guide. I suggest that you look for a study guide to help you with your self-study. I recommend the *PMP Training Kit* and the *PMP Rapid Review*, both books I've written and both available from all good book retailers.

10. Schedule an exam date. Nothing focusses your study like having a confirmed exam date. If you don't lock it in, you may be a perpetual student.

Here are my six steps to help you answer the questions:

1. Read the question fully!

2. Reread the question!

3. Eliminate any obviously wrong answers.

4. Place the answers on a spectrum of most right to most wrong, and choose the most right one.

5. Organize the answers in order of which would be done first to last, and choose the one you would do first.

6. Guess! Leave no question unanswered.

For up-to-date PMP® examination eligibility, pricing, and scheduling information, please visit the Project Management Institute web site, www.pmi.org.

Finally, it is important that if you get a question wrong, you understand why. Use the following sheet to record the reason you marked an incorrect answer. See if you can spot patterns or issues that need adjusting in your test-taking technique.

With the benefit of hindsight I could have got more questions correct if I had...	No. of Questions
Carefully read the entire question and made sure I understood what was being asked.	
Carefully read all of the alternative answers provided and understood what each meant before answering the question.	
Eliminated the obviously wrong answers.	
Had a thorough knowledge of the appropriate definitions from the PMBOK® Guide.	
Had a working knowledge and understanding of the appropriate and relevant formula from the PMBOK® Guide.	
Double-checked my mathematical results before selecting an answer.	
Answered the questions as per the PMBOK® Guide perspective instead of my own perspective.	
Reviewed how I answered tough questions after completing other related questions to see if my memory was any better.	
Had more time to complete the examination questions and didn't rush to answer each question.	

Please visit my web site for free games, tools, and study aids you can download to help with your study. Here is the list of what you can download for free:

- How to Pass the PMP® Exam Guide
- The PMBOK® Guide Process Mapping Game
- PMP® Examination Domain Tasks Puzzle Game

- PMBOK® Guide Blank Mind Maps
- Key Terms and Definitions
- Formulae to Remember

Good luck!

sean@seanwhitaker.com
www.seanwhitaker.com

CHAPTER 1

Questions

The purpose of this book is to provide essential support to your study for the Project Management Professional (PMP®) examination. There are many ways to study for the exam, and you should spend some time learning exactly what works for you.

Answering questions written in the style and format of the actual exam questions is a good way to study, for two main reasons. First, it tests the extent of your knowledge, exposing any holes in your knowledge so that you can revise your studying appropriately.

Second, it helps you get accustomed to answering exam-style questions, which will take away a bit of the nerves you may face during the exam, particularly if you put yourself under the same time limits of 200 questions in 4 hours.

With this in mind, I have crafted a book offering the flexibility to meet these particular needs. This first chapter provides over 400 multiple choice questions grouped by topic. The second chapter restates the questions and provides a brief explanation of why three of the answers are wrong and one is correct.

There are many ways you can use this book. You can to answer the questions in each section immediately after reviewing material associated with the section. You can also pick questions at random from different sections of the chapter, as the exam will be fully randomized.

Whichever method you choose, you will find that these questions will add to your knowledge and contribute to your success in passing the exam.

Foundational Concepts

Question 1: Your team is confused because they use terminology and words in project communications that appear to have interchangeable meanings, but other teams treat these terms as though they have specific, unique meanings. How can your team find out what the terms mean?

> **A:** The best way to differentiate between similar project terms is to ask the project sponsor.
>
> **B:** Direct your team to a defined and standardized glossary such as the PMBOK® Guide.
>
> **C:** Have your project team vote on what definitions they would like to use for common terms.
>
> **D:** Project management terms have different meanings in different countries, so consult your nearest PMI community.

© Sean Whitaker 2016
S. Whitaker, *PMP® Examination Practice Questions*, DOI 10.1007/978-1-4842-1883-9_1

Question 2: You are delivering an introduction to a project management training session to new team members. One team member appears confused about the exact definition of a *project*. What is the BEST definition of a project?

> **A:** A temporary endeavor undertaken to create a unique product, service, or result.
>
> **B:** A body of work constrained by finances and time.
>
> **C:** An organized effort of work by a team managed by a project manager.
>
> **D:** The ongoing management of a business enterprise to achieve profitability.

Question 3: Your team seems confused about whether the work they are doing meets the definition of a project. To help them understand the difference between projectized and operational work you give them the following examples. Which of the following is not an example of a project?

> **A:** Designing a new software solution.
>
> **B:** Building a new house.
>
> **C:** Regularly achieving 3% growth on last year's sales figures.
>
> **D:** Implementing a new business process or procedure.

Question 4: You are planning to sit the PMP® examination and as part of your study are referring to the PMBOK® Guide for help in defining the project process groups. Which of the following is not one of the five process groups in the PMBOK® Guide?

> **A:** Closing
>
> **B:** Checking
>
> **C:** Initiating
>
> **D:** Executing

Question 5: You are the project manager on a project to develop a new piece of customer management software for an external client. Through your approved change control process you are considering a request to alter the scope of the project. While considering the impact of the request on the project scope, you must also consider the impact on other areas of the project such as quality, schedule, budget, and risk. These other areas that you are considering represent what to the project?

> **A:** Opportunities
>
> **B:** Constraints
>
> **C:** Constrictions
>
> **D:** Risks

Question 6: The process of continuously updating, improving, and detailing a project management plan, or parts of a project management plan, as more specific information becomes available is known as what?

    A: Iterative expectation management

    B: Project life cycle

    C: Continuous improvement

    D: Progressive elaboration

Question 7: While delivering a presentation to senior management on the ways in which portfolio management can help your organization achieve strategic success, you realize that not everyone in the room understands what portfolio management is. Portfolio management is BEST defined as what?

    A: A group of projects managed by a project director.

    B: A collection of projects grouped together to take advantage of effective management to meet strategic business objectives.

    C: A group of related projects managed in a coordinated way.

    D: A collection of projects relating to a single business unit within an organization.

Question 8: A group of projects that must be managed in a coordinated manner to ensure that common goals and potential resource conflicts are managed effectively is known as what?

    A: Program

    B: Portfolio

    C: PMO

    D: Life cycle

Question 9: The CEO of your organization is considering the strategic reasons the company has for approving your project proposal. At times he seems confused about the definition of *strategic consideration*. Which of the following is not a strategic consideration for authorizing a project?

    A: Strategic opportunity

    B: Return on investment (ROI)

    C: Customer demand

    D: Market demand

Question 10: The team, or function, assigned responsibility for the centralized and coordinated management of projects within an organization is known as what?

> **A:** Project headquarters
>
> **B:** Program management office
>
> **C:** Project management office
>
> **D:** War room

Question 11: Your organization has employed a person to head the PMO. During your first meeting with her, you discuss the extent of her roles and responsibilities to fully explain what tasks she will be responsible for and those she won't be responsible for. Which of the following is not a primary function of a project management office?

> **A:** Providing a project manager with daily progress reports on a specific project.
>
> **B:** Managing shared resources across several projects.
>
> **C:** Identifying and developing project management methodologies, best practices, and standards.
>
> **D:** Coordinating communication across projects.

Question 12: All of the following are points where projects can intersect with operational activity during the product life cycle except?

> **A:** During development of a new product.
>
> **B:** While monitoring and controlling.
>
> **C:** During improvements in operations.
>
> **D:** In closeout phases.

Question 13: What is the best description of the relationship between project management and organizational strategy?

> **A:** Organizational strategy ensures that projects are delivered successfully due to the way in which it appoints a qualified project manager.
>
> **B:** Organizational strategy enables a project manager to provide appropriate governance to the entire project life cycle.
>
> **C:** Organizational strategy and project management don't interact because one is operational in nature and the other is project based.
>
> **D:** Organizational strategy should provide guidance and direction to project management, and project management should deliver organizational strategy by successful project delivery.

Question 14: Your team seems confused about roles and responsibilities in the project that you are leading. They are particularly confused about your role as project manager. How would you explain the primary purpose of your role?

>   **A:** The person responsible for budget control.

>   **B:** The person responsible for delivery of technical tasks.

>   **C:** The person assigned by the performing organization to achieve the project objectives.

>   **D:** The person responsible for sharing resources among projects.

Question 15: While using the PMBOK® Guide to help you define and carry out processes on your project, you notice that a very common input into nearly all the processes is enterprise environmental factors. Which of the following examples would not be considered an enterprise environmental factor?

>   **A:** Government or industry standards or regulations

>   **B:** Political climate

>   **C:** Net present value of investment

>   **D:** Project management information systems

Question 16: You have volunteered your time to help your organization's PMO carry out an assessment of your organization using the OPM3 tool. What does OPM3 measure?

>   **A:** The interdependency of projects within a program of work.

>   **B:** The level of variance between project management best practice and the actual application.

>   **C:** The ability of a project manager to successfully deliver a project.

>   **D:** An organization's project management maturity level.

Question 17: The internal and external environmental factors that surround and influence, and sometimes constrain, a project are known as what?

>   **A:** Enterprise organizational assets

>   **B:** Environmental process assets

>   **C:** Environmental enterprise constraints

>   **D:** Enterprise environmental factors

Question 18: The collection of generally sequential and sometimes overlapping project phases differentiated by a distinct work focus is known as what?

    A: Project management information systems

    B: Project management methodology

    C: Project management office

    D: Project life cycle

Question 19: All of the following are basic characteristics of the project life cycle except?

    A: Closing the project.

    B: Checking the project work.

    C: Starting the project.

    D: Carrying out the project work.

Question 20: Divisions within a project where extra control is needed to effectively manage the completion of a major deliverable are commonly known as what?

    A: Phases

    B: Stage gates

    C: Decision trees

    D: Sub-projects

Question 21: You are explaining to your project sponsor that the best approach to managing your project is a phase-to-phase relationship. Which of the following is not an example of a phase-to-phase relationship?

    A: Sequential

    B: Overlapping

    C: Iterative

    D: Progressive

Question 22: You are the project manager working in an organization where the functional manager, to whom some of your staff answer when not working on your project, controls the project budget and resource availability. This type of organization is commonly referred to as what?

    A: Projectized

    B: Strong matrix

    C: Functional

    D: Weak matrix

Question 23: You work in an organization where staff members are grouped according to their specialty, such as production, engineering, and accounting, and projects are generally undertaken within these respective groupings. What is this type of organizational structure known as?

> **A:** Projectized

> **B:** Weak matrix

> **C:** Strong matrix

> **D:** Functional

Question 24: All of the following are examples of Organizational Process Assets that can assist your project except?

> **A:** Government regulations

> **B:** Lessons learned from previous projects

> **C:** A template for a work breakdown structure

> **D:** Configuration management knowledge bases

Question 25: The process of determining which of the PMBOK® Guide processes are appropriate to use on your project and the appropriate degree of rigor to be applied in any given project is known as what?

> **A:** Customizing

> **B:** Prudency

> **C:** Tailoring

> **D:** Standardization

Question 26: The process group consisting of those processes performed to define a new project, or a new phase of an existing project, by obtaining authorization to start the project or phase is known as what?

> **A:** Closing

> **B:** Executing

> **C:** Initiating

> **D:** Planning

Question 27: You are completing the work defined in the project management plan to satisfy the project specifications. Which process group would your activities fall under?

> **A:** Monitoring and Controlling

> **B:** Planning

> **C:** Initiating

> **D:** Executing

Question 28: Your team members are not aware of the differences between a framework, such as the PMBOK® Guide, and a methodology, such as Kanban or Lean. How would you best explain this?

> **A:** A framework is a toolbox containing a series of structured best practices used across a profession; it is not prescriptive. A methodology prescribes how a project should be delivered, using certain procedures and techniques.

> **B:** A framework prescribes how a project should be delivered, using certain procedures and techniques. A methodology is a toolbox containing a series of structured best practices used across a profession; it is not prescriptive.

> **C:** A framework is used during the planning phase of a project, whereas a methodology is used during the execution phase of a project.

> **D:** There is no difference. They are both concepts used to manage the delivery of a project.

Question 29: You have been asked to lead a project to improve the operations of a major company. The sponsor has requested you to apply Lean principles to facilitate the improvement program. Which of the following is not a principle of Lean?

> **A:** Seek Perfection.

> **B:** Identify the value-add.

> **C:** Eliminate waste.

> **D:** Reduce team size.

Question 30: What does *eliminating waste* refer to under the practice of applying Lean?

> **A:** Not having project meetings because it is more important for staff to be working on delivery.

> **B:** Avoiding project documentation where appropriate because it consumes unnecessary time.

> **C:** Keeping a clear work area to avoid risks associated with health and safety.

> **D:** Assessing a process to understand if value can still be achieved without the inclusion of certain components.

Question 31: You are working through the planning phase for a project that will improve the production output of your employer's automotive factory by 7.5%. As part of your approach to managing the engagement of your stakeholders, you are educating them on the benefits of Lean. What are the key benefits realized from applying Lean practices?

> **A:** Reduced duration, minimized costs.
>
> **B:** Increased duration, minimized costs.
>
> **C:** Increased duration, maximized costs.
>
> **D:** Reduced duration, maximized costs.

Question 32: Delays, duplication, over-production, and errors are all forms of what?

> **A:** WIP
>
> **B:** Waste
>
> **C:** Risks
>
> **D:** Issues

Project Integration Management

Question 33: You are in the process of developing your project closure checklist and selecting those items and actions that need to be completed to ensure your project is closed properly. A team member asks to help you do this work and asks how you know a project can be closed. A project can be considered finished under all of the following conditions except?

> **A:** When the project manager resigns.
>
> **B:** When the project objectives have been achieved.
>
> **C:** When the project is terminated because its objectives will not or cannot be met.
>
> **D:** When the need for the project no longer exists.

Question 34: During the preparation of the business case for your project you outline and document several different compelling reasons why your project should proceed. These reasons include the high ROI, delivering strategic value, and an increase in business value. What is the BEST definition of business value?

> **A:** The value of company's tangible assets, which can be liquidated to provide working capital.
>
> **B:** The value added to the business by projects that are completed successfully.
>
> **C:** The value of the total sum of all tangible and intangible elements of the business.
>
> **D:** The value of all of the projects that the company is currently completing.

Question 35: You are explaining to your team that all changes on your project must be documented and assessed in relation to any extra costs incurred. This is particularly important at what point in a project's timeline?

      A: At the beginning of the project.

      B: Towards the end of the project.

      C: During the project execution.

      D: It is equal throughout a project.

Question 36: While studying towards the PMP® examination, you memorize the processes in the PMBOK® Guide. How many processes are there in the Project Integration Management knowledge area in the PMBOK® Guide?

      A: 7

      B: 5

      C: 4

      D: 6

Question 37: You are involved in making choices about resource allocation on your project, making trade-offs among competing objectives and alternatives, and managing the interdependencies among the different project management knowledge areas. Of which of the PMBOK® Guide knowledge areas will it be most useful to have an in-depth understanding?

      A: Develop Project Management Plan

      B: Project Integration Management

      C: Project Risk Management

      D: Perform Integrated Change Control

Question 38: One of your team members has recently discovered the PMBOK® Guide and is intent on doing a project using each and every process, tool, and technique. You take this team member aside and explain to her that the knowledge and processes described in the PMBOK® Guide should be applied in what way?

      A: You should apply the project management knowledge, skills, and required processes in whatever order is appropriate and with varying degrees of rigor to achieve the desired project performance.

      B: Rigorously and exactly as shown in the PMBOK® Guide.

      C: The PMBOK® Guide is only a guide, and you should only apply the parts you understand fully.

      D: You should apply all the different knowledge areas and processes to your project at the level required to achieve project success.

Question 39: You are newly appointed to a project and are currently reading the project charter to gain an understanding of what is known about the project at this point. The project charter should contain enough information to do all of the following except?

    A: Complete the WBS.

    B: Initiate the project.

    C: Describe the high-level project scope.

    D: Appoint the project manager.

Question 40: You have been called in to evaluate a project that is experiencing some performance challenges. The team seems disorganized, and when you ask to meet the project sponsor, the project manager replies that she doesn't know who the sponsor is. She also shares with you that the planned value (PV) is $20,000, earned value (EV) is $14,500, and the actual cost (AC) is $36,000. You decide that you should really go back to the beginning and figure out how this project got started. What document should you request?

    A: The project plan

    B: The project charter

    C: The cost performance analysis and report

    D: The project authorization memo

Question 41: You and your team are currently developing the project charter and are looking for valuable inputs you can use to complete it. All of the following are inputs in the Develop Project Charter process except?

    A: Business case

    B: Project management plan

    C: Enterprise environmental factors

    D: Project statement of work

Question 42: You have completed a business case and project charter for your project and are presenting it to senior management for consideration and approval. Which of the following have you included in this document?

    A: The project management plan

    B: A copy of the stakeholder register

    C: Any blank templates your organization has to assist in completing the project charter

    D: A description of the expected market demand for the product of the project

Question 43: There are many ways to describe the work to be done on a project. What is the high-level, narrative description of products or services to be delivered by the project more commonly referred to as?

    A: Project statement of work

    B: Project scope statement

    C: Project scope

    D: Product scope description

Question 44: Which of the following is not a method you would expect to see used in a business case to justify a project on financial grounds?

    A: External rate of investment (ERI)

    B: Return on investment (ROI)

    C: Net present value (NPV)

    D: Internal rate of return (IRR)

Question 45: You are a project manager working for an organization and have been asked to help evaluate some potential projects and draft the statement of work (SOW) to be given to potential solution providers. One of the projects has an expected value of $50,000 in three years. Another project has an expected value of $60,000 in four years. The discount rate is 8.2%. You will want to make sure your statement of work indicates all the following except?

    A: Staffing plan

    B: Business need

    C: High-level project scope description

    D: Strategic plan

Question 46: You are in the process of developing a project charter for your project. Which of the following is a tool or technique that you would find useful to complete this work?

    A: Delphi technique

    B: Expert judgment

    C: Analytical techniques

    D: Business case preparation

Question 47: You have just taken over a project that has been underway for 10 months. The previous project manager left the project for health reasons. The project is performing well but you would like to become familiar with the way in which this particular project is being executed, monitored and controlled, and closed. What document will help you in this instance?

> **A:** Quality management plan

> **B:** Project statement of work

> **C:** Project charter

> **D:** Project management plan

Question 48: You and your team are carrying out the development of the project management plan for your project. You are unsure about which inputs are best to use to develop it. All of the following may be of assistance to you except?

> **A:** Communications management plan

> **B:** Project charter

> **C:** Process improvement plan

> **D:** Work performance information

Question 49: After completing most of your project management plan, your project sponsor is so impressed that she comments, "With this level of planning and detail, we know exactly where the project will be nine months from now." What is the BEST response you should give to the sponsor?

> **A:** "Projects seldom run exactly according to the project management plan, which is why we have the integrated change control process."

> **B:** "Projects that are planned and scheduled using the critical chain method will completely eliminate any possible changes."

> **C:** "That's correct. Good planning gives us precise knowledge about how our project will perform."

> **D:** "These are exactly the type of results that are achieved through professional project management as defined in the PMBOK® Guide."

Question 50: Which of the following would your project sponsor not expect to see in your project management plan?

> **A:** The project management plan can be either summary or detailed.

> **B:** The project management plan sets out the business case for the project, the project manager, and approval from the project sponsor.

> **C:** The project management plan describes how work will be executed to accomplish the project objectives.

> **D:** The project management plan integrates and consolidates all of the subsidiary management plans.

Question 51: You and your project team are busy putting together a first iteration of your project management plan. One of your team members seems confused about what exactly a project management plan is. Which of the following answers would be your best response to this team member?

> **A:** The project management plan includes the actions necessary to define, integrate, and coordinate all subsidiary plans into a project management plan. This is a deliverable that is rarely used in real practice.

> **B:** The project management plan includes the actions necessary to define, integrate, and coordinate all subsidiary plans into a project management plan. The content will be very similar regardless of the complexity of the project.

> **C:** The project management plan includes the actions necessary to define, integrate, and coordinate all subsidiary plans into a project management plan. The content will vary depending on the complexity of the project.

> **D:** The project management plan includes the actions necessary to define, integrate, and coordinate all subsidiary plans into a project management plan. The content will be very high level and further refined in the project charter.

Question 52: Which of the following tools or techniques would you find useful when developing your project management plan?

> **A:** Project scope analysis

> **B:** Project management information systems

> **C:** Expert judgment

> **D:** Business case preparation

Question 53: Your project management plan describes your performance measurement baseline against which you will measure project performance in several interrelated areas. This baseline is most commonly a combination of what other baselines?

    A: Procurement, scope, and cost baselines

    B: Schedule, cost, and risk baselines

    C: Communications, cost, and schedule baselines

    D: Scope, schedule, and cost baselines

Question 54: You and your project team are implementing a variety of approved changes to your project. Which of the following would not be a type of approved change?

    A: Lessons learned

    B: Preventative action

    C: Corrective action

    D: Defect repair

Question 55: The activities involved in performing the work defined in the project management plan to achieve the project's objectives include all of the following except?

    A: Issue change requests and adapt approved changes into the project's scope, plan, and environment.

    B: Manage risks and implement risk response activities.

    C: Staff, train, and manage the team members assigned to the project.

    D: Complete the business case and use it as an input into the development of the project charter.

Question 56: You are in the process of directing and managing the work to be done on the project. Which of the following would not be of use to you during this process?

    A: Project management plan

    B: Work performance data

    C: Approved change requests

    D: Enterprise environmental factors

Question 57: You are in the process of directing and managing the work to be done on the project. Which of the following would not be a useful type of Organizational Process Asset to use during this process?

    A: Issue and defect management procedures

    B: Process measurement database

    C: Stakeholder risk tolerances

    D: Standardized guidelines and work instructions

Question 58: You are the sponsor on a time-constrained project that must deliver the expected output by a defined date or your organization will face severe financial penalties. You meet with the project manager 20 days after the kick-off of the project and ask to have an update on schedule progress, schedule activities that have been started, and the extent to which quality standards are being met. The project manager looks at you somewhat uncomfortably and tells you that he doesn't have any of that information. What output from Direct and Manage Project Work process is the project manager missing?

A: Change requests

B: Project management plan updates

C: Deliverables

D: Work performance data

Question 59: The process of tracking, reviewing, and regulating the progress of your project to meet the performance objectives defined in the project management plan is known as what?

A: Perform Integrated Change Control process

B: Direct and Manage Project Work process

C: Monitor and Control Project Work process

D: Develop Project Management Plan process

Question 60: You and your team are completing work to monitor and control project work. Which of the following tools or techniques would not be of use to you to complete this work?

A: Expert judgment

B: Delphi technique

C: Analytical techniques

D: Meetings

Question 61: You and your team are completing work to monitor and control project work. As part of this effort you are producing a variety of outputs. Which of the following is not one of these outputs?

A: Project management plan updates

B: Work performance information

C: Change requests

D: Project documents updates

Question 62: You and your team are considering making an early change to a part of the project management plan when one of your team members says that it is too early to be considering any changes. At what points in the project would you perform integrated change control?

A: During project execution

B: From project inception to completion

C: During project monitoring and control

D: From project execution through to project closure

Question 63: Your client has requested a change to the project and as a result you are preparing a change request according to the approved change control process that your project management methodology prescribes. A project administrator on your project asks to assist in the preparation and assessment of the change request but seems confused about the key characteristics of a change request. You explain that all of the following are characteristics of a change request except?

A: Every documented change request must be approved or rejected.

B: All change requests should be considered by the change control board.

C: They may be initiated verbally.

D: They may involve assessing impacts on several knowledge areas.

Question 64: You have developed a formal documented system and set of processes to assist with technical and administrative direction, control, and iteration management of project documents, records, accountability, physical characteristics, and required materials. What is this system called?

A: A work authorization system

B: A risk management system

C: A project management information system (PMIS)

D: A configuration management system

Question 65: You are carrying out project-wide application of the configuration management system in order to accomplish three main objectives. Which of the following is not one of these objectives?

A: Establishing an evolutionary method to consistently identify and request changes to established baselines.

B: Providing a documented process to enable the assessment of requested changes to the project.

C: Providing opportunities to continuously validate and improve the project by considering the impact of each change.

D: Providing a mechanism for the project management team to consistently communicate all approved and rejected changes to the stakeholders.

Question 66: The configuration management system is a collection of formal documented procedures. Which of the following is not an objective of configuration management?

> **A:** Prevent any changes to functional characteristics.

> **B:** Record and report each change to the functional characteristics.

> **C:** Identify and document the functional characteristics of a product.

> **D:** Support the audit of the products to verify conformance to requirements.

Question 67: You are in the process of documenting, assessing, and making a decision on a requested change to your project. Which of the following configuration management activities would you not find useful at this time?

> **A:** Configuration control and assessment

> **B:** Configuration identification

> **C:** Configuration status accounting

> **D:** Configuration validation and audit

Question 68: As an experienced project manager, you have been asked to review a project with an SPI of 0.86 and a CPI of 0.83. You quickly identify a number of changes that are required to fix defects and meet some critical customer needs. Which of the following PMBOK® Guide processes will you need to perform first?

> **A:** Perform Integrated Change Control

> **B:** Direct and Manage Project Work

> **C:** Monitor and Control Project Work

> **D:** Develop Project Management Plan

Question 69: You are carrying out work to document and assess requested changes to your project. Which of the following would you find least helpful to you as an input as you complete this work?

> **A:** Organizational Process Assets

> **B:** Change requests

> **C:** Project documents updates

> **D:** Work performance reports

Question 70: Your client has requested a change that is considered feasible but is outside of the already approved project scope, and your project is already significantly advanced. What should occur if the change is approved?

A: The project sponsor should be consulted.

B: The request should not be approved.

C: The relevant baseline will require changing.

D: The person making the change request should be removed from the project to avoid conflict of interest.

Question 71: You and your project team are carrying out the work described in the Close Project or Phase process in the PMBOK® guide. You want your team to understand the exact characteristics of this work, so you tell them that the process includes all of the following except?

A: Establishing the procedures to investigate and document the reasons for actions taken if a project is terminated before completion.

B: Finalizing all activities across all of the project management process groups.

C: Closing and finalizing any contracts for providing goods or services.

D: It includes all of the activities necessary for administrative closure of the project or phase.

Question 72: While carrying out the work to close the design phase of your project you are using a variety of useful inputs. Which of the following is not a useful input to you?

A: Organizational Process Assets

B: Accepted deliverables

C: Work performance information

D: Project management plan

Question 73: You are a project manager and you have just been informed that due to budget cuts your project has been cancelled and your team should cease work immediately. The project was doing very well and will likely be restarted at a later time when organizational finances are better. What is the BEST action to take next?

A: Formally document why the project was terminated and set up the procedures to transfer finished and unfinished deliverables to others.

B: Ignore the request since your charter has been approved and it commits organizational resources to your project.

C: Release your team to the functional organization, shred most of your documents, and ask for a new project.

D: See if more money is available from another project.

Question 74: You are just about to complete administrative closure of your project and are updating the relevant Organizational Process Assets for your company. Which of the following is not an example of an Organizational Process Asset that you would update?

> **A:** Project closure documents

> **B:** Project files

> **C:** Stakeholder risk tolerance register

> **D:** Historical information

Question 75: Your project is reporting a CPI of 1.02 and a SPI of 1.1. The project you are delivering is for a customer who is notoriously difficult to please. Your team comes up with a way to deliver more functionality in the project than the customer is expecting, at a lower cost, and the change will result in improvements to the schedule. What is your BEST course of action?

> **A:** Do not do the extra work because it is not included in the project scope.

> **B:** Contact the customer and explain the situation to them.

> **C:** Carry out the work and surprise the customer.

> **D:** Do not do the extra work because the customer will not appreciate it.

Question 76: You are a project manager that is involved with the preparation of a business case to justify whether a particular project should go ahead. You are using net present value as a key financial filter. Your project will spend $100,000 in the first year, and then it will generate revenue of $33,000 in the first year, $62,000 in the second year, and $85,000 in the third year. Assuming a discount rate of 10%, what is the net present value?

> **A:** $100,000

> **B:** $45,101

> **C:** $80,000

> **D:** $280,000

Question 77: You are choosing between two potential projects that your organization could undertake. The first project, Project Eagle, will cost $500,000 and will have a NPV of $50,000. The second project, Project Falcon, will cost $420,000 and will have a NPV of $48,000. Which of the two projects should you do?

> **A:** Do not have enough information to answer this question.

> **B:** Project Falcon.

> **C:** Project Eagle.

> **D:** Neither project meets NPV criteria.

Question 78: After measuring expected project benefits, your project management office has four projects from which to choose. Project A has a NPV of $160,000 and will cost $10,000. Project B has a NPV of $470,000 and will cost $220,000. Project C has a NPV of $265,000 and will cost $33,000. Project D has a NPV of $335,000 and will cost $57,000. Which project would be BEST?

> **A:** Project C
>
> **B:** Project A
>
> **C:** Project B
>
> **D:** Project D

Question 79: You are assisting your portfolio manager in making a decision about which of two possible projects should be given approval to proceed. Project A would generate $75,000 in benefit. Project B would generate $225,000 in benefit. Unfortunately, due to limited resources, your company can only perform one project, and they choose Project B because of the higher benefit. What is the opportunity cost of performing Project B?

> **A:** $225,000
>
> **B:** $75,000
>
> **C:** $300,000
>
> **D:** $150,000

Project Scope Management

Question 80: The processes that describe the work required to ensure that the project includes all the work and only the work required to complete the project successfully are collectively known as what?

> **A:** Project scope management
>
> **B:** Project baseline delivery
>
> **C:** Project specification delivery
>
> **D:** Project management execution

Question 81: You are completing the work defined in the project scope statement of a new software development project when a team member points out that you have an opportunity to deliver enhanced capability to the client at no extra cost, time, or risk to the project. What should you do NEXT?

> **A:** Decline to make the changes and proceed to deliver exactly what the scope statement sets out.
>
> **B:** Assess the change via the change control process and, if approved, amend the project scope statement.
>
> **C:** Go ahead and make the changes, and surprise the client with the extra capability.
>
> **D:** Ask the team member to keep quiet about the changes and ignore her recommendation because it presents too many risks to the project.

Question 82: You are new to a project that has been underway for some time. One of your first jobs as project manager is to familiarize yourself with and understand the scope baseline. What documents will you require in order to do this?

> **A:** The project scope statement, the WBS, and the WBS dictionary
>
> **B:** The project scope statement, the WBS, and the risk register
>
> **C:** The WBS, the change register, and the project scope statement
>
> **D:** The WBS, the project management plan, and the change register

Question 83: You are a project manager and you are working with your sponsor to define and plan a complex project. You plan to complete your initiation and planning documents sequentially to make sure the organization really understands and supports the project. What key deliverables will you produce in the correct order?

> **A:** First the project management plan, then then project charter, and then the project scope statement.
>
> **B:** First the project charter, then the requirements documentation, and then the project scope statement.
>
> **C:** First the project charter, then the project scope statement, and then the requirements documentation.
>
> **D:** First the project management plan, then the requirements documentation, and then the project charter.

Question 84: What is the name of the planning document that describes how requirements will be analyzed, documented, and managed?

    A: Requirements traceability matrix

    B: Scope management plan

    C: Requirements management plan

    D: Requirements scope statement

Question 85: Completion of the project scope is measured against the scope management plan. What is completion of the product scope measured against?

    A: Client expectations

    B: Scope management plan

    C: Project management plan

    D: Product requirements

Question 86: As part of your ongoing commitment to mentoring the next generation of professional project managers you have taken on an intern on your software development project. You are explaining to her the key differences between project requirements and product requirements. How would you best explain this to her?

    A: Project requirements relate to the detail contained in the individual components of the project management plan and the processes that make them up, while product requirements relate to the specifications provided by the client and their expectations for the project delivery methodology.

    B: Project requirements can include tools and techniques for completing the appropriate project process groups, while product requirements can include the method of delivery and manufacturing quality specifications.

    C: Project requirements relate to the detail included in the project management plan, while product requirements are defined by the client's expectations.

    D: Project requirements can include business requirements, project management requirements, and delivery requirements, while product requirements can include technical requirements, security requirements, and performance requirements.

Question 87: You are carrying out the work to define and document the project stakeholders' needs to meet the project objectives. What PMBOK® Guide process describes this work best?

      A: Determine stakeholder expectations.

      B: Project integration management.

      C: Project scope management.

      D: Collect requirements.

Question 88: A team member on your project has questioned whether the project is delivering as per the original high-level requirements and narrative high-level product description, and is concerned that what you are doing has deviated from this. What is your BEST course of action?

      A: Check the project scope statement.

      B: Check the project management plan.

      C: Check the project charter.

      D: Have the team member assigned to another project because she is clearly not a team player.

Question 89: You are carrying out the work to define and document the project stakeholders' needs to meet the project objectives. All of the following are tools or techniques that would be useful to you except?

      A: Focus groups

      B: Requirements traceability matrix

      C: Group decision-making techniques

      D: Interviews

Question 90: You have decided to use a technique to help get a comprehensive set of project requirements that involves getting a group of experts to answer a series of questionnaires anonymously and provide feedback on information received in an iterative manner. What technique are you using?

      A: Mind mapping

      B: Nominal group technique

      C: Brainstorming

      D: The Delphi technique

Question 91: You have just completed the work of gathering, documenting, and prioritizing the project and product requirements, and mapping them back to original project objectives. Which PMBOK® Guide process best describes this work?

> **A:** Scope Definition
>
> **B:** Develop Project Charter
>
> **C:** Project Scope Management
>
> **D:** Collect Requirements

Question 92: An experienced team member has taken responsibility for compiling the requirements documentation for the project. Which of the following components would you not expect to see included in this documentation?

> **A:** Business rules stating the guiding principles of the organization
>
> **B:** Business need
>
> **C:** Acceptance criteria
>
> **D:** Configuration management activities

Question 93: You are a project manager working on a complex construction project and have begun the process of planning your project. You have the project charter, which is guiding you in preparing your project management plan. Using your requirements documentation, you begin the process of developing a detailed description of the project and product. What process are you completing?

> **A:** Collect Requirements
>
> **B:** Define Scope
>
> **C:** Plan Scope Management
>
> **D:** Define Activities

Question 94: You are the project manager for a large project and have recently taken over the project from another project manager. On review of the project schedule, you learn that two major deliverables are missing. Your sponsor reminds you how important it is to complete this project on time and within budget. What part of scope management was likely not done properly and should be reviewed and perhaps even repeated?

> **A:** Decomposition
>
> **B:** Critical path analysis
>
> **C:** Integrated change control
>
> **D:** Stakeholder analysis

Question 95: You are completing the work to define the scope of your project. This work is best performed with a certain variety of documents and processes already available to you. Which of the following is not a useful input for you to have in order to complete this work?

> **A:** Project scope statement

> **B:** Project charter

> **C:** Requirements documentation

> **D:** Your organization's project management methodology

Question 96: You have been assigned as a new project manager for a multi-phase project that is midway through phase 3 of 5 phases. While the overall work of the team seems pretty good, you feel that phase 3 is starting to drift from the original plan. You set up a meeting with the project sponsor to discuss your concerns. The sponsor is surprised and agrees that phase 3 includes work that was not documented in the original agreement. To prove this, the sponsor refers you to which document?

> **A:** Requirements traceability matrix

> **B:** Project management plan

> **C:** Statement of work

> **D:** Project scope statement

Question 97: You and your project team have spent time decomposing the project scope statement using your organization's work breakdown structure template. What is the lowest level of the work breakdown structure called?

> **A:** Tasks

> **B:** Work packages

> **C:** Activities

> **D:** Units

Question 98: The PMBOK® Guide process of subdividing project deliverables and project work into smaller components is known as what?

> **A:** Collect Requirements

> **B:** Define Activities

> **C:** Define Scope

> **D:** Create WBS

Question 99: You have just completed a workshop with all of your senior project technicians to break the project work down into its component parts and produce the first iteration of your work breakdown structure. All of the following are true about the work breakdown structure except?

> **A:** The planned work within the lowest levels can be scheduled, cost estimated, monitored, and controlled.

> **B:** It is a deliverable-oriented hierarchical decomposition of the work to be executed by the project team in order to accomplish the project objectives and create the required deliverables.

> **C:** Each descending level of the WBS represents an increasingly detailed definition of the project work.

> **D:** It is an output of the Define Scope process in the PMBOK® Guide.

Question 100: The point in the decomposition of the WBS at which cost and activity durations for the work can be reliably estimated and managed is called what?

> **A:** Tasks

> **B:** Activities

> **C:** WBS dictionary elements

> **D:** Work packages

Question 101: You are consulting with senior technicians working on your project in order to decompose the project scope into its component parts to produce a work breakdown structure for your project. One team member with extensive experience and a focus on detail wishes to continue decomposing the project scope further but you advise him against doing this because excessive decomposition of the WBS can lead to all of the following except?

> **A:** Non-productive management effort

> **B:** Inefficient use of resources

> **C:** Decreased efficiency in performing the work

> **D:** Added value

Question 102: You have a new team member on board and she is new to the profession of project management. How would you explain the work breakdown structure to her?

> **A:** The WBS is a list of categories and sub-categories within which risks may arise for a typical project.

> **B:** The WBS is a hierarchically organized depiction of the resources by type to be used on the project.

> **C:** The WBS defines the scope of the contract.

> **D:** The WBS represents the work specified in the current approved project scope statement.

Question 103: Your project team has largely completed the creation of the WBS. However, some deliverables have not been decomposed because clarity is lacking. The project team decides to leave them and wait until more details are available. What is this an example of?

       A: Rolling wave planning

       B: Progressive decision making

       C: Iterative expectation management

       D: Poor project management planning

Question 104: You are having trouble understanding some of the detail associated with your WBS work packages. To help you understand the components of your WBS in greater detail, which document would you use?

       A: Project scope statement

       B: Project charter

       C: WBS dictionary

       D: Activity list

Question 105: A team member responsible for validating the scope of the project seems to be confusing this work with quality control work. How would you explain the difference between scope validation and quality control work on the project?

       A: Scope validation is primarily concerned with acceptance of the deliverables, while quality control is primarily concerned with correctness of the deliverables and meeting the quality requirements specific for the deliverables.

       B: Scope validation involves checking the output from the project, whereas quality control means checking the output from the product.

       C: Scope validation is primarily concerned with ensuring the scope management plan is being followed, while quality control is ensuring that the product is fit for its purpose.

       D: Scope validation involves checking that the requirements documentation reflects the project charter, whereas quality control means checking the amount of defects in the deliverable.

Question 106: You are currently completing work associated with the process called Validate Scope in the PMBOK® Guide. What is this process primarily focused on?

> **A:** Performing variance analysis on the expected and actual deliverables.
>
> **B:** Finalizing the project and product scope statement.
>
> **C:** Formalizing acceptance of the completed project deliverables.
>
> **D:** Accepting approved change requests and amending the project scope baseline.

Question 107: You are using your project management plan, requirements documentation, and requirements traceability matrix, and you are undertaking inspection to validate the project and product. What PMBOK® Guide process group are you involved in?

> **A:** Closing
>
> **B:** Monitoring and Controlling
>
> **C:** Planning
>
> **D:** Executing

Question 108: The customer has contacted you and has requested a change to the scope of your project, which is already well underway. They are in a hurry to get the change implemented and they tell you that they are prepared to pay whatever extra cost is associated with the change so you should just get on and do it. What is your BEST course of action?

> **A:** Tell the customer it is too late because the scope is already defined.
>
> **B:** Refer to your change control process for controlling scope and submit the request as detailed.
>
> **C:** Incorporate the change into the project because the customer has agreed to it.
>
> **D:** Send the customer a written agreement for them to sign before you accept the change into the project.

Question 109: Your team is receiving a large number of small change requests and some are being adopted without being fully documented and assessed. These uncontrolled scope changes are often referred to as what?

> **A:** Scope amendment
>
> **B:** Scope variance
>
> **C:** Scope change
>
> **D:** Scope creep

Question 110: A team member is concerned that you have not documented how requirements activities will be planned, tracked, and changed. What document will you show this team member to show him how you did the work?

A: Requirements management plan

B: Change control plan

C: Project management plan

D: Scope management plan

Question 111: You are assessing the magnitude of variation of actual work performed from the original scope baseline. What technique are you utilizing?

A: Scope baseline analysis

B: Change control assessment

C: Variance analysis

D: Variation change analysis

Question 112: You are leading a PMP® study group within your organization. You are widely respected within the organization for your theoretical and practical knowledge, particularly in those areas required to pass the PMP®. Several of the students in the class are struggling with some of the concepts in the recommended study material, particularly the PMBOK® Guide. An area of concern to most of the class relates to the distinction between the focus of the Validate Scope and Quality Control processes. They look to you for clarification and a clear explanation. How do you best describe the difference between these two processes?

A: Quality Control is performed in the Monitoring and Controlling part of the project, while Validate Scope is performed at the Executing part of the project.

B: Quality Control is concerned with the correct acceptance of the deliverables; Validate Scope is concerned with the completeness of the deliverables.

C: Quality Control is concerned with the correctness of the deliverables; Validate Scope is concerned with the acceptance of the deliverables.

D: Validate Scope is performed by the project sponsor, while Quality Control is performed by the team members.

Project Time Management

Question 113: You are helping a colleague study for the PMP® exam, and as part of his study plan he is using the PMBOK® Guide as one of his reference books. He is having difficulty understanding the Time Management knowledge area processes, particularly how inputs from one process are often outputs from other processes and as such there is an order in which the processes are generally performed. You offer some advice and describe the generally correct order of schedule development activities in the Time Management knowledge area in the PMBOK® Guide. What is your answer?

A: Define Activities, Sequence Activities, Estimate Activity Resources, Estimate Activity Durations, Develop Schedule

B: Sequence Activities, Develop Schedule, Estimate Activity Resources, Estimate Activity Durations, Define Activities

C: Define Activities, Estimate Activity Resources, Estimate Activity Durations, Sequence Activities, Develop Schedule

D: Sequence Activities, Define Activities, Estimate Activity Resources, Estimate Activity Durations, Develop Schedule

Question 114: You are using the work packages from your WBS to assist with creating your project schedule. You begin breaking the work packages down into the actual work necessary to complete the work package. What are you in the process of defining?

A: WBS dictionary items

B: Project tasks

C: Activities

D: Work package assignments

Question 115: You are the project manager on a project that is currently in the planning stage. You are working on your project schedule and beginning the process of defining your activity list. Involving your team members in this process would result in what outcome?

A: Better and more accurate results

B: Project inefficiencies due to delays experienced in building consensus

C: Bad team morale due to disagreements between experts

D: Extra cost to the project

Question 116: You have your activity list completed and are explaining to your team members what it contains. Which of the following is not contained on the activity list?

A: Milestone list

B: Scope of work description

C: All schedule activities required on the project

D: Activity identifier

Question 117: You and your project management team are conducting the activity sequencing for a new project. The team has determined that Task A takes 3 days. Task B is dependent on Task A finishing and has a duration of 1 day. Task C takes 4 days. Task D is dependent on Task C starting and has a duration of 7 days. Task E is dependent on both Task C and Task D finishing and has a duration of 2 days. Task F is dependent on both Task E and Task B finishing and has a duration of 4 days. What is the duration of the project?

    A: 10 days

    B: 13 days

    C: 17 days

    D: 8 days

Question 118: You are leading your team in the preparation of your project schedule and are currently sequencing the activities and determining which type of precedence relationship exists between them. Which of the following is the most commonly used type of precedence relationship that you will use?

    A: Start-to-start

    B: Start-to-finish

    C: Finish-to-finish

    D: Finish-to-start

Question 119: You are using the precedence diagramming method to construct your project schedule network diagram. What other name is sometimes used to describe the precedence diagramming method?

    A: Activity-on-node diagram

    B: Activity-on-arrow diagram

    C: Critical chain methodology

    D: Critical path methodology

Question 120: After talking with your team and the people responsible for completing the activity, you schedule two activities in your project so that the successor activity is able to start a week before the predecessor activity. What is this is an example of?

    A: Lag

    B: Lead

    C: Slack

    D: Float

Question 121: You are leading your project scheduling specialists in the completion of your project schedule and you wish to add leads and lags into your schedule to accurately reflect the total project duration. Some members of your team are confused about the two terms. How would you describe the difference between a lead and a lag to them?

> **A:** A lead means a successor activity can be started prior to the completion of a predecessor activity. A lag directs a delay in the successor activity.

> **B:** A lead means that both activities can start at the same time. A lag means that neither can start until the other one starts.

> **C:** A lead means that the successor activity must start prior to the predecessor activity finishing. A lag means the successor activity has a mandatory dependency and can not start until the predecessor activity is complete.

> **D:** A lead means the amount of time free on the critical path between activities. A lag is the amount of delay that can occur between activities that will not adversely affect the final project delivery date.

Question 122: You are completing the sequence of activities and note that one of your activities can not proceed until consent is granted by the local government agency. This is an example of what sort of dependency?

> **A:** Discretionary

> **B:** External

> **C:** Environmental

> **D:** Mandatory

Question 123: You have successfully completed the first iteration of your project schedule network diagram. This indicates that you have completed the work in which PMBOK® Guide process?

> **A:** Control Schedule

> **B:** Define Activities

> **C:** Develop Schedule

> **D:** Sequence Activities

Question 124: Your project sponsor has asked to see your resource calendar. What sort of information is included in this document?

> **A:** The length of time the project will require input from external resources.

> **B:** The dates of annual holidays for project team members.

> **C:** The duration of each activity in the project resource diagram.

> **D:** When and how long project resources will be available during the project.

Question 125: You are estimating your activity resources and breaking down the work within each activity to its lowest level and then aggregating these estimates to get a total quantity for each activity's resources. What tool or technique are you using?

> **A:** Published estimating data

> **B:** Bottom-up estimating

> **C:** Expert judgment

> **D:** Parametric estimating

Question 126: You are about to begin the work to estimate activity durations on your project. Which of the following would not be an input you could use to complete this work?

> **A:** Activity attributes

> **B:** Activity duration estimates

> **C:** Project scope statement

> **D:** Activity list

Question 127: While estimating the activity durations on your project, you come across a similar project completed by your organization last year. To save time, you use information from this project to help estimate activity durations. This is an example of which tool or technique?

> **A:** Bottom-up estimating

> **B:** Analogous estimating

> **C:** Parametric estimating

> **D:** Three-point estimating

Question 128: As a result of a brainstorming session, your team determines that the most likely duration of an activity will be 8 days, the optimistic duration is 6 days, and the pessimistic duration is 16 days. What it the expected activity duration?

> **A:** 10 days
>
> **B:** 5 days
>
> **C:** 9 days
>
> **D:** 30 days

Question 129: There is some uncertainty over the duration of a particular activity on your project. You call your team together, all of whom have experience in completing the activity. After a brainstorming session, they are able to determine a most likely duration, an optimistic duration, and a pessimistic duration. You then use these numbers to calculate the expected activity duration. This is an example of which sort of tool or technique?

> **A:** Bottom-up estimating
>
> **B:** Three-point estimating
>
> **C:** Analogous estimating
>
> **D:** Parametric estimating

Question 130: To estimate the amount of time it will take to install 500 meters of cable on your project, you divide the number of meters required by how many meters an hour the person laying the cable can lay. This is an example of which sort of tool or technique?

> **A:** Three-point estimating
>
> **B:** Bottom-up estimating
>
> **C:** Analogous estimating
>
> **D:** Parametric estimating

Question 131: You are leading your team members in the development of your project schedule. You have just started the process and are checking that you have all the appropriate inputs required. Which of the following would not be an input into this process?

> **A:** Resource calendar
>
> **B:** Project schedule network diagram
>
> **C:** Activity list
>
> **D:** Project schedule

Question 132: What is the PMBOK® Guide process of analyzing activity sequences, durations, resource requirements, and scheduled constraints to create the project schedule?

> **A:** Project Schedule Development
>
> **B:** Create Project Schedule
>
> **C:** Develop Schedule
>
> **D:** Schedule Management

Question 133: You are completing a network diagram with the following information: Task A has a duration of 3 days and has the start as a predecessor; Task B has a duration of 5 days and also has the start as a predecessor; Task C has a duration of 4 days and has Task A as a predecessor; Task D has a duration of 4 days and has Task B as a predecessor; Task E has a duration of 6 days and has Tasks C and D as predecessors; Task F has a duration of 5 days and has Task D as a predecessor; the finish milestone has a duration of zero days and has Tasks E and F as predecessors. Using this data, what is the duration of the project?

> **A:** 16
>
> **B:** 14
>
> **C:** 13
>
> **D:** 15

Question 134: You are completing a network diagram with the following information: Task A has a duration of 3 days and has the start as a predecessor; Task B has a duration of 5 days and also has the start as a predecessor; Task C has a duration of 4 days and has Task A as a predecessor; Task D has a duration of 4 days and has Task B as a predecessor; Task E has a duration of 6 days and has Tasks C and D as predecessors; Task F has a duration of 5 days and has Task D as a predecessor; the finish milestone has a duration of zero days and has Tasks E and F as predecessors. What is the critical path for this network diagram?

> **A:** Start-B-D-F-Finish
>
> **B:** Start-B-D-E-Finish
>
> **C:** Start-A-C-E-Finish
>
> **D:** Start-A-C-F-Finish

Question 135: According to Goldratt's critical chain theory, what should you do in order to reduce risk in project schedules?

> **A:** Start activities in the feeder chains as late as possible.
>
> **B:** Add buffers to the critical chains.
>
> **C:** Start activities in the critical chains as early as possible.
>
> **D:** Start activities in the feeder chains as early as possible.

Question 136: During a discussion with a fellow project manager you realize that she is using the terms *critical path method* and *critical chain method* incorrectly. You offer some pieces of advice and insight into how the two methods are different. Which of these statements about the critical path method and the critical chain method is FALSE?

> **A:** The critical path method schedules early start and late start dates to planned activities, whereas the critical chain method schedules only late start dates to planned activities.

> **B:** The critical chain method initially uses non-conservative estimates, whereas the critical path method is concerned with using more accurate estimates.

> **C:** The critical path method focuses on managing the total float of network paths, whereas the critical chain method focuses on managing the buffer activity durations and the resources applied to planned schedule activities.

> **D:** The critical chain method accounts for resource availability, whereas the critical path method does not.

Question 137: You are adding duration buffers that are non-workable schedule activities to manage uncertainty in your project schedule. What tool or technique are you using?

> **A:** Parametric estimating

> **B:** Critical path method

> **C:** Three-point estimating

> **D:** Critical chain method

Question 138: You are using a methodology that calculates the amount of float on various paths in the network diagram to determine the minimum project duration. What tool or technique are you using?

> **A:** Critical path method

> **B:** Critical chain method

> **C:** Parametric estimating

> **D:** Three-point estimating

Question 139: In the first attempt at resource leveling the project schedule, what would you expect to occur?

> **A:** The overall project duration will increase.

> **B:** The number of required resources will decrease during certain time periods of the project.

> **C:** The number of required resources will increase during certain time periods of the project.

> **D:** The overall project duration will decrease.

Question 140: You are the project manager on a software project. While examining your schedule you see that there has been a delay in completing a task. The sensible choice seems to move a person, someone who is an expert on the work that is behind, from another task. There is a choice between two people who are working on different tasks. One person is working on a task that has 5 days of free float and the other is working on a task that has 8 days of total float and no free float. What is your BEST course of action?

A: A person should be brought in from outside the project.

B: The person working on the task with total float of 8 days.

C: Either person can be used.

D: The person working on the task with free float of 5 days.

Question 141: You are using a computer-based modelling technique that examines possible outcomes based on a range of potential probabilities if a particular situation occurs. What is this technique called?

A: Parametric estimating

B: Schedule compression

C: Critical chain methodology

D: What-if scenario analysis

Question 142: Your project team is behind schedule and has decided to compress the schedule. They have requested extra budget to bring in the additional resources required. Which schedule compression technique are they seeking to use?

A: Compressing

B: Crashing

C: Fast tracking

D: Resource leveling

Question 143: You have managed to bring forward the predicted completion date for your project by doing in parallel several of the activities that were scheduled to be done in sequence. What is this technique called?

A: Acceleration

B: Increasing priorities

C: Fast tracking

D: Crashing

Question 144: You are working on a project to build a new house. Usually you would wait until the concrete foundation dried and then erect the wall on top of it. To speed up the project, you start putting the wall frame together off site while the concrete foundation is drying. This is an example of which schedule compression technique?

    A: Fast tracking

    B: Compressing

    C: Crashing

    D: Resource leveling

Question 145: Your project sponsor asks you to attend a senior management meeting and present a brief update on your project progress. Which of the following would be best to use in the presentation?

    A: Bar chart

    B: Project management plan

    C: Work performance information

    D: Schedule network diagram

Question 146: What is the name of the process in the PMBOK® Guide that monitors the status of the project to update project progress and manage changes to the schedule baseline?

    A: Develop Schedule

    B: Monitoring and Controlling

    C: Verify Schedule

    D: Control Schedule

Question 147: Your project is underway and you are measuring the forecast schedule against the actual schedule, checking for variances between the two and initiating corrective actions if required. To successfully complete this work, you require a range of inputs. Which of the following is not one of these inputs?

    A: Project management plan

    B: Work performance information

    C: Project schedule

    D: Work performance data

Question 148: While using the earned value management technique to measure project schedule progress on your project, you discover that your project's schedule performance index (SPI) is 0.9. What does this mean?

    A: The amount of buffer in your critical chain methodology is less than optimal.

    B: The project network diagram was incorrectly put together.

    C: The project is behind schedule and in need of schedule compression.

    D: The project is ahead of schedule.

Question 149: You are a project manager on a project where your SPI has been calculated at .95. Your earned value (EV) has been calculated at $10,000, and your actual cost (AC) is $10,400, so what is your planned value (PV)?

    A: $10,000

    B: $10,526

    C: $9,500

    D: $10,947

Question 150: As part of the development of your project schedule, you are informed that a particular activity has an estimated optimistic duration of 7 days, an estimated pessimistic duration of 15 days, and will most likely take 10 days to complete. Using PERT analysis, what is the standard deviation?

    A: 0.5

    B: 10.33

    C: 1.76

    D: 1.33

Question 151: As part of the development of your project schedule, you are informed that a particular activity has an estimated optimistic duration of 7 days, an estimated pessimistic duration of 15 days, and will most likely take 10 days to complete. Your sponsor asks you the activity duration range in which you are 95% confident that the activity will be delivered. What is your response?

    A: 8–12 days

    B: 7.67–12.99 days

    C: 9–11.66 days

    D: 10 days

Question 152: Yvette is the project manager for a software project. She and her team are determining the activity duration estimates for the project. She has requested that each team member determine the estimates by multiplying the quantity of work to be performed by the known historical productivity rate of the individual department. Yvette has asked her team to generate the estimates using what technique?

A: Parametric estimating

B: Analogous estimating

C: Three-point estimating

D: Expert judgment

Question 153: Consider the following information. What is the critical path? Task A has a duration of 3 days and is a starting activity. Task B has a duration of 6 days and has Task A as a predecessor. Task C has a duration of 5 days and has Tasks A and B as predecessors. Task D has a duration of 4 days and has Task B as a predecessor. Task E has a duration of 1 day and has Task C as the predecessor. Task F has a duration of 6 days and has Tasks D and E as predecessors. Task G has a duration of 4 days and has Tasks E and F as predecessors.

A: A-B-C-E-F-G

B: A-D-F-G

C: A-C-D-E-F-G

D: A-B-D-F-G

Question 154: Consider the following information. How many tasks have a slack of 2 days? Task A has a duration of 3 days and is a starting activity. Task B has a duration of 6 days and has Task A as a predecessor. Task C has a duration of 5 days and has Tasks A and B as predecessors. Task D has a duration of 4 days, and has Task B as a predecessor. Task E has a duration of 1 day and has Task C as a predecessor. Task F has a duration of 6 days and has Tasks D and E as predecessors. Task G has a duration of 4 days and has Tasks E and F as predecessors.

A: 4

B: 2

C: 3

D: 1

Project Cost Management

Question 155: You have finished putting together your project budget and notice that there is a point at which cost and staffing levels are highest. At which point in the project would this generally be?

> **A:** Starting the project.
>
> **B:** Organizing and preparing.
>
> **C:** Carrying out the work.
>
> **D:** Closing the project.

Question 156: You are completing the work of aggregating the estimated costs of individual activities or work packages to establish an authorized cost baseline. What PMBOK® Guide process are you completing?

> **A:** Cost Performance Baseline
>
> **B:** Estimate Costs
>
> **C:** Control Costs
>
> **D:** Determine Budget

Question 157: You have completed the work required to develop your cost management plan and are introducing it to your team members so that they are aware of its purpose and limitations. The cost management plan can establish all of the following except?

> **A:** Units of measure
>
> **B:** Level of accuracy
>
> **C:** Activity definition
>
> **D:** Control thresholds

Question 158: Costs that cannot be directly traced to a specific project and are accumulated and allocated equitably over multiple projects are known as what?

> **A:** Indirect costs
>
> **B:** Direct costs
>
> **C:** Allocatable costs
>
> **D:** Non-projectized costs

Question 159: While completing the processes required to develop an approved project budget, you have started the work required to estimate costs on your project. In order to do this successfully, you should have access to several important inputs. Which of the following is not an input you would find useful to complete this work?

A: Activity cost estimates

B: Project schedule

C: Risk register

D: Scope baseline

Question 160: Which of the following is not an Organizational Process Asset you would consider when estimating costs on your project?

A: Historical information

B: Cost-estimating templates

C: Market conditions

D: Lessons learned

Question 161: You are estimating the costs in your project and are using information from a previous, similar project as the basis for estimating in your current project. What technique are you using?

A: Parametric estimating

B: Analogous estimating

C: Three-point estimating

D: Published estimating data

Question 162: You and your team are currently breaking down all the project deliverables into the smallest useful unit so that you can then estimate costs for each of these units and then aggregate these estimates into a total project cost estimate. What is the name of the technique you are using to estimate costs?

A: Parametric estimating

B: Bottom-up estimating

C: Low-level estimating

D: Project management software

Question 163: While developing individual costs estimates for work packages on your project, you use a technique that requires you to use a statistical relationship between historical data and other variables to calculate a cost estimate for a schedule activity resource. What is this estimating technique more commonly referred to as?

A: Statistical estimating

B: Bottom-up estimating

C: Parametric estimating

D: Top-down estimating

Question 164: Your project sponsor has asked you to provide a cost estimate quickly to give the project steering group an idea of what the costs for a particular work package will be. Which of the following estimating techniques would you choose to use?

    A: Analogous estimating

    B: Parametric estimating

    C: Resource rate estimating

    D: Bottom-up estimating

Question 165: While completing the cost estimating process for a particular activity in your project, several members of your team disagree over the estimate to do the work. After a discussion with the team, you determine that the most likely cost of the activity will be $25, the optimistic cost of the activity will be $15, and the pessimistic cost will be $70. Using the three-point estimating technique, what is the expected cost of the activity?

    A: $110

    B: $36.66

    C: $30.83

    D: $25.83

Question 166: While completing the cost estimating for a particular activity in your project, several members of your team disagree over the estimate to do the work. After a discussion with the team, you determine that the most likely cost of the activity will be $50, the optimistic cost of the activity will be $30, and the pessimistic cost will be $70. Using the three-point estimating technique, what is the expected cost of the activity?

    A: $150

    B: $25

    C: $70

    D: $50

Question 167: During your cost estimating you include a figure for cost uncertainty on your project, and the project sponsor agrees to give you delegated authority to manage this reserve. What is this figure generally known as?

    A: Reserve analysis

    B: Contingency reserve

    C: Management reserve

    D: Slush fund

Question 168: You are using the three-point estimating method of scheduling for a project. The variance for the project is found to be 16 days and the duration of the project is found to be 90 days. What is the range of values for the project duration such that there will be at least a 95% probability that the actual project completion will fall between the high and low value of the range of values?

A: 58-122 days

B: 74-106 days

C: 82-98 days

D: 86-94 days

Question 169: You are aggregating the cost estimates of individual activities and work packages to establish an authorized cost baseline. Which PMBOK® Guide process are you engaged in?

A: Budget Preparation

B: Determine Budget

C: Estimate Costs

D: Cost Performance Baseline

Question 170: You have spent time with your team developing individual cost estimates and are now using the project schedule to determine your project budget. Which of the following inputs would you not find helpful to complete this work?

A: Cost baseline

B: Basis of estimates

C: Activity cost estimates

D: Scope baseline

Question 171: What is the authorized time-phased budget at completion used to measure, monitor, and control overall cost performance on the project more commonly known as?

A: Approved project budget

B: Cost baseline

C: Activity cost estimate

D: Total funding requirements

Question 172: You are monitoring the status of the project to update the project budget and manage changes to the cost baseline. Which PMBOK® Guide process best describes the work are you carrying out?

A: Determine Budget

B: Control Costs

C: Earned Value Management

D: Cost Aggregation

Question 173: While using a technique that gathers a number of key metrics to assess, track, and forecast variances in both project cost and time, you discover that the tool is being used without all the required inputs. Which of the following inputs would you not require to use this particular technique?

> **A:** Work performance information
>
> **B:** Earned value
>
> **C:** Planned value
>
> **D:** Actual cost

Question 174: After measuring your project performance you note that your schedule variance is $75,000. What would your BEST course of action be?

> **A:** Immediately begin fast tracking the schedule to catch up time.
>
> **B:** Ask your project sponsor for extra funds to crash the schedule to catch up time.
>
> **C:** Congratulate your project team on doing well with the project but also submit the information through the approved change control process so that any updates required can be made to the schedule baseline documents.
>
> **D:** Do nothing because everything is going well on your project and you are obviously a good project manager.

Question 175: The earned value on your project is $15,000, the planned value is $20,000, and the actual cost is $18,000. What is your schedule variance?

> **A:** -$3,000
>
> **B:** $5,000
>
> **C:** $3,000
>
> **D:** -$5,000

Question 176: The earned value on your project is $18,000, the planned value is $20,000, and the actual cost is $15,000. What is your cost variance?

> **A:** $3,000
>
> **B:** -$3,000
>
> **C:** $2,000
>
> **D:** -$2,000

Question 177: The earned value on your project is $26,000, the planned value is $20,000, and the actual cost is $18,000. What is your schedule variance?

A: $6,000

B: $8,000

C: -$8,000

D: $2,000

Question 178: The earned value on your project is $52,000, the planned value is $51,000, and the actual cost is $49,000. What is your cost variance?

A: $3,000

B: $2,000

C: $1,000

D: -$1,000

Question 179: A new junior project manager seems to be having some difficulty understanding key terms used in the reports being prepared for the project. He is particularly confused by the earned value management system and the approved project budget. You explain to him that there are easy ways to understand what each element means and demonstrate this by point out that the total planned value of the project is better known as what?

A: Approved project budget

B: Cost baseline

C: Actual cost

D: Budget at completion

Question 180: What is the term for the measurement of the authorized work that has been completed and the authorized budget for such completed work?

A: Cost baseline

B: Earned value

C: Actual cost

D: Budget at completion

Question 181: You are a project manager on a large software project using the earned value reporting system to manage your project. At this point in time, the EV is $24,000, the BAC is $97,000, the PV is $29,000, and the AC is $45,000. What is the percent complete?

A: 30%

B: 25%

C: 46%

D: 53%

Question 182: You are working on a large project and have determined that your CV is $50,000 and your EV is $125,000. What is your AC?

    A: $75,000

    B: $50,000

    C: $175,000

    D: $125,000

Question 183: The earned value on your project is $20,000, the actual cost is $18,000, and the planned value is $25,000. What is your SPI?

    A: -$5,000

    B: 1.11

    C: 0.8

    D: $5,000

Question 184: The earned value on your project is $25,000, the actual cost is $20,000, and the planned value is $20,000. What is your SPI?

    A: 0.75

    B: 1.25

    C: 1

    D: 0.8

Question 185: The planned value on your project is $120,000, the earned value is $100,000, the actual cost is $90,000, and your cost variance is $10,000. What is your cost performance index (CPI)?

    A: 1.2

    B: 3

    C: 0.83

    D: 1.11

Question 186: The planned value on your project is $9,000, the earned value is $9,000, the actual cost is $8,000, and your cost variance is $1,000. What is your cost performance index?

    A: 1

    B: 1.125

    C: 0.88

    D: 8

CHAPTER 1 ▓ QUESTIONS

Question 187: You are working on a large project and have determined that your cost variance is $50,000 and your earned value is $125,000. What is your cost performance index?

      A: 2.5

      B: 1.5

      C: 0.4

      D: 1.666

Question 188: Your project control measurements show a CPI of 0.89. What does this show about your project?

      A: That your project is only spending 89% of the money need to get 100% of the job done.

      B: That your project is experiencing a cost overrun for the work completed.

      C: That your project is experiencing a cost underrun for the work completed.

      D: That your project is running behind schedule and over budget.

Question 189: Your project has a CPI of 1.1 and a SPI of .9. What does this mean?

      A: You are experiencing a cost underrun and are ahead of schedule.

      B: You are experiencing a cost overrun and are behind schedule.

      C: You are experiencing a cost underrun and are behind schedule.

      D: You are experiencing a cost overrun and are ahead of schedule.

Question 190: You are forecasting your estimate to complete your project and are incurring extra costs to do this work. What sort of estimating technique are you using?

      A: Earned value management

      B: Bottom-up EAC estimating

      C: Estimate to complete (ETC) forecast

      D: To Complete Performance Index (TCPI)

Question 191: Your actual costs on your project are $75,000, the budget at completion is $100,000, and the earned value is $85,000. Your project has experienced some atypical variances to date which have affected its financial performance but from this point forward you expect it to perform at the originally budgeted rate. What is your estimate at completion?

     A: $90,000

     B: $110,000

     C: $100,000

     D: $105,000

Question 192: Your budget at completion is $50,000, your earned value is $40,000, and your actual cost is $45,000. Using an estimate at completion forecast for ETC work performed at the present CPI, what is your estimate at completion?

     A: $47,666

     B: $50,000

     C: $56,818

     D: $53,225

Question 193: The calculated projection of cost performance that must be achieved on the remaining work to meet a specified management goal such as the BAC or the EAC is known as what?

     A: Earned value

     B: Estimate to complete

     C: Cost baseline

     D: To Complete Performance Index

Question 194: Your actual cost on the project is $10,000, the budget at completion is $20,000, the earned value is $8,000, the cumulative CPI is 0.8, and the cumulative SPI is 0.9. Using both your CPI and SPI factors, what is your estimate at completion forecast?

     A: $18,750

     B: $25,000

     C: $22,666

     D: $26,666

Question 195: You are approximately halfway through a complex construction project and are presenting the data from earned value management analysis of the project to your team. You have a BAC of $50,0000, an EV of $2,800,000, an AC of $260,000, and a PV of $250,000. The team members are happy with these figures and want to know the rate at which they have to work to achieve the revised estimate at completion. What is your answer?

A: 1.0

B: 0.92

C: 1.08

D: 0.5

Question 196: As part of the work to check if you are achieving your expected and approved spend on the project, you are completing a process of controlling project costs. Which of the following is not an output from this process?

A: Work performance information

B: Variance analysis

C: Cost forecasts

D: Change requests

Question 197: You are managing a project and the original scope baseline of the project was budgeted at $100,000. Since work on the project started there have been 13 authorized and approved changes to the project. The changes have a value of $12,000 and the cost of investigating them prior to their approval was $1,500. What is the current budget for the project?

A: $113,500

B: $109,500

C: $112,000

D: $100,000

Question 198: The project you are managing is going well and you are using the earned value management system to assess historical information and forecast a likely future financial state of the project. You have a budget at completion of $120,000, an earned value of $50,000, a planned value of $55,000, and an actual cost of $45,000. What is your To Complete Performance Index to achieve the budget at completion?

A: 1

B: 1.07

C: 0.93

D: $5,000

Question 199: You are nearing the end of a residential remodeling project and are presenting the data from earned value management analysis of the project to your team. You have a BAC of $300,000, an EV of $2,500,000, an AC of $260,000, and a PV of $250,000. The team members are happy with these figures and want to know the rate at which they have to work to achieve the budget at completion. What is your answer?

> **A:** 1.25
>
> **B:** 0.95
>
> **C:** 1.1
>
> **D:** 0.85

Project Quality Management

Question 200: Customer satisfaction means that customer requirements are met. Meeting customer requirements requires a combination of what two factors?

> **A:** Continuous improvement and prevention over inspection
>
> **B:** Conformance to requirements and prevention over inspection
>
> **C:** Continuous improvement and fitness for use
>
> **D:** Conformance to requirements and fitness for use

Question 201: You are successful using the FMEA approach to assess implications of quality decisions on your project. Your client asks you what FMEA stands for. What is your answer?

> **A:** Failure model of effective analysis
>
> **B:** Failed measurement and effect analysis
>
> **C:** Failed measurement and effective assurance
>
> **D:** Failure mode and effect analysis

Question 202: Modern quality management complements project management very highly, with both disciplines recognizing the importance of all the following characteristics except?

> **A:** Customer satisfaction
>
> **B:** Prevention over inspection
>
> **C:** Continuous improvement
>
> **D:** Total quality management (TQM)

Question 203: Quality is planned, designed, and built into your project instead of being inspected in. What is the main reason that prevention of mistakes in quality is preferred over finding the mistakes via inspection?

> **A:** Because finding defects via inspection should be avoided at all costs.
>
> **B:** Because if you are a good project manager and perform prevention well, you won't have to deal with inspection.
>
> **C:** Because the cost of preventing mistakes is generally much less than the cost of correcting them when they are found by inspection.
>
> **D:** Because your quality management plan focuses on prevention.

Question 204: How would you best describe to your client the difference between precision and accuracy?

> **A:** Precision means the degree to which there is conformance to requirements. Accuracy refers to fitness for use.
>
> **B:** Precision means the values of the repeated measurements are clustered and have little scatter. Accuracy means that the measured value is very close to the true value.
>
> **C:** Precision is the degree to which the project quality assurance processes are being met. Accuracy is the degree to which the product meets customer specifications.
>
> **D:** Precision is the ability to provide information to a six sigma level. Accuracy is the process of ensuring that the six sigma target is met.

Question 205: A member of your project team seems confused about the differences between quality approaches to the project and product. How would you best explain these differences?

> **A:** Quality in relation to the project relates to the processes and procedures that run the project. Quality in relation to the product looks at conformance to requirements and fitness of use.
>
> **B:** There is no difference between the two.
>
> **C:** Quality in relation to the project is focused on ensuring the project control and reporting are accurate. Quality in relation to the product ensures that it stays within the upper and lower control limits.
>
> **D:** Quality in relation to the project is focused on the preparation and execution of the quality management plan. Quality in relation to the product is set solely by the customer.

Question 206: Your project is behind schedule and you have asked your project team to work longer hours to make up the time so that the customer's needs are met as planned. As project manager, you should monitor your quality management plan for what reason?

> **A:** Meeting customer requirements by overworking the project team may result in increased employee attrition, errors, or rework.
>
> **B:** The customer requirements and specifications can change rapidly during periods of rework as the customer sees opportunities to make changes.
>
> **C:** Achieving customer needs is not the primary focus of the quality management plan, and you need to make sure your team is working on project quality, not product quality, at these times.
>
> **D:** The overtime cost incurred will take away the project budget assigned to the implementation of the quality management plan.

Question 207: Your project team has completed a check of the project and the product you are managing. They discover that although you are meeting the quality requirements, the product is of a low grade. What should you do FIRST?

> **A:** Keep the project running as normal with no changes as a result of this discovery.
>
> **B:** Check the quality management plan on what to do when discovering a low-grade product.
>
> **C:** Immediately stop work to discover the source of the low grade, and proceed to fix it.
>
> **D:** Keep the project running so that you don't lose time, but assign a team member with experience in the area of the product to discover the reason behind the low grade.

Question 208: What is the method of modern quality management that relies on continuing small improvements involving everyone from the top management to the lowest-level worker in the organization more most commonly known as?

> **A:** Kampai
>
> **B:** Kanban
>
> **C:** Kawasaki
>
> **D:** Kaizen

Question 209: The PMBOK® Guide process groups of initiating, planning, executing, monitoring, and controlling a project are based on the work of Shewhart and Deming. What is their quality improvement model known as?

    A: Six Sigma

    B: Organizational Project Management Maturity Model (OPM3)

    C: Plan-do-check-act cycle

    D: Total quality management

Question 210: You are explaining to your project sponsor that the decision made to lower the quality of deliverables on the project to save money will have long-lasting cost impacts beyond the project. The project sponsor does not seem convinced so you refer to the concept of cost of quality to make your point. How would you best describe cost of quality to your sponsor?

    A: The total cost of the quality effort throughout the project life cycle

    B: The amount of money required to complete your project quality management plan

    C: The total cost of all efforts related to quality throughout the product life cycle

    D: The total cost of implementing a prevention and inspection regime

Question 211: The PMBOK® Guide process that is focused on identifying quality requirements and standards for the project and product is known as what?

    A: Control Quality

    B: Cost of Quality

    C: Plan Quality Management

    D: Perform Quality Assurance

Question 212: You are completing the work to identify and document quality requirements and standards for your project. Which of the following would you not use as an input into this process?

    A: Requirements documentation

    B: Stakeholder register

    C: Risk register

    D: Quality checklists

CHAPTER 1 ▓ QUESTIONS

Question 213: When considering the cost of quality on your project you should consider all of the following characteristics except?

    A: Destructive testing loss.

    B: Investment in preventing non-conformance to requirements.

    C: Appraising the product or service for conformance to requirements.

    D: Failing to meet requirements.

Question 214: Which of the following is not an example of a cost of conformance?

    A: Testing

    B: Equipment

    C: Training

    D: Rework

Question 215: You and your team are checking data that has been gathered and presented in a control chart to determine if the product you are producing is meeting the required quality objectives. What is your main objective in completing this work and representing it in this way?

    A: To measure if the cost of quality is providing the forecast cost benefit analysis.

    B: To determine if your quality management plan is achieving the objectives.

    C: To measure if your product is meeting the goal of fitness for use.

    D: To determine if a process is stable or has predictable performance.

Question 216: Control limits for the production rates for the machines your project is building are set at 3 and 9, with a mean value of 6 units per hour. The results this week are as follows: 4, 7, 10, 5, and 6. What should you do first?

    A: Investigate the third result.

    B: Continue working.

    C: Investigate the tenth result.

    D: Investigate the first result.

Question 217: You have received the results of statistical sampling performed on the product of your project. The control chart shows nine data points in a row just under the mean. What should you do first?

> **A:** Change the control limits and the mean so the process is under control.
>
> **B:** Find an assignable or special cause using an Ishikawa diagram.
>
> **C:** Nothing. If the data points are not outside the control limits, then the process is in control.
>
> **D:** Fire the quality assurance team.

Question 218: Upper and lower control limits on a control chart are generally set at how many standard deviations above and below the acceptable mean?

> **A:** 1 standard deviation
>
> **B:** 2 standard deviations
>
> **C:** 3 standard deviations
>
> **D:** 6 standard deviations

Question 219: Your project data, as shown on the control chart, indicates the latest seven consecutive points are above the mean but within the upper control limit. What is your BEST course of action?

> **A:** Stop work immediately and investigate the root cause of the problem.
>
> **B:** Do nothing because the data clearly indicates that the process is above the lower specification limit.
>
> **C:** Initiate corrective action in accordance with your quality management plan.
>
> **D:** Lower the lower control limit so that the data is now above the limit.

Question 220: Your project is generating useful data for your control chart. The latest data indicates that the process of manufacturing the product has produced units below the lower control limit but above the lower specification limit. What is your BEST course of action?

> **A:** Initiate corrective action in accordance with your quality management plan.
>
> **B:** Do nothing because the data clearly indicates that the process is above the lower specification limit.
>
> **C:** Stop work immediately and investigate the root cause of the problem.
>
> **D:** Lower the lower control limit so that the data is now above the limit.

Question 221: While working on the project to assess and measure quality, you are determining the number and type of tests and their impact on cost of quality. What technique are you using?

> **A:** Design of experiments
>
> **B:** Analogous estimating
>
> **C:** Benchmarking
>
> **D:** Cost of quality

Question 222: You are comparing actual or planned project practices to those of comparable projects to identify best practices and generate ideas for improvement for your project. What quality technique are you using?

> **A:** Cost of quality
>
> **B:** Analogous estimating
>
> **C:** Design of experiments
>
> **D:** Benchmarking

Question 223: A quality technique that chooses only a part of a population of interest for studying, and is often used to reduce cost, is called what?

> **A:** Inspection
>
> **B:** Flowcharting
>
> **C:** Statistical sampling
>
> **D:** Budget control chart

Question 224: Your project team is working on a software project with over two million lines of code and has just randomly selected a number of lines of code for inspection. What quality technique are they using?

> **A:** Benchmarking
>
> **B:** Design of experiments
>
> **C:** Statistical sampling
>
> **D:** Random inspection

Question 225: During a project to deliver a complex set of requirements for a wide range of stakeholders, you and your team have placed a great deal of importance on the quality of the project. You have decided to use a wide variety of tools and techniques to help you achieve the desired quality standards. Which of the following is not an example of a quality planning tool that you would find useful in this endeavor?

> **A:** Affinity diagram
>
> **B:** Force field diagram
>
> **C:** Matrix diagram
>
> **D:** Quality checklist

Question 226: While completing work associated with ensuring quality in a project, it is important that you know the difference between several different quality related terms. Several of your team members regularly get confused about the difference between the different terms, particularly understanding exactly what a quality metric is. To demonstrate to your team the difference, you point out that one of the following is not a quality metric. Which one do you point out?

A: Failure rate

B: Budget control

C: Defect frequency

D: Upper control limit

Question 227: You have completed the work to plan and document your particular approach to quality on your project. Which of the following is not an output you would expect to produce as a result of this work?

A: Quality metrics

B: Flowcharting

C: Process improvement plan

D: Quality management plan

Question 228: The process of continuous process improvements to reduce waste and eliminate activities that do not add value to a project is known as what?

A: Progressive elaboration

B: Plan quality management

C: Control quality

D: Perform quality assurance

Question 229: You are using your quality management plan to guide the work being done to ensure that project quality assurance expectations are being met. Which of the following would not be a useful input to you?

A: Process improvement plan

B: Quality audits

C: Quality metrics

D: Quality control measurements

Question 230: A project administrator has asked for guidance on completing a project audit as per the approved quality management plan for your project. They are seeking your guidance on what exactly a quality audit is. How is a quality audit best defined?

    A: A structured, independent review to determine whether product specifications comply with organizational and project policies, processes, and procedures.

    B: A structured, independent review to determine whether project activities comply with organizational and project policies, processes, and procedures.

    C: An examination of the product specifications to test whether they are fit for use and conform to requirements.

    D: A review of the project management plan to ensure it contains the appropriate quality management plan.

Question 231: You are completing the work to ensure the required quality assurance levels are met on your project. Which of the following is an output of this work?

    A: Quality audits

    B: Quality metrics

    C: Change requests

    D: Process analysis

Question 232: What is the process of monitoring and recording results of executing the quality activities to assess performance and recommend necessary changes known as?

    A: Perform quality assurance

    B: Control quality

    C: Plan quality management

    D: Statistical sampling

Question 233: During a workshop to define quality control processes on your project, you sense that team members are confused abut the difference between prevention and inspection. What is the BEST description of the difference between prevention and inspection?

    A: Prevention is focused on keeping errors out of the process. Inspection is focused on keeping errors out of the hands of the customer.

    B: Prevention is concerned with the implementation of the quality process at the start of the project. Inspection is done once the project is underway.

C: Prevention is the systematic adoption of rigorous quality standards during the planning phase. Inspection is carried out during the monitoring and control process group.

D: Prevention is focused on the quality of the project. Inspection is focused on the quality of the product.

Question 234: What is the BEST description of the difference between tolerances and control limits?

A: Tolerances are concerned with project quality. Control limits are concerned with product quality.

B: Tolerances can indicate if the process is out of control. Control limits specify a range of acceptable results.

C: Tolerances are a specified range of acceptable results. Control limits are thresholds that can indicate if the process is out of control.

D: Tolerances are concerned with product quality. Control limits are concerned with project quality.

Question 235: All of the following are an example of one of Ishikawa's seven tools of quality except?

A: Flowcharting

B: Inspection

C: Run chart

D: Control charts

Question 236: You are the project manager for a project where quality is an important constraint, and you are trying to correct a problem with a machine that makes parts that are used in complex medical imaging equipment. As a result of carrying our your Control Quality process, you discover that unfortunately these parts are frequently made with defects. You have decided to hold a meeting to discuss the process of making the parts. You create a diagram that has branches that show the possible causes of the problems. Each of the branches breaks the cause down into more and more detail. What is this diagram called?

A: Fishbowl diagram

B: Cause and effect diagram

C: Pareto diagram

D: Scatter diagram

Question 237: You are trying to find the cause of an identified problem on your project by examining the various factors that might be linked to potential problems. What technique are you using?

A: Ishikawa diagram

B: Control chart

C: Pareto chart

D: Run chart

Question 238: The quality manager on your project wishes to analyze the data that is being received in the form of a list of defects that have occurred in the manufacturing department. The report comes with defects listed chronologically as they occurred, the cost of the repair necessary to correct each defect, the person involved, and a description of the defect. The quality manager would like to determine which of the defects should be corrected first according to the frequency of the defect occurring. Which of the following tools should she use?

A: Pareto diagram

B: Sampling inspection

C: Cause and effect diagram

D: Quality critical path

Question 239: You are explaining to your project team the ranking of causes for defects on your project to enable them to focus their corrective actions on those causes that are responsible for the greatest defects. What sort of diagram would you use for this?

A: Pareto chart

B: Scatter diagram

C: Control chart

D: Histogram

Question 240: While performing quality control inspections, you note down relevant data and use a vertical bar chart to show how often a particular variable state occurred. What is this sort of bar chart more commonly called?

A: Histogram

B: Pareto chart

C: Control chart

D: Scatter diagram

Question 241: While performing quality control inspections, you note down relevant data and use a chart similar to a control chart without displayed limits, which shows the history and pattern of a variation. What sort of chart are you using?

A: Fishbone diagram

B: Control charts

C: Pareto chart

D: Run chart

Question 242: A visual presentation of quality data gathered showing the relationship between a dependent and independent variable is known as what?

A: Run chart

B: Pareto chart

C: Control chart

D: Scatter diagram

Question 243: Your team members have completed work to perform quality control on the project. Which of the following outputs would you not expect them to produce as a result of doing this work?

A: Quality metrics

B: Validated changes

C: Change requests

D: Quality control measurements

Question 244: You and your team are working hard to produce a quality wireless headphone product capable of high-quality audio transmission. You are discussing an approach with your Quality Assurance Team Leader that will aim to reduce the variation the team is experiencing with the prototype headsets being produced. What technique are you discussing?

A: Six Sigma

B: Lean

C: Scrum

D: Kanban

Question 245: If a process is considered to have only 3.4 defects per million opportunities, which sigma class is this defined as?

A: Two Sigma

B: Three Sigma

C: Six Sigma

D: Twelve Sigma

Question 246: The terms Yellow Belt, Green Belt, and Black Belt are terms given to individuals that practice which methodology?

    A: Rapid Application Development

    B: Six Sigma

    C: Scrum

    D: Kanban

Question 247: You have been asked by senior management to focus on eliminating any bottlenecks that exist in your project's processes. What methodology will be most effective in highlighting bottlenecks?

    A: Prince2

    B: MPMM

    C: Lean

    D: Kanban

Question 248: Your Quality Assurance Manager has requested that you assist her in mapping the value stream for the assembly of a new combustion engine. Value stream mapping is part of which methodology?

    A: Waterfall

    B: Scrum

    C: Lean

    D: Kaizen

Project Human Resource Management

Question 249: The PMBOK® Guide processes that organize, recruit, reward, manage, and lead the project team are collectively known as what?

    A: Project Human Resource Management

    B: Project Team Management

    C: Project Management

    D: Project Team Building and Development

Question 250: The project sponsor has several responsibilities while working with the project management team. Which of the following is not a responsibility of the project sponsor?

> **A:** Influencing others in support of the project.
>
> **B:** Completing the WBS.
>
> **C:** Monitoring progress.
>
> **D:** Project funding.

Question 251: A team member is studying towards obtaining the PMP® credential and has asked for your assistance with her study. She is having difficulty remembering the generally correct order of activities in the PMBOK® Guide Project Human Resource Management knowledge area. What is your answer to this question?

> **A:** Plan Human Resource Management, Acquire Project Team, Develop Project Team, Manage Project Team
>
> **B:** Develop Project Team, Acquire Project Team, Plan Human Resource Management, Manage Project Team
>
> **C:** Acquire Project Team, Plan Human Resource Management, Develop Project Team, Manage Project Team
>
> **D:** Plan Human Resource Management, Develop Project Team, Acquire Project Team, Manage Project Team

Question 252: You have completed your human resource management plan for your project. You recognize that the profession of project management features a lot of interdependencies, and you want to make sure that the human resource plan is used in other appropriate parts of your project work. This plan is used as an input into all of the following processes except?

> **A:** Identify Risks
>
> **B:** Estimate Costs
>
> **C:** Estimate Activity Resources
>
> **D:** Acquire Project Team

Question 253: While completing initial planning work on your project, you begin to develop your human resource plan. Which of the following inputs would not be of use to you to complete this plan?

> **A:** Activity resource requirements
>
> **B:** WBS
>
> **C:** Enterprise environmental factors
>
> **D:** Organizational process assets

Question 254: You are showing your project team members the organizational structure, and you point out where in the structure their role is located. What tool would be useful to you in preparing this information?

    A: Responsibility assignment matrix (RAM)

    B: Work breakdown structure (WBS)

    C: Resource breakdown structure (RBS)

    D: Organizational breakdown structure (OBS)

Question 255: You are using a matrix-based chart to give a clear indication of the connection between work packages and team members. Additionally, the chart shows who is responsible, accountable, consulted, and informed about the work. What is the common name of this type of chart?

    A: RACI chart

    B: Organizational breakdown structure

    C: Work breakdown structure

    D: Responsibility assignment matrix

Question 256: As a competent project manager you should be aware of the leading and foundational theories relating to the management of human resources and their practical application. Which of the following is not one of these theories?

    A: Colbin's Intuitive Behavior Modification Theory

    B: Maslow's Hierarchy of Needs

    C: McGregor's Theory X and Theory Y

    D: Herzberg's Motivation-Hygiene Theory

Question 257: As a competent project manager you should be aware of the leading and foundational theories relating to the management of human resources and their practical application. Which of the following is not one of these theories?

    A: Vroom's Expectancy Theory

    B: Ouchi's Theory Z

    C: McLachlan's Theory of External Motivation

    D: McClelland's Human Motivation, Achievement, or Three Needs Theory

Question 258: While completing initial planning work on your project, you begin to develop your human resource management plan. The human resource management plan can include all the following information except?

A: Project organization charts

B: Staffing management plan

C: Cost estimates for staff time

D: Roles and responsibilities

Question 259: What does a resource calendar show?

A: The annual leave for staff throughout the project

B: The cost of staff members over time

C: The human resource level, constraints, and commitment over time

D: Any programmed team-building activities throughout the project

Question 260: You are currently attempting to acquire project team members on a project that is just about to start. You are meeting resistance from the functional managers of the staff you want to use on your project, and it appears that you may have to seek help from external consultants. Your project sponsor is concerned about the impact this process is having on the project. All of following are potential adverse effects of not acquiring your project team except?

A: Reduced quality

B: Decreased customer satisfaction

C: Reduced project costs

D: Delays to project schedules

Question 261: Your construction manager approaches you about a particular team member that has just been assigned to the project. She thinks that he does not have the required skills to complete the work expected of him and suggests that this team member be assigned to a different project. What is your BEST course of action?

A: Arrange for the team member to get the necessary training.

B: Tell your construction manager to fire the team member immediately.

C: Tell your construction manager that it is ok if the team member learns on the job.

D: Arrange for the team member to be assigned to another project.

Question 262: You are in the process of obtaining the staff members you require on your project from other functional areas within your organization. You have made a request to a particular functional manager to have one of her staff members assigned part time to your project. The functional manager is concerned about the effect this will have on her operational goals and suggests instead that the staff member be assigned to your project for 30% of her time instead of 50%. What technique are you engaged in?

    A: Negotiation

    B: Pre-assignment of staff

    C: Acquisition

    D: Acquire project team

Question 263: The software project you are working on is using developers from different geographic areas around the world because the high level of experience required for this project could not be obtained locally. With the different time zones you are having difficulty organizing regular meetings between all the project team members. What would be the BEST thing you could do to improve communication between your virtual team?

    A: Only meet with those team members in your office and tell them to let the other team members know what was discussed.

    B: Insist they all make themselves available at 10 AM your time once a week.

    C: Run multiple meetings on the same topic so that everyone gets the same message.

    D: Use real-time and recorded web-based video conferencing.

Question 264: What is the PMBOK® Guide process of improving the competencies, team interaction, and the overall team environment to enhance project performance known as?

    A: Acquire Project Team

    B: Plan Human Resource Management

    C: Develop Project Team

    D: Manage Project Team

Question 265: You are holding a weekly project meeting when a disagreement between two members of the project team begins. The disagreement is over a technical detail of the project. It is important that the conflicting opinions of the two team members be resolved as quickly as possible. It is even more important that the difference of opinion be resolved correctly. What is your BEST course of action?

> **A:** You should make the decision right away to save time and not let the two disagreeing parties stay in disagreement very long.
>
> **B:** End the meeting and give everyone a few days to cool off.
>
> **C:** Assign someone to find out more factual information about the problem.
>
> **D:** You should suggest a compromise between the two disagreeing team members.

Question 266: Which of the following is not an objective of developing your project team?

> **A:** Improve team members' knowledge and skills.
>
> **B:** Get everyone to align themselves with the culture of the project office.
>
> **C:** Improve trust and agreement between team members.
>
> **D:** Create a dynamic and cohesive team culture.

Question 267: The Tuckman theory of team development states that team development generally follows a sequence of stages. Which is the correct order of those stages?

> **A:** Storming, Norming, Forming, Performing, Adjourning
>
> **B:** Forming, Storming, Norming, Performing, Adjourning
>
> **C:** Forming, Norming, Storming, Performing, Adjourning
>
> **D:** Performing, Forming, Norming, Storming, Adjourning

Question 268: You have offered everyone on your team an individual financial bonus if they are the first to complete a particular piece of work. Instead of motivating the team, your offer has caused unhealthy competition in some staff and apathy in others. What could be the problem with your offer?

> **A:** Your team does not respect you as project manager.
>
> **B:** You offered too little money.
>
> **C:** You offered too much money.
>
> **D:** Your team culture does not support individualism.

Question 269: You have decided that all of your project team members must move into their own space within the organization's main headquarters to improve efficiency and team building. What is this commonly called?

> **A:** Assignment

> **B:** Project team residential compatibility

> **C:** Co-location

> **D:** War room

Question 270: After completing some work required to develop your project team members, you have noted several outputs that have been produced. Which of the following is an output that you would expect to produce?

> **A:** Team performance assessments

> **B:** Team building activities

> **C:** Staff assignments

> **D:** WBS dictionary elements

Question 271: As a project manager, your greatest challenge has been managing your project team. You have decided to gain extra skills to help you in this task. All of the following are areas you should focus on except?

> **A:** Negotiation

> **B:** Communication

> **C:** Remuneration

> **D:** Leadership

Question 272: Your project is more than halfway through and you have a CPI of 1.08 and an SPI of 1.03. You attribute a lot of the success so far to the work being done by the team and the way in which they are working together. This has been as a result of the work you have done as project manager in managing the project team. In order to complete the work associated with managing the project team successfully, you have used a variety of inputs to help your efforts. Which of the following is not an input that you would have used?

> **A:** Team performance assessments

> **B:** Project staff assignments

> **C:** Project management plan

> **D:** Project performance appraisals

Question 273: In his theory of motivation of employees, Herzberg divided motivation factors into two classes: satisfiers and dissatisfiers. Which of the following are examples of satisfiers according to Herzberg?

    A: Vacation time, assignment of a personal staff assistant

    B: Work satisfaction, fringe benefits

    C: Plush office space, performance-based salary raise

    D: Sense of personal achievement, work satisfaction

Question 274: As a project manager, you understand how important effective management of your team is to the success of the project. Which of the following is not a key interpersonal skill that you should have as a project manager to help you manage your team?

    A: Strong leadership skills with the ability to communicate the vision and inspire the project team to achieve high performance

    B: The ability to be persuasive and have high levels of active and effective listening skills

    C: A focus on prevention over inspection and an eye for detail when reporting your project status reports

    D: Effective decision-making skills

Question 275: Your project has been underway for 18 months and currently has a CPI of 1.02 and an SPI of 1.07. During the project, two of your project team members have disagreed constantly over non-technical issues and on occasion have shown open hostility towards each other, often in front of other team members. Lately the situation has escalated, and during your last project team status meeting they openly shouted at each other. As project manager, you decide to call both team members into your office and explain to them that the best way to resolve this conflict is a give-and-take attitude and open dialogue. What conflict resolution technique are you using?

    A: Collaborating and forcing

    B: Confronting and problem solving

    C: Smoothing and accommodating

    D: Withdrawing and avoiding

Question 276: As part of your own professional development plan, you have approval from your senior manager to undertake leadership training. As part of your training, you have asked your team members for their opinion on what constitutes the key elements and characteristics of an effective leader. What are the key elements of effective leadership?

    A: Fear and submission

    B: Friendship and admiration

    C: Vision and humor

    D: Respect and trust

Question 277: Which of the following is not one of the four basic decision-making styles normally used by project managers?

> **A:** Ideas to action
>
> **B:** Coin flip
>
> **C:** Command
>
> **D:** Consensus

Question 278: You are faced with a large decision to make on your project. After fully defining the problem, you call in your team to brainstorm multiple solutions. You then define the evaluation criteria and rate the pros and cons of different options. Prior to making a decision, you go through a process of problem definition, solution generation, ideas to action, solution action planning, solution evaluation planning, and evaluation of the outcome and process. What process are you using?

> **A:** Kouzes and Posner six-step decision making process
>
> **B:** Shewhart and Deming's plan-do-check-act cycle
>
> **C:** Six-phase decision making model
>
> **D:** Turner and Muller's six-phase decision making process

Project Communications Management

Question 279: It is commonly acknowledged that one of the most important sets of skills a project manager should develop is their communication skills. All of the following are examples of communication skills except?

> **A:** Reviewing the work breakdown structure to ensure team members know what has to be done.
>
> **B:** Setting and managing expectations.
>
> **C:** Persuading a person or organization to perform an action.
>
> **D:** Listening actively and effectively.

Question 280: Your project is experiencing a range of variations that require one of the contracts you are using to engage an external vendor to be amended. What sort of communication is most appropriate when dealing with changes to a contract?

> **A:** Informal written
>
> **B:** Formal written
>
> **C:** Formal verbal
>
> **D:** Electronic

Question 281: After conducting your stakeholder analysis, you determine that there are, excluding you, 7 stakeholders on the project. How many communication channels are there?

    A: 7

    B: 21

    C: 28

    D: 35

Question 282: There are 12 stakeholders including yourself on the project, so how many communication channels are there?

    A: 66

    B: 144

    C: 78

    D: 12

Question 283: All of the following are factors that influence the method of communication disbursement between team members except?

    A: Availability of technology

    B: Duration of the project

    C: Local government regulations

    D: Urgency of the need for information

Question 284: You are leading a team on a complex project that requires constant communication with influential stakeholders. Despite your best efforts, the message that you send to the stakeholders is disrupted and misunderstood. Communication between the sender and the receiver is often affected by communication barriers or noise. These include all of the following except?

    A: Educational differences

    B: Differences in motivation

    C: Lack of a communications device

    D: Cultural differences

Question 285: You are having difficulty concentrating on what a stakeholder is saying during a business meeting and you feel you are not fully understanding them. What technique could help you to understand them better?

    A: Repeat the message back to the stakeholder.

    B: Ask them to write everything down.

    C: Ask to postpone the meeting until you feel better.

    D: Ask them to speak slower.

Question 286: Your project team is scattered over three countries in three different time zones. Each project office has a different language as its first language, so to improve communication you have asked that all correspondence be conducted in English. In doing this, what are you trying to minimize in your team's communication?

    A: Environmental constraints

    B: Cultural differences

    C: Noise

    D: Foreign accents

Question 287: The skill of listening involves more than just hearing the sounds. Which of the following is a characteristic of a good listener?

    A: Takes good notes.

    B: Repeats some of the things said.

    C: Finishes the speaker's sentences.

    D: Agrees with the speaker.

Question 288: You are in the process of sending out your weekly project update to a wide range of stakeholders. This is an example of what sort of communication method?

    A: Stakeholder management strategy

    B: Pull communication

    C: Interactive communication

    D: Push communication

Question 289: You are using your intranet site to post large amounts of information that team members can log into to read. This is an example of what sort of communication method?

    A: Encoding and decoding

    B: Push communication

    C: Interactive communication

    D: Pull communication

Question 290: Your project team has spent a considerable amount of time and energy completing the stakeholder analysis and putting together the communications management plan but is now disagreeing what, how, and when different communication methods are to be used. Who should take responsibility for determining this?

    A: Stakeholder representative

    B: Project team

    C: Project sponsor

    D: Project manager

Question 291: You are regularly referring to your communications management plan to help guide your project communications. Which of the following would you not expect to find in your communications management plan?

    A: The person responsible for authorizing the release of confidential information

    B: Team members' addresses and phone numbers

    C: Glossary of common terminology

    D: Stakeholder communication requirements

Question 292: As part of your project, you regularly hold status meetings with project team members and influential stakeholders. You endeavor at all times to ensure that these meetings are productive and contribute to successful communication on the project. All of the following are techniques to ensure your project meetings are more productive except?

    A: Teleconferencing

    B: Ground rules

    C: A set start and finish time for the meeting

    D: An agenda

Question 293: While carrying out the work described in your project communications plan, you go to great lengths to ensure that relevant information is disseminated to the correct stakeholders in the right way at the right time. As a senior project manager, you know that effective information distribution is a key factor in project success. This is because effective information distribution includes all of the following techniques except?

    A: Writing style

    B: Presentation techniques

    C: Issue log

    D: Choice of media

Question 294: You have decided to study for the PMP® credential and are currently learning the way in which the project life cycle can be described in terms of process groups associated with initiating, planning, executing, monitoring and controlling, and closing activities. You then move on to studying the ways in which successful communication occurs in a project. In order to demonstrate how much you have learned, you are able to describe to a colleague how some aspect of project communication occurs in different process groups. The Manage Communications process occurs within which PMBOK® Guide process group?

    A: Initiating

    B: Planning

    C: Executing

    D: Monitoring and Controlling

Question 295: You and your project team have been in negotiations with a potential supplier for several hours over an important contract that will deliver a large part of the one product required to complete your project. You and your team are getting frustrated at the slow rate of progress on the negotiations but know it is important that they are done thoroughly. How important is non-verbal communication to the negotiations?

    A: Very important

    B: Not very important

    C: Only important when the other party is silent

    D: Only important during negotiations over cost

Question 296: You have called a team member into your office to deal with unacceptable behavior towards other project team members. After the meeting you decide to follow up to make clear what was discussed. What is the best form of communication to use in this instance?

    A: Formal written

    B: Formal verbal

    C: Informal written

    D: Informal verbal

Question 297: Your project sponsor has asked you to present a detailed project update to some high-level stakeholders who are concerned that the project is not meeting its agreed timeframes, its agreed budget, nor delivering the quality the customer is expecting. What information and method would be BEST to use in this situation?

    A: A verbal presentation during a 10-minute meeting

    B: A summary milestone report tabled as an agenda item at their next scheduled meeting

    C: A PowerPoint presentation outlining the major issues, given in your office

    D: A detailed performance report in writing with an accompanying presentation and time for questions and answers

Question 298: You are attempting to communicate with various project stakeholders and, despite your best efforts, you find that the information that you send to them is misunderstood. Cultural differences and using unfamiliar technology are the main problems contributing to this lack of understanding. What is the best term to describe these characteristics?

    A: Decoding

    B: Feedback

    C: Noise

    D: Transmission

Question 299: You are actively monitoring and controlling the project communications according to your approved communications management plan and are seeking to generate work performance information about the effectiveness of your project communications. Which of the following would be least useful to you?

    A: Project communications

    B: Issue log

    C: Work performance data

    D: Change requests

Question 300: You are using historical data about your project to forecast an estimated future outcome in your project performance reporting. This is an example of what forecasting method?

    A: Budget forecasts

    B: Judgmental methods

    C: Econometric method

    D: Time series methods

Question 301: Your project team has just finished the first round of soliciting information from experts about what they think the forecasted future performance on your project will be using information supplied to them. You are currently assessing the information supplied anonymously by the respondents and plan to request a second round of opinions to use in your project forecasts. What forecasting method are you using?

    A: Judgmental method

    B: Causal method

    C: Earned value

    D: Econometric method

Question 302: Which of the following would you not expect to see in a detailed project performance report?

    A: Current status of risks and issues

    B: Staff performance reviews

    C: Forecasted project completion

    D: Summary of changes approved in the period

Question 303: Several of your stakeholders are raising issues with you, and you are documenting their issues in an issue log and providing feedback to the stakeholders about the status and any resolution of the issues. Furthermore, you are using the issue log as an input into a process because it provides a repository for what has already happened in the project and a platform for subsequent communication to be delivered. Which process are you involved in?

      A: Control Communications

      B: Manage Communications

      C: Plan Communications Management

      D: Monitor and Control Project Work

Question 304: A project manager should spend approximately how much of their time communicating to team members and stakeholders to effectively contribute to project success?

      A: 50%

      B: 5%

      C: 90%

      D: 70%

Question 305: Which of the following has been identified as one of the single biggest reasons for project success or failure?

      A: Enterprise environmental factors

      B: Financial accountability and accuracy

      C: Appropriate communication

      D: The nature of the working relationship between project sponsor and the project manager

Question 306: There are 36 communications channels on a project. How many stakeholders are there in the project?

      A: 6

      B: 36

      C: 18

      D: 9

Project Risk Management

Question 307: What is the best description of the objectives of the risk management work you will undertake on your project?

> **A:** Increase the probability and impact of positive events and decrease the probability and impact of negative events.
>
> **B:** Decrease the probability and impact of positive events and increase the probability and impact of negative events.
>
> **C:** Decrease the probability and impact of any risks occurring on the project.
>
> **D:** Assess the qualitative and quantitative probability and impact of positive and negative risk to the project.

Question 308: All of the following are characteristics of risks except?

> **A:** Risk is always in the future.
>
> **B:** Risk is an uncertain event or condition.
>
> **C:** If a risk occurs, it will have an effect on at least one project objective.
>
> **D:** Risk cannot be avoided.

Question 309: When completing your risk management plan you also decide to create a contingency plan. What is the main reason for creating a risk contingency plan?

> **A:** Unknown risks that cannot be managed proactively.
>
> **B:** To deal with known risks with a large uncertainty about the probability of occurrence.
>
> **C:** Unknown risks that have been identified in the risk management plan.
>
> **D:** Known risks that if they occur can have a larger-than-anticipated impact on your project.

Question 310: While completing your risk management plan you also decide to create a fallback plan. What is the main reason for creating a fallback plan?

> **A:** To deal with known risks with a large uncertainty about the probability of occurrence.
>
> **B:** Unknown risks that cannot be managed proactively.
>
> **C:** Unknown risks that have been identified in the risk management plan.
>
> **D:** Known risks that if they occur can have a larger-than-anticipated impact on your project.

Question 311: The willingness to accept varying degrees of risk is called what?

A: Risk tolerance

B: Risk acceptance

C: Risk planning

D: Risk analysis

Question 312: When should you begin risk management on a project?

A: When you are completing the monitoring and controlling.

B: Once project planning has commenced.

C: Once project execution has commenced.

D: As soon as a project is initiated or conceived.

Question 313: During a meeting to develop your risk management plan, a senior team member questions whether you have all the required inputs to develop a robust risk management plan that is appropriate for your project. Which of the following is not an input that you could use to complete this work successfully?

A: Risk management plan

B: Project charter

C: Stakeholder register

D: Project management plan

Question 314: You and your project team are currently involved in the process to plan your particular approach to risk management on your project and are using a variety of tools and techniques to assist you in producing the risk management plan. Which of the following is not a tool or technique used during the Plan Risk Management process?

A: Risk probability and impact assessment

B: Analytical techniques

C: Expert judgment

D: Meetings

Question 315: As part of your risk management planning, you develop a diagram showing the hierarchy of project risks arranged by risk category and subcategory. What is this diagram commonly called?

A: Risk assessment register

B: Risk breakdown structure

C: Probability and impact matrix

D: Risk register

Question 316: Your risk management planning session has produced definitions of risk probability and impact. These are used during which PMBOK® Guide process?

    A: Perform Quantitative Risk Analysis

    B: Identify Risks

    C: Perform Qualitative Risk Analysis

    D: Plan Risk Management

Question 317: Your team is carrying out the process of determining which risks may affect the project and documenting their characteristics. You are using a variety of tools and techniques, including documentation, reviews, information gathering techniques, checklist analysis, and SWOT analysis. What is the name of this process?

    A: Perform Qualitative Risk Analysis

    B: Identify Risks

    C: Perform Quantitative Risk analysis

    D: Plan Risk Management

Question 318: You are congratulating your team for the time and effort taken to develop the first iteration of your project risk register. You are now contemplating the many uses that your risk register will have in your project and the many different areas in which it can be used as an input into the work being done. Which of the following PMBOK® Guide processes does not use the risk register as an input?

    A: Control Risks

    B: Manage Stakeholder Engagement

    C: Plan Procurement Management

    D: Perform Qualitative Risk Analysis

Question 319: You and your team are in the process of identifying all potential uncertainty and risk on your project. You wish to ensure that your risk register is as comprehensive as possible; as such you are looking for as many relevant inputs as possible to assist you in this process. Which of the following is not an input into this process?

    A: Activity duration estimates

    B: Assumptions analysis

    C: Stakeholder register

    D: Activity cost estimates

Question 320: You are using your risk management plan to guide the work needed to identify both positive and negative risks on your project. Which of the following is not a tool or technique you would find useful to complete this work?

      A: Assumptions analysis

      B: Information gathering techniques

      C: Risk urgency assessment

      D: Diagramming techniques

Question 321: You and your team are completing the process of identifying risks on your project, and you wish to use a particular type of diagram to represent risk characteristics. All of the following are diagramming techniques used during the Identify Risks process except?

      A: Process flow chart

      B: Cause and effect diagram

      C: Pareto diagram

      D: Influence diagram

Question 322: Your team has successfully identified many categories of risks, and within each category they have identified specific risk events that may impact your project. You have documented all of this information in an initial list of identified risks as part of the iterative development of your risk register. At this early stage, this document will generally have all of the following information on it except?

      A: Cause

      B: Event

      C: Consequence

      D: Probability

Question 323: Your team is carrying out the process to identify the risks to the project and is identifying strengths and weaknesses of the organization by looking at the way these strengths offset threats and opportunities that may serve to overcome weaknesses. What technique are they using?

      A: SWOT analysis

      B: Expert judgment

      C: PERT analysis

      D: PEST analysis

CHAPTER 1 ▓ QUESTIONS

Question 324: As project manager on a project, you have begun the process of qualitatively assessing the probability and impact to risks that have been identified on your project. Which of the following is not an input you would find useful in completing this work?

> **A:** Project charter
>
> **B:** Risk management plan
>
> **C:** Risk register
>
> **D:** Scope baseline

Question 325: Your team is using the project risk register and has started a quantitative assessment of the risks. You tell your team that it is better to start with qualitative analysis first. What reasons do you give your team for this decision?

> **A:** Quantitative analysis takes the numerical values assigned during the qualitative process and adds a more intuitive interpretation of the risks.
>
> **B:** Qualitative analysis provides accurate numerical values based on probability and impact that can then be quantified.
>
> **C:** There is no particular reason why one should be done before the other. It is just the way your organizational processes require the process to be completed.
>
> **D:** Qualitative analysis provides a subjective and rapid means of prioritizing risks and indicating which risk can have quantitative analysis applied to them.

Question 326: Your team is using your risk register to prioritize risks for further analysis by assessing their probability of occurrence and impact. What PMBOK® Guide process best describes the work they are carrying out?

> **A:** Plan Risk Management
>
> **B:** Perform Quantitative Risk Analysis
>
> **C:** Identify Risks
>
> **D:** Perform Qualitative Risk Analysis

Question 327: While completing your assessment of the risks on your project, you begin to examine the ones with the greatest potential threat to your project. You are using a diagram to help you complete this task, and you are currently looking at the high priority risks for further analysis. What diagram would best help you?

> **A:** Probability and impact matrix
>
> **B:** Scatter diagram
>
> **C:** Pareto chart
>
> **D:** Risk register

83

Question 328: An important aspect of your qualitative risk analysis is determining the validity of the information you are using. What is this technique commonly called?

    A: Risk data quality assessment

    B: Assumption analysis

    C: Risk urgency assessment

    D: Risk categorization

Question 329: Your team is completing the process of numerically analyzing the effect of identified risks on your project objectives. Which PMBOK® Guide process best describes the work they are carrying out?

    A: Plan Risk Response

    B: Perform Qualitative Risk Analysis

    C: Perform Quantitative Risk Analysis

    D: Identify Risks

Question 330: After completing work to perform qualitative risk analysis on identified risks in your risk register, you have produced several updates to your risk register. Which of the following processes described in the PMBOK® Guide indirectly uses these updates?

    A: Identify Risks

    B: Project Integration Management

    C: Project Time Management

    D: Plan Risk Responses

Question 331: Three-point estimating is a commonly used technique for gathering and analyzing data. It is used in all of the following project areas except?

    A: Project risk management

    B: Project time management

    C: Project quality management

    D: Project cost management

Question 332: If a project has a 40% chance of achieving a $17,000 profit and a 60% chance of achieving a $20,000 loss, what is the expected monetary value of the project?

    A: -$3,000

    B: $37,000

    C: $5,200

    D: -$5,200

Question 333: If a project has a 65% chance of a $200,000 profit and a 35% chance of a $100,000 loss, what is the expected monetary value for the project?

  A: -$100,000

  B: $100,000

  C: $165,000

  D: $95,000

Question 334: If a risk event has a 80% chance of occurring, and if it does occur, the consequence will be a $10,000 cost to the project, what does -$8,000 represent to the project?

  A: Quantified risk

  B: Probabilistic risk assessment

  C: What-if analysis result

  D: Expected monetary value

Question 335: After completing your risk register and a quantitative assessment of the financial value of prioritized risks on your project, you have a dollar amount added to your project budget. What is this amount typically called?

  A: Contingent response strategy

  B: Management reserve

  C: Slush fund

  D: Contingency reserve

Question 336: Which of the following is not an example of a probability distribution?

  A: Normal distribution

  B: Obtuse distribution

  C: Triangular distribution

  D: Beta distribution

Question 337: Your team is completing an exercise to determine which risks have the greatest potential impact on your project. They are assessing the extent to which the uncertainty of each element of the project affects the risk being examined when all other uncertain elements are held at static baseline values. What is this technique commonly known as?

  A: Tornado diagram

  B: Expected monetary value analysis

  C: Sensitivity analysis

  D: Modeling and simulation

Question 338: You are currently performing risk analysis on a large and extremely complex project. Your project team decides that the most comprehensive way to approach the process of risk analysis is to examine all the possible outcomes using an iterative computer simulation process to model a range of variables taken from a probability distribution. What is this technique known as?

> **A:** Sensitivity analysis
>
> **B:** Expected monetary value analysis
>
> **C:** Monte Carlo analysis
>
> **D:** Ishikawa analysis

Question 339: You have documented and quantitatively assessed the risk to your project and the potential outcomes in a diagram to show the different outcomes of events should a particular probability occur, in order to determine the expected monetary value. What is this technique generally called?

> **A:** What-if scenario analysis
>
> **B:** Decision tree analysis
>
> **C:** Ishikawa diagram
>
> **D:** Tornado diagram

Question 340: Your team has completed the process of assessing and documenting risks that may occur on your project. What is the next step to complete?

> **A:** Identify risks.
>
> **B:** Control risks.
>
> **C:** Plan risk responses.
>
> **D:** Execute the project tasks.

Question 341: A project manager is faced with making a large decision about a risk that her project team has identified. The risk involves the design of a car component. It has been found that the weld of the component where the load-bearing flange is located will corrode in a high salt environment. If this takes place, the component may fail and injure the driver and passenger. The project team decides that the design of the component should be modified by using corrosion-resistant materials. This will eliminate the risk from consideration. What is this risk response technique called?

> **A:** Risk rejection
>
> **B:** Risk acceptance
>
> **C:** Risk avoidance
>
> **D:** Risk transference

Question 342: You are managing a project to build a large hydro dam for electrical power generation, which will be built over a known seismically active area. Your team decides to strengthen the core structure of the dam to better tolerate any earth movements that may occur. This is an example of what sort of risk response?

A: Accept

B: Transfer

C: Avoid

D: Mitigate

Question 343: You have decided to take out insurance on your project to cover your project financially if a risk occurs. This is an example of what sort of risk response?

A: Transference

B: Mitigation

C: Sharing

D: Avoidance

Question 344: All of the following are acceptable responses to positive risks except?

A: Accept

B: Mitigate

C: Enhance

D: Exploit

Question 345: You are about to tender for a large, multi-billion dollar infrastructure project, and your general manager has just announced a joint venture with another company to help with risk management. This is an example of what sort of risk response?

A: Sharing

B: Avoidance

C: Mitigation

D: Exploiting

Question 346: You and your project team have completed your risk register, including planned responses to identified risks. What is your next step?

A: Update the work breakdown structure.

B: Begin the Control Risks process.

C: Perform another iteration of the risk register.

D: Update your project sponsor on the planned risk responses.

Question 347: You have completed the final steps to develop a complete risk register with identified risks, a priority assessment, a qualitative assessment of all risks, a quantitative assessment of the top priority risks, and you have also identified appropriate risk responses for each risk. Which of the following is not an expected output from completing this work?

    A: Project document updates

    B: Project management plan updates

    C: Updates to the cost management plan

    D: Contingent response strategies

Question 348: Your project has been underway for 9 months when a major problem occurs that is not included in the risk register. What is your BEST course of action?

    A: Begin the process of evaluating the risk qualitatively, then quantitatively.

    B: Begin the process of evaluating the risk quantitatively, then qualitatively.

    C: Create a workaround.

    D: Contact your project sponsor.

Question 349: Despite your best efforts at anticipating and documenting all risk and uncertainty on your project, you have encountered a completely unforeseeable risk that will incur significant extra cost to your project. You decide to approach your project sponsor and ask for permission to get these extra funds from a pool of money that they control. What is this pool of money generally referred to as?

    A: Slush fund

    B: Contingency reserve

    C: Management reserve

    D: Control account

Question 350: The project you are working on is over halfway through, and you have begun to measure that price increases on the steel that you require for the project have gone 8% over your estimate for price increases over the timeframe of the project. As a result, you put in place a policy to procure all the remaining steel required for the project and pay for it to be stored in a warehouse instead of ordering the steel as you require it. This is an example of what?

    A: Contingent response strategy

    B: Mitigation

    C: Transference

    D: Exploiting

Question 351: You are using your risk management plan and your risk register to check if your assessment of risks is accurate, if there are any new risks, or if new information is available about existing risks. Which of the following inputs would not be of use to you to complete this work?

    A: Project management plan

    B: Quality control measurements

    C: Work performance reports

    D: Risk register

Question 352: You are conducting the process of implementing your risk response plans, tracking identified risks, monitoring residual risks, and identifying new risks. What is this PMBOK® Guide process called?

    A: Assess and Control Risks

    B: Risk Management

    C: Risk Assessment

    D: Control Risks

Question 353: During your regular monitoring of the risks identified on your project, you examine and document the effectiveness of risk responses in dealing with identified risks and their root causes. What technique are you using?

    A: Ishikawa analysis

    B: Risk audits

    C: Risk urgency assessment

    D: Trend analysis

Question 354: The project team members assigned responsibility for controlling risks on your project are doing a great job. Which of the following is not an expected output of the work they are completing?

    A: Project management plan updates

    B: Change requests

    C: Organizational Process Assets updates

    D: Work performance data

Project Procurement Management

Question 355: During the process of procurement management, the organization you work for can be all of the following except?

>   **A:** Buyer and seller of products or services
>
>   **B:** Seller of services
>
>   **C:** Insolvent
>
>   **D:** Buyer of products

Question 356: As part of your commitment to advancing the profession of project management you are tutoring candidates wishing to sit the PMP® examination. The session you are about to give is focused on the Project Procurement Management knowledge area in the PMBOK® Guide. What is the generally accepted correct sequence of processes in the Project Procurement Management knowledge area?

>   **A:** Plan Procurement Management, Conduct Procurements, Control Procurements, Close Procurements
>
>   **B:** Conduct Procurements, Plan Procurement Management, Control Procurements, Close Procurements
>
>   **C:** Plan Procurement Management, Conduct Procurements, Close Procurements, Control Procurements
>
>   **D:** Plan Procurement Management, Control Procurements, Conduct Procurements, Close Procurements

Question 357: You are carrying out the Contract Management and Change Control processes required to develop and administer contracts for you project. What is this PMBOK® Guide knowledge area called?

>   **A:** Plan Procurement Management
>
>   **B:** Close Procurements
>
>   **C:** Project Integration Management
>
>   **D:** Project Procurement Management

Question 358: All of the following are examples of legally binding agreements except?

>   **A:** Agreement
>
>   **B:** Subcontract
>
>   **C:** Organizational process assets
>
>   **D:** Purchase order

Question 359: You are just about to begin the process of procuring services from external providers and you think there may be a standard set of rules governing this process. Where would it be BEST to look for these rules?

> **A:** Lessons learned
>
> **B:** Organizational Process Assets
>
> **C:** The PMBOK® Guide
>
> **D:** Your organization's legal team

Question 360: You have completed the work described in the contract as per the required specifications but the customer is complaining that the product is not what they wanted. What is your BEST course of action?

> **A:** Ask your project sponsor to clarify the scope of the project.
>
> **B:** Restart the project and complete the work the way the customer wants it.
>
> **C:** Ask the customer to note their concerns in writing and present them to your project team at the next team meeting.
>
> **D:** Enter the Close Procurements process.

Question 361: Which of the following is not a term used to describe the buyer in a contract?

> **A:** Client
>
> **B:** Entrepreneur
>
> **C:** Service requestor
>
> **D:** Prime contractor

Question 362: Which of the following is not a term used to describe the seller in a contract?

> **A:** Service provider
>
> **B:** Vendor
>
> **C:** Dealer
>
> **D:** Contractor

Question 363: You and your project team are completing the process of producing your procurement management plan and want to make sure that you have completed a robust process and used all possible and appropriate inputs. Which of the following is not an input into the work to plan procurement management on your project?

> **A:** Requirements documentation
>
> **B:** Activity resource requirements
>
> **C:** Stakeholder register
>
> **D:** Make-or-buy decisions

Question 364: You are carrying out the procurement of services necessary for your project. After consulting with your Organizational Process Assets, specifically the procurement guidelines, which specify that you are to use the most commonly used contract type, you offer the seller what type of contract?

> **A:** Time and materials
>
> **B:** Firm-fixed-price
>
> **C:** Fixed-price-incentive-fee
>
> **D:** Cost-plus-incentive-fee

Question 365: You discover that there is a part of the project that contains some risk. Your strategy to deal with this risk is to subcontract the work to an outside supplier by using a firm-fixed-price contract. Which of the following must you do?

> **A:** You should assign a member of the project team to monitor the activity of the supplier to make sure that the supplier deals with the risk properly if it occurs.
>
> **B:** You should make every effort to make sure that the supplier is made aware of the risk after the contract is signed.
>
> **C:** You should make certain that the project team does not reveal the risk to the supplier until the contract is signed.
>
> **D:** You should make sure that the supplier understands the risk before the contract is signed.

Question 366: You are the project manager for a project that is well underway. You are using a contractor that has agreed to a fixed-price contract that calls for a single, lump sum payment on completion of the contract. The contractor's project manager contacts you and informs you that cash flow problems are making it difficult for the contractor to pay employees and subcontractors. The contractor then asks you for a partial payment for work accomplished to date. What is your best course of action?

> **A:** Make no payments to the contractor until all the work is completed as per the terms of the agreed contract.
>
> **B:** Negotiate a change to the contract to allow payments to the contractor.
>
> **C:** Pay for work accomplished to date.
>
> **D:** Start making partial payments to the contractor.

Question 367: Your organization is providing services to another organization as part of a project. Which of the following contract types would your organization most prefer to engage in to carry out the work?

> **A:** Fixed-price-incentive-fee contract
>
> **B:** Fixed-price with economic price adjustment
>
> **C:** Firm-fixed-price
>
> **D:** Cost-plus-incentive-fee

Question 368: Your project has begun with a planned series of iterations that will gradually define the scope of work required. You are negotiating with a potential supplier of services. What is the BEST form of contract to enter into?

    A: Fixed-price-incentive-fee

    B: Time and materials

    C: Cost-plus-fixed-fee

    D: Firm-fixed-price

Question 369: During your project there has been an unforeseen amount of work that requires urgent and immediate attention from an external contractor to ensure it does not adversely affect the project. What sort of contract for services is BEST to use in this instance?

    A: Fixed-price incentive fee

    B: Time and materials

    C: Cost-plus-fixed-fee

    D: Cost-plus-incentive-fee

Question 370: You are leading your team through the process of making procurement decisions and selecting the appropriate procurement documentation to use when procuring services from external contractors. Which of the following is not a form of procurement document?

    A: Request for fixed price contract (RFPC)

    B: Request for proposal (RFP)

    C: Request for quotation (RFQ)

    D: Request for information (RFI)

Question 371: Several procurement specialists on your team have completed the procurement management plan for your project. Which of the following is not an output you would expect from them?

    A: Source selection criteria

    B: Procurement statement of work

    C: Procurement management plan

    D: Project scope statement

Question 372: You are the project manager on a large project to develop a new customer information database for your organization. You are currently assessing the merits of developing key components of the required software in-house by your own development team compared to getting an external contractor to complete the work. What technique are you using?

> **A:** Risk-related contract decisions

> **B:** Make-or-buy analysis

> **C:** Source selection criteria

> **D:** Expert judgment

Question 373: You are letting your project team analyze responses received to some of your procurement documents and you are beginning the process of selecting the successful seller. Which of the following is not an example of selection criteria used to select sellers?

> **A:** Technical capability

> **B:** Make-or-buy decision

> **C:** Management approach

> **D:** Proprietary rights

Question 374: You are currently obtaining seller responses to an RFP you issued and, after assessing the responses, you expect to select a seller and award a contract for delivery for services on your project. What process are you carrying out?

> **A:** Close Procurements

> **B:** Plan Procurement Management

> **C:** Conduct Procurements

> **D:** Control Procurements

Question 375: You are carrying out the process of obtaining seller responses, selecting a seller, and an awarding a contract. You wish to make sure that you complete the process thoroughly and use any and all inputs that may be useful to you. Which of the following is not an input into the Conduct Procurements process?

> **A:** Procurement statement of work

> **B:** Source selection criteria

> **C:** Resource calendars

> **D:** Project management plan

Question 376: You have just finished preparation of an exhaustive RFP for your project and are about to send it out to potential service providers. Based on past acceptable performance, you decide to send the RFP to a small group of potential suppliers and not all of the suppliers who may be interested in providing a response. What technique are you using?

    A: Bidder conference

    B: Qualified seller list

    C: Procurement management plan

    D: Proposal evaluation technique

Question 377: After soliciting responses from prospective sellers, you are in the process of considering each seller's response against a set of criteria in order to determine who will be the seller selected to provide the required services. The process is giving a greater weight to previous experience in this type of work than it is giving to the price submitted. What technique are you using?

    A: Weighted average calculation

    B: Weighted criteria

    C: Expert judgment

    D: Procurement negotiations

Question 378: You are carrying out a bidder conference that is attended by five potential sellers of services to your project. You have spent a considerable amount of time explaining the statement of work and answering questions from the sellers at the bidder conference. During a break in the afternoon, one of the sellers approaches you and asks a question relating to the statement of work. What is your BEST course of action?

    A: Ask the seller to leave the room and remove him from the process.

    B: Refuse to provide an answer to the seller.

    C: Provide an answer to the seller.

    D: Explain to the seller that they should wait until the session begins again and then submit their question.

Question 379: You are in the process of ensuring that the seller you have engaged to provide a product for your project is meeting the contractual requirements expected of them. What PMBOK® Guide process are you carrying out?

    A: Conduct Procurements

    B: Control Procurements

    C: Close Procurements

    D: Plan Procurement Management

Question 380: As part of your project, you are looking to make sure that you complete the Control Procurements process properly in order to ensure that you are managing procurement relationships, monitoring contract performance, and making changes and corrections to contracts as appropriate. As part of this process, you want to make sure that you are using all the appropriate inputs. Which of the following processes does not provide an input into the work to control procurements?

    A: Control costs

    B: Monitor and Control Project Work

    C: Perform Integrated Change Control

    D: Direct and Manage Project Work

Question 381: As part of your project, you are looking to make sure that you complete the Control Procurements process properly in order to ensure that you are managing procurement relationships, monitoring contract performance, and making changes and corrections to contracts as appropriate. In order to do this process thoroughly, you have decided to review all the possible tools and techniques that you could use. All of the following are tools or techniques used in the Control Procurements process except?

    A: Inspections and audits

    B: Performance reporting

    C: Work performance information

    D: Claims administration

Question 382: You are the project manager on a large project that has been underway for five years. Your project has consistently reported a CPI of 1.2 and an SPI of 1.3. Delivery of the expected product of the project has been in accordance with the customer's expectations and you are beginning the process of closing the project. Your project team is confused about which process to complete first, the Close Procurements process or the Close Project process. What is your BEST advice to your project team?

    A: Complete the Close Project process first and then the Close Procurements process so that any final payments incurred by the Close Project process can be made.

    B: Only complete the Close Project process because it incorporates the Close Procurements process.

    C: Complete the Close Procurements process first because the contracts need to be closed before the project can be closed by the Close Project process.

    D: It does not matter which order they are completed in as long as they are both completed according to the organization's project management guidelines.

Question 383: You and your project team are completing the work required by contract with a buyer when your general manager decides to suddenly terminate the contract due to factors that are outside of your control. What is your BEST course of action?

      A: Contact the buyer and explain the situation to them.

      B: Begin the Close Procurements process.

      C: Review the WBS for errors in the scope of work.

      D: Explain to your manager that you are contractually bound to carry out the work.

Question 384: As part of closing out all contracts used on a project, you want to make sure that you demonstrate to your team what is considered best practice in this area and have available to you all of the potential tools and techniques that could assist. Which of the following is not a tool or technique used in the Close Procurements process?

      A: Bidder conferences

      B: Procurement negotiations

      C: Procurement audits

      D: Records management system

Question 385: You are completing the Close Procurements process and are informing sellers that the contract has been completed. What is the BEST way to do this?

      A: At the completion party

      B: In person

      C: Via email

      D: By written letter

Question 386: You have entered into an agreement with a seller to provide the goods you require for your project. You have selected to use a fixed-price-incentive-fee form of contract with a target cost of $100,000, a target price of $120,000, a ceiling price of $140,000, with a sharing ratio of 80/20 to the buyer. What is your point of total assumption?

      A: $125,000

      B: $140,000

      C: $120,000

      D: $130,000

Project Stakeholder Management

Question 387: You are putting together your stakeholder management plan and have identified the need to gather information about all of the different project stakeholders as soon as possible. This recognizes that the ability of stakeholders to influence the project is greatest at which point in the project?

      A: During the project execution.

      B: At the close of the project.

      C: At the beginning of the project.

      D: It is equal throughout a project.

Question 388: You are compiling a register of all people, groups, and organizations that can potentially and actually be affected by the project. What is the collective term for this group?

      A: Sponsor

      B: Customers

      C: Team members

      D: Stakeholders

Question 389: During work to initiate your project you have begun to identify stakeholders and gather information about them to allow you to successfully manage their expectations. All of the following are stakeholder attributes you should analyze as part of this work to identify stakeholders except?

      A: Their interest in the project.

      B: Their expectations of the project.

      C: Their influence on the project.

      D: Their personal conflict resolution style.

Question 390: During work to initiate your project you have begun to identify stakeholders and gather information about them to allow you to successfully manage their expectations. Which of the following is not an input you would use to complete this work?

      A: Procurement documents

      B: Project charter

      C: Stakeholder register

      D: Lessons learned

Question 391: With the help of your project team, you identify all potential project stakeholders and information about them. You then interview all of the stakeholders you have identified in an effort to learn more about their interaction with your project and also to gain knowledge of any other stakeholders you may not be aware of. After completing this process, you then identify the potential impact or support each stakeholder could generate. Finally, you assess how the key stakeholders are likely to react in various situations so you can plan for this. What are you carrying out?

A: Stakeholder management strategy

B: Stakeholder analysis

C: Stakeholder register assimilation

D: Stakeholder communications analysis

Question 392: You are showing your team the relative interest and power each identified stakeholder has in your project. What is the BEST way to show this information?

A: Salience model

B: Control chart

C: Stakeholder register template

D: Power/interest grid

Question 393: You have just taken over a project that has been underway for 8 months. The project is performing well and is currently reporting a CPI of 1.2 and an EAC of $1.2 m. As part of your familiarization process, you want to understand who the stakeholders on the project are. Where would you find this information?

A: Stakeholder management strategy

B: Organizational process assets

C: Stakeholder register

D: Email distribution list

Question 394: You have just taken over a project that is nearing the end of its life cycle. Shortly after taking control of the project you note that a particular stakeholder is having a negative impact on the project. You decide that this presents an unacceptable risk to the project and look for a way to manage the stakeholder. Which document will you look for to help you do this?

A: Stakeholder analysis matrix

B: Stakeholder analysis

C: Stakeholder register

D: Stakeholder management appropriation register

Question 395: After considerable effort involving your project team members and experts with experience in communications, you have developed your project communications management plan. This can now be used as an input into which of the following PMBOK® Guide processes?

    A: Estimate Costs

    B: Plan Quality Management

    C: Manage Stakeholder Engagement

    D: Close Project or Phase

Question 396: You are completing the process of communication and working with stakeholders to meet their needs and addressing issues as they occur. Which process are you completing?

    A: Stakeholder Analysis

    B: Manage Communications

    C: Manage Stakeholder Engagement

    D: Control Communications

Question 397: Your project is halfway through its expected duration and has a CPI of 1.3 and an SPI of 1.2. Your project sponsor has told you during a meeting that in her eyes the project is a failure because of the feedback she has been getting from important stakeholders on the project. You are surprised at this because the project is performing well financially and is ahead of schedule and you are sure the quality of the work you are completing is of a high standard and meets customer requirements. As the meeting closes, your project sponsor asks what you intend to do about the situation. Your BEST response would be what?

    A: Revisit the manage stakeholder expectation process in your communications management plan.

    B: Quit the project.

    C: Say nothing.

    D: Send out an e-mail to all stakeholders telling them how great the project is performing financially and time-wise.

Question 398: What is your primary goal in managing and identifying stakeholder expectations?

    A: Your primary goal in identifying and managing stakeholder expectations is to be able to introduce key stakeholders to each other so they can exchange project information.

    B: Your primary goal in identifying and managing stakeholder expectations is to be able to contact stakeholders when you need to send project communications.

C: Your primary goal in identifying and managing stakeholder expectations is to either get stakeholders to support your project or at least not to oppose it.

D: Your primary goal in identifying and managing stakeholder expectations is to be able to determine which of the stakeholders can be most easily influenced and which will require a greater amount of effort.

Question 399: You and your project team are systematically gathering and analyzing quantitative and qualitative information to determine which stakeholder's interests should be taken into account throughout the project. You have identified the interests, expectations, and influence of individual stakeholders and related to them the purpose of the project. What tool or technique are you using?

A: Meetings

B: Expert judgment

C: Information gathering techniques

D: Stakeholder analysis

Question 400: You are using a classification model for stakeholder analysis that describes classes of stakeholders based on their power, urgency, and legitimacy. What is the name of this particular model of stakeholder analysis?

A: Pareto chart

B: Power/interest grid

C: Influence/impact grid

D: Salience model

Question 401: As part of your analysis of stakeholder engagement, you have classified each stakeholder as either being unaware, resistant, neutral, supportive, or leading when it comes to the level of their engagement with the project. This is an example of what sort of technique?

A: Stakeholder analysis

B: Information gathering technique

C: Analytical technique

D: Expert judgment

Question 402: As a senior project manager on a complex project with many stakeholders, you are consistently having to coordinate and harmonize stakeholders towards supporting the project and accomplishing the project objectives. In order to do this, you are using your skills to facilitate consensus, influence people, negotiate agreements, and modify organizational behavior to accept the project outcomes. These are examples of what?

>   **A:** Information gathering techniques

>   **B:** Interpersonal skills

>   **C:** Communication methods

>   **D:** Management skills

Question 403: You are managing a complex project with many stakeholders, each with their own interest in the project. You have begun the process of monitoring overall project stakeholder relationships and adjusting your stakeholder expectation management strategies and plans for engaging stakeholders to suit the changing project circumstances. Your goal is to increase the efficiency and effectiveness of stakeholder engagement activity. What process are you are engaged in?

>   **A:** Manage Stakeholder Engagement

>   **B:** Control Stakeholder Engagement

>   **C:** Control Communications

>   **D:** Manage Communications

Question 404: While controlling stakeholder engagement on your project, you are generating a number of updates relating to the state of project stakeholder relationships and their level of engagement and satisfaction with your project. Which of the following is not an Organizational Process Asset that would be updated as a result of this process?

>   **A:** Issue log

>   **B:** Project records

>   **C:** Project presentations

>   **D:** Stakeholder notifications

Professional Ethics

Question 405: A colleague of yours, who was your mentor in your earlier career, still claims to have the PMP® credential but you know that it expired several years ago. What should you do FIRST?

>   **A:** Let your manager know and let them deal with it.

>   **B:** Report your colleague to PMI.

C: Approach your colleague and ask them to remove any reference to the credential.

D: Do nothing as it does not affect your colleague's work performance.

Question 406: A project is nearing the end and is reporting a CPI of 1.01 and a SPI of 1.3. The project manager has been reassigned to another more urgent project, and you have been brought in to close the project. While reviewing the financial accounts for the project, you discover that the previous project manager made a large payment that was not approved in accordance with the policies of your company. What is the BEST thing you can do?

A: Notify the project sponsor.

B: Do nothing as the project has come in under budget.

C: Confront the previous project manager and ask him to explain.

D: Carry on as if nothing had happened.

Question 407: The project administrator working for you on the project does not have the level of skills you assumed he had. What is your BEST course of action?

A: Assign him lower-level tasks and bring in another more qualified person.

B: Do nothing; he will learn on the job.

C: Assign the project administrator to another project.

D: Organize training for him.

Question 408: You and your project administrator have been working on a detailed project progress report to present to high-level stakeholders. You leave it up to the project administrator to complete the report, and he e-mails it to you on the day of the meeting. You are having a busy day and don't get a chance to read the report, but as you walk into the meeting you notice some large errors in the financial reporting section of the report. What is your BEST course of action?

A: Get the project administrator to appear before the stakeholders to explain the mistakes.

B: Give the report to the stakeholders and point out the project administrators errors.

C: Give the report in the meeting and accept the blame personally for any errors.

D: Reschedule the meeting for another time to give you the chance to fix the errors.

Question 409: You are completing a large infrastructure project in a foreign country. The government officials of the country are extremely grateful for the work you are doing and one of them sends a large cash payment to you to thank you and your team for the work they have done. What should you do?

> **A:** Gratefully accept the payment and send a thank you card to the donor.
>
> **B:** Accept the payment and divide it up among team members.
>
> **C:** Refuse the payment.
>
> **D:** Ask the government official if you can have a car instead of cash.

Question 410: You are currently preparing monthly status reports for your project and you are planning on reporting that the project has an SPI of 1.02 and a CPI of .83. Your project sponsor approaches you and says that she has been given a directive by the CEO of the company to report only positive figures or else he is afraid the shareholders in the company will demand changes to the organization. You are confident that the next month's status report will show a CPI greater than 1. What should you do?

> **A:** Explain to your project sponsor the reasons why you believe the project reporting should be honest.
>
> **B:** Report the CPI based on what you believe next months figures will be.
>
> **C:** Resign from the project.
>
> **D:** Report the project sponsor's behavior to the CEO.

Question 411: You are the project manager for a large project that has been completed on time and on budget. The customer and all of the stakeholders are very pleased with the results. As a direct result of the successful completion of the project, your project sponsor approves a bonus of $10,000 to you. There are twelve members on your project team. However, one of the people on the project team has been a very low contributor to the project; the other eleven have all been above standard. What should you do with the money?

> **A:** Divide the money equally among all the team members.
>
> **B:** Ask the team members how they would divide the money.
>
> **C:** Keep the money yourself; you deserve it, and the manager gave it to you.
>
> **D:** Divide the money equally among the team members except for the substandard team member.

Question 412: You are the project manager for a large software implementation project that is nearing completion when you discover that one of your technicians has been taking shortcuts with the code being written and it is below the standard required in the technical specification. You and a senior team member review the code and form the opinion that it will probably not affect the functionality of the final software product. What is your NEXT course of action?

> **A:** Carry on as planned and submit a change request.
>
> **B:** Stop the project and start again, this time writing the code as per the specification.
>
> **C:** Record the discrepancy, inform the customer, and look for ways to ensure the project won't be affected.
>
> **D:** Ignore the problem.

Question 413: You are the project manager for a project that has high visibility, and your project sponsor wants you to prepare a presentation for her to present at a conference. Most of the material in the presentation will be facts that are the results of your project. Your sponsor intends to present the material under her own name, and your name will not appear. What is your BEST course of action?

> **A:** Do the work as you were told by your manager.
>
> **B:** Explain to the sponsor that the correct thing to do is to acknowledge all authors and contributors to the work and, if necessary, refuse to work on the presentation unless you are listed as a co-author.
>
> **C:** Present your own presentation.
>
> **D:** Meet with your project sponsor's manager and discuss the problem.

Question 414: You are working in a foreign country delivering a reconstruction project after a large natural disaster. It is normal in this country for government officials to request bribes to assist with processing the consents you require. During a meeting with a government official, he mentions that if you pay a $500 bribe you can have the consent you require tomorrow. What is your BEST course of action?

> **A:** Pay the $500 out of your own pocket.
>
> **B:** Refuse to pay the bribe.
>
> **C:** Ask the official for an invoice so the payment can be made by the project.
>
> **D:** Report the official to his manager.

Question 415: You are working on a project to construct a new water treatment plant and are waiting on consents required from the government before you can proceed with the work. During a meeting with a government employee to discuss the required consent, the employee mentions that the consent can be processed faster if you are willing to pay a processing fee. What is your BEST course of action?

A: Walk out of the meeting and notify your project sponsor.

B: Explain that you are not permitted to pay bribes.

C: Pay the fee if your project budget has allowed for it.

D: Ask the employee if he will accept goods instead of cash so you can hide the transaction better.

Question 416: You have just completed the selection of a preferred seller for an upcoming project and have scheduled a meeting in 2 days to finalize the contract when your manager informs you that due to current economic conditions the project will now probably not be going ahead but the definite answer will be provided by the CEO in 3 days. What is your BEST course of action?

A: Go ahead with the meeting and complete the negotiations, knowing you can use the termination clause to end it.

B: Postpone the meeting until the fate of the project is clear.

C: Go ahead with the meeting, but make an excuse to not sign the contract.

D: Cancel the meeting and let the other party know why.

CHAPTER 2

Answers

Foundational Concepts

Question 1: Your team is confused because they use terminology and words in project communications that appear to have interchangeable meanings, but other teams treat these terms as though they have specific, unique meanings. How can your team find out what the terms mean?

> **The correct answer is B.**

> **A:** This answer is incorrect because you are trying to get a standardized terminology and the sponsor may have their own words. The promotion of the profession of project management is part of your professional responsibilities and using internationally recognized and standardized publications like the PMBOK® Guide is an example of this.

> **B:** The promotion of the profession of project management is part of your professional responsibilities and using internationally recognized and standardized publications like the PMBOK® Guide is an example of this.

> **C:** This answer is incorrect because you are trying to get a standardized terminology and having the team develop a terminology in this way does not mean it will necessarily align with international best practice. The promotion of the profession of project management is part of your professional responsibilities and using internationally recognized and standardized publications like the PMBOK® Guide is an example of this.

> **D:** This answer is incorrect because you are trying to get a standardized terminology and using an internationally recognized and standardized publication like the PMBOK® Guide is the best way to achieve this.

© Sean Whitaker 2016
S. Whitaker, *PMP® Examination Practice Questions*, DOI 10.1007/978-1-4842-1883-9_2

Question 2: You are delivering an introduction to a project management training session to new team members. One team member appears confused about the exact definition of a *project*. What is the BEST definition of a project?
The correct answer is A.

> **A:** A project is differentiated from operational activity by the fact that it is designed to deliver a unique product within a specified time period whereas operational work is ongoing and repetitive.

> **B:** This answer is not correct because there are projects and operational activities that are constrained by finances and time. It must also have a unique product, service, or result to be a project.

> **C:** This answer is not correct because it does not refer to the temporal nature of the work being completed.

> **D:** This answer is not correct because it describes operational work that is repetitive and ongoing.

Question 3: Your team seems confused about whether the work they are doing meets the definition of a project. To help them understand the difference between projectized and operational work you give them the following examples. Which of the following is not an example of a project?
The correct answer is C.

> **A:** Designing a new software solution is an example of a project because it has a defined beginning and end, and a unique deliverable.

> **B:** Building a new house is an example of a project because it has a defined time and delivers a unique product, service, or result.

> **C:** Achieving 3% growth on last year's sales figures is an operational goal in line with on-going repetitive company activity and as such it is not an example of a project.

> **D:** Implementing a new business process is an example of a project because it has a defined beginning and end, and a unique deliverable.

Question 4: You are planning to sit the PMP® examination and as part of your study are referring to the PMBOK® Guide for help in defining the project process groups. Which of the following is not one of the five process groups in the PMBOK® Guide?
The correct answer is B.

> **A:** Closing is one of the five PMBOK® Guide process groups.

> **B:** Checking is not the correct answer because it is not the right term. You may have thought this described the Monitoring and Controlling process group.

> **C:** Initiating is one of the five PMBOK® Guide process groups.

> **D:** Executing is one of the five PMBOK® Guide process groups.

Question 5: You are the project manager on a project to develop a new piece of customer management software for an external client. Through your approved change control process you are considering a request to alter the scope of the project. While considering the impact of the request on the project scope, you must also consider the impact on other areas of the project such as quality, schedule, budget, and risk. These other areas that you are considering represent what to the project?

The correct answer is B.

> **A:** Opportunities is not correct because opportunities are the opposite of constraints.

> **B:** Constraints is correct because central to any successful project management is an awareness that a project manager must balance competing constraints on the project. A change in one area can and usually does also mean a potential change in another area.

> **C:** Constrictions is not correct because the correct terminology is constraint, not constriction.

> **D:** Risks is not correct because risks refer to any areas of positive or negative uncertainty on the project.

Question 6: The process of continuously updating, improving, and detailing a project management plan, or parts of a project management plan, as more specific information becomes available is known as what?

The correct answer is D.

> **A:** Iterative expectation management is not correct because it is not a term referenced within the PMBOK® Guide.

> **B:** Project life cycle is not correct because it refers to the entire project life cycle, which is subject to progressive elaboration.

> **C:** Continuous improvement is not correct because it is a concept from the project quality management processes that seeks to improve all aspects of project quality.

> **D:** Progressive elaboration is correct because very rarely will you encounter a project where every detail is known at the beginning of a project and there are no changes to the project. It is typical for a project management plan to be iterative in response to this potential for change. The process of knowing more detail as the project develops is known as progressive elaboration.

Question 7: While delivering a presentation to senior management on the ways in which portfolio management can help your organization achieve strategic success you realize that not everyone in the room understands what portfolio management is. Portfolio management is BEST defined as what?
The correct answer is B.

> **A:** A group of projects managed by a project director is not correct because a project director can manage projects, programs, or portfolios.

> **B:** This answer is correct because portfolio management is typically used by more mature companies to align projects with their strategic aspirations in order to increase the chances of project success and of meeting strategic goals.

> **C:** A group of related projects managed in a coordinated way is not correct because a group of projects managed in a related way is referred to as a program.

> **D:** A collection of projects relating to a single business unit within an organization is not correct because they may be managed as individual projects or a program.

Question 8: A group of projects that must be managed in a coordinated manner to ensure that common goals and potential resource conflicts are managed effectively is known as what?
The correct answer is A.

> **A:** Program is correct because a program is a group of projects that are interrelated in some way. A project may be part of a program, but a program will always have projects.

> **B:** Portfolio is not correct because a portfolio describes all projects that an organization is undertaking and they may not be related in some way.

> **C:** PMO is incorrect because a project management office (PMO) describes the center for excellence in project management for an organization.

> **D:** Life cycle is not correct because a life cycle is a concept describing either a project or product from inception to completion.

Question 9: The CEO of your organization is considering the strategic reasons the company has for approving your project proposal. At times he seems confused about the definition of *strategic consideration*. Which of the following is not a strategic consideration for authorizing a project?
The correct answer is B.

> **A:** The chance to achieve a strategic opportunity is a clear strategic consideration for authorizing a project.

> **B:** Return on investment is not a strategic consideration. It is a method of calculating whether a project should proceed from a financial rather than a strategic point of view.

> **C:** Customer demand is a strategic consideration because it is a forecast of what the customer will want in the future and the company's strategic goals should include the desire to fulfill this demand.

> **D:** Market demand is a strategic consideration because it is a forecast of how the market will be behaving in the future and the company's strategic goals should include the desire to fulfill this demand.

Question 10: The team, or function, assigned responsibility for the centralized and coordinated management of projects within an organization is known as what?
The correct answer is C.

> **A:** Project headquarters is not correct. Although the term may be used by some organizations, it is not part of the standardized terminology offered by the PMBOK® Guide.

> **B:** Although sometimes the acronym PMO does stand for program management office, it is more commonly used to refer to a project management office, which is the most correct answer in this instance.

> **C:** A project management office takes responsibility for providing organization-wide project management support functions, including common standards, templates, and processes. It is also directly responsible for project delivery.

> **D:** A war room is a specific meeting room for project team members to be co-located and focus on doing the project work.

CHAPTER 2 ▓ ANSWERS

Question 11: Your organization has employed a person to head the PMO. During your first meeting with her, you discuss the extent of her roles and responsibilities to fully explain what tasks she will be responsible for and those she won't be responsible for. Which of the following is not a primary function of a project management office?

The correct answer is A.

> **A:** A PMO provides high-level support across several projects. It does not provide lower-level detail to a single project but instead provides a rolled-up summary report of the project.

> **B:** A clear role of a mature PMO is to oversee and manage shared resources across several projects.

> **C:** A role of a PMO is to develop and improve an organization's project management methodology.

> **D:** One very clear role of any sort of PMO is to ensure that communication across projects is done effectively.

Question 12: All of the following are points where projects can intersect with operational activity during the product life cycle except?

The correct answer is B.

> **A:** The project life cycle and the product life cycle certainly do intersect during the development of a new product, because it is a project.

> **B:** Notice that this question uses the product life cycle, not the project life cycle. You will need to look out for this style of question and make sure you read it properly. The product life cycle covers all aspects of the product from inception, design, and manufacture to end of life, recycling, and obsolescence. Monitoring and Controlling is one of the five process groups.

> **C:** Improvements in operations can be delivered by defining them as a project, and as such projects do intersect with operational activities at this point.

> **D:** During closeout phases, the deliverable is handed over to operations, and as such there is a clear intersection between the project and operational activities.

Question 13: What is the best description of the relationship between project management and organizational strategy?

The correct answer is D.

> **A:** Organizational strategy will not operate at a level that influences the appointment of the project manager.

> **B:** Organizational strategy does not directly link to project governance.

112

C: Organizational strategy and project management do interact because project management as seen as a strategic enabler for organizations.

D: Successful projects enable organizations to deliver their strategic goals.

Question 14: Your team seems confused about roles and responsibilities in the project that you are leading. They are particularly confused about your role as project manager. How would you explain the primary purpose of your role?
The correct answer is C.

A: While a project manager does have responsibility for controlling the budget in most instances, this is not the best description offered from the available answers.

B: A project team member would be responsible for delivery of the technical tasks.

C: The project manager is the person vested with the authority by the performing organization to achieve the objectives of the project.

D: A program manager is responsible for sharing resources among projects.

Question 15: While using the PMBOK® Guide to help you define and carry out processes on your project you notice that a very common input into nearly all the processes is enterprise environmental factors. Which of the following examples would not be considered an enterprise environmental factor?
The correct answer is C.

A: Government standards and industry regulations are a great example of enterprise environmental factors because they can affect a project.

B: The political climate that a project operates in is an enterprise environmental factor.

C: Net present value of investment is a tool for project selection.

D: Project management information systems are an example of Organizational Process Assets, not enterprise environmental factors.

Question 16: You have volunteered your time to help your organization's PMO carry out an assessment of your organization using the OPM3 tool. What does OPM3 measure?
The correct answer is D.

A: The interdependency of projects within a program of work is an example of an organization's program management, not OPM3.

B: An assessment of the level of variance between project management best practices and the actual application of these practices would be part of an assessment of project management maturity, but it is not the best description of OPM3.

C: The ability of a project manager to successfully deliver a project is an example of a individual project manager's level of professional development and not OPM3.

D: OPM3 stands for Organizational Project Management Maturity Model, and part of the model is used to assess where on a scale an organization sits in relation to its adoption and application of project management practices.

Question 17: The internal and external environmental factors that surround and influence, and sometimes constrain, a project are known as what?
The correct answer is D.

A-C: Theses answers are not correct because they are made-up terms and they are not terms referenced within the PMBOK® Guide.

D: Enterprise environmental factors are a constant input into many of the processes. They can be thought of as the environment in which the project must operate and by which it will be influenced.

Question 18: The collection of generally sequential and sometimes overlapping project phases differentiated by a distinct work focus is known as what?
The correct answer is D.

A: The project management information system is an example of an Organizational Process Asset and does not refer to a collection of overlapping phases.

B: A project management methodology is a prescribed and standardized approach to project management and does not describe overlapping project phases.

C: A project management office is the center of excellence for project management within an organization and does not refer to a collection of overlapping phases.

D: Knowing the project life cycle and how projects and project management fit gives you context and provides a basic framework for managing a project, regardless of the specific work involved. Do not get this confused with PRODUCT life cycle.

Question 19: All of the following are basic characteristics of the project life cycle except?
The correct answer is B.

A: Closing the project is the final step in the project life cycle.

B: The generic level of the project life cycle features four key characteristics of starting the project, organizing and preparing, carrying out the project work, and closing the project. Checking the project is part of the Shewhart and Deming plan-do-check-act cycle, which elaborates more on a specific part of the project life cycle.

C: Starting the project is the first step in the project life cycle.

D: Carrying out the project work is a characteristic of the project life cycle.

Question 20: Divisions within a project where extra control is needed to effectively manage the completion of a major deliverable are commonly known as what?
The correct answer is A.

A: You may decide to initiate phases in a project due to the size, complexity, or presence of defined major deliverables. Breaking such projects down into phases gives a greater level of control.

B: Stage gate may be a common term but it is not the term used in the standardized terminology offered by the PMBOK® Guide.

C: Decision trees are ways of assessing quantifiable risk and do not refer to divisions within a project.

D: Sub-projects is an informal term used to describe smaller subsets of work but it does not refer to divisions in the project.

Question 21: You are explaining to your project sponsor that the best approach to managing your project is a phase-to-phase relationship. Which of the following is not an example of a phase-to-phase relationship?
The correct answer is D.

A: Sequential projects are an example of a phase-to-phase relationship because each sequence forms a distinct phase.

B: Overlapping is an example of a phase-to-phase relationship and refers to the way in which the end of one phase may overlap with the beginning of another phase.

C: Iterative is an example of a phase-to-phase relationship because they can be repeated as necessary before moving on to the next phase.

D: The three types of phase-to-phase relationships are overlapping, iterative, and sequential. Progressive is not one of these.

Question 22: You are the project manager working in an organization where the functional manager, to whom some of your staff answer when not working on your project, controls the project budget and resource availability. This type of organization is commonly referred to as what?
The correct answer is D.

A: In a projectized structure, the project manager has full responsibility and authority.

B: In a strong matrix, the project manager, not the functional manager, has the most power.

C: The question refers to some staff working for you, implying there are other staff from other functional areas working for you, and as such it indicates a matrix form of organization, specifically a weak matrix.

D: This situation describes a matrix organization where the functional manager retains most of the power. Therefore, it is a weak matrix, reflecting the small amount of power the project manager has to influence resources and budget on the project.

Question 23: You work in an organization where staff members are grouped according to their specialty, such as production, engineering, and accounting, and projects are generally undertaken within these respective groupings. What is this type of organizational structure known as?
The correct answer is D.

A: In a projectized structure, the project manager has full responsibility and authority.

B: A weak matrix is a matrix organization where the project manager has less power than a functional manager but still has some.

C: A strong matrix is a matrix organization where the project manager has more power than the functional manager.

D: This situation describes an organization divided into its functional responsibilities. A project manager often has to deal with staff and resources from different areas across the organization that are ultimately controlled by the functional manager. As such, the project manager has little or no power in this type of organization.

Question 24: All of the following are examples of Organizational Process Assets that can assist your project except?
The correct answer is A.

A: Government regulations are an example of enterprise environmental factors. The other three are examples of Organizational Process Assets, which belong to the company, are the property of the company, and reflect the organizational culture.

B: Lessons learned are an example of Organizational Process Assets because they are owned by the organization and can be used to assist projects.

C: Any sort of templates are an example of Organizational Process Assets because they are owned by the organization and can be used to assist projects.

D: Configuration management knowledgebases are an example of Organizational Process Assets because they are owned by the organization and can be used to assist projects.

Question 25: The process of determining which of the PMBOK® Guide processes are appropriate to use on your project and the appropriate degree of rigor to be applied in any given project is known as what?
The correct answer is C.

> **A:** Customizing may generally describe the process of tailoring but it is not the terminology offered in the PMBOK® Guide.

> **B:** Taking a prudent view when deciding which processes, tools, and techniques are appropriate would be correct but tailoring is the term used to describe the process of doing this.

> **C:** The processes described in the PMBOK® Guide are not to be universally applied to every project. Each project is different. It is the responsibility of the project manager and project team to determine which processes are appropriate and how rigorously they should be applied to any project depending on its size, complexity, and impact.

> **D:** Standardization is not correct because every project is different.

Question 26: The process group consisting of those processes performed to define a new project or a new phase of an existing project by obtaining authorization to start the project or phase is known as what?
The correct answer is C.

> **A:** The Closing process closes the project.

> **B:** The Executing process carries out the work planned.

> **C:** The Initiating process group is always the first performed in any project or phase of a project. It is the process group that formally establishes the project.

> **D:** The Planning process builds on the work done during the initiating process.

Question 27: You are completing the work defined in the project management plan to satisfy the project specifications. Which process group would your activities fall under?
The correct answer is D.

> **A:** The Monitoring and Controlling process checks that the work being done matches what was planned and manages any requested changes.

> **B:** The Planning process builds on the work done during the initiating process.

> **C:** The Initiating process group is always the first performed in any project or phase of a project. It is the process group that formally establishes the project.

> **D:** The Executing process group consists of those processes that complete the work defined in the project management plan.

Question 28: Your team members are not aware of the differences between a framework, such as the PMBOK® Guide, and a methodology, such as Kanban or Lean. How would you best explain this?

The correct answer is A.

> **A:** A framework is an international standard of best practices and it to be used as a toolbox from which you choose processes, tools, and techniques to help you deliver projects successfully. A methodology has already taken the processes, tools, and techniques and developed them into a standardized approach to managing projects in a certain way.

> **B:** This answer is incorrect because a framework does not prescribe how a project should be delivered whereas a methodology is prescriptive. This answer has presented the defintion of the terms in reverse order.

> **C:** This answer is incorrect because a framework is not just used during the planning phase of a project and a methodology during the execution phase. Frameworks can be used to develop methodolgies to be used at any stage in a project life cycle.

> **D:** This answer is incorrect because there is a difference between the two terms. It is important that you understand that a framework is a non-prescriptive collection of best practices, while a methodology is a specific set of processes, tools, and techniques taken from the framework.

Question 29: You have been asked to lead a project to improve the operations of a major company. The sponsor has requested you to apply Lean principles to facilitate the improvement program. Which of the following is not a principle of Lean?

The correct answer is D.

> **A:** Seeking perfection, particularly through Kaizen or continous improvement, is a key principle of a Lean appproach to managing projects.

> **B:** Identifying the value-add, especially as defined by the customer, is a foundational principle of a Lean approach.

> **C:** By eliminating waste, seeking perfection, and identifying the value add activities, you are creating an incredibly efficient environment - allowing value to be delivered through each activity you action.

> **D:** Reducing the team size is not one of the key principles behind Lean. This may help if the team has identified waste associated with the team size, but it is not one of the principles.

Question 30: What does *eliminating waste* refer to under the practice of applying Lean? **The correct answer is D.**

> **A:** Not having project meetings could be an example of waste that could be eliminated, but this answer does not explain the concept of eliminating waste.

> **B:** Avoiding documentation could be an example of waste that could be eliminated, but this answer does not explain the concept of eliminating waste.

> **C:** Keeping a clear work area is not a practice usually associated with Lean. It is more of a Health and Safety matter.

> **D:** Eliminating waste is the act of reducing or minimizing any unnecessary part of a process. This can include waiting times, meetings, documentation, or duplicated activities. If a process can be completed without a specific component, and the result still provides the value that is required/specified, then it is better that component to be removed.

Question 31: You are working through the planning phase for a project that will improve the production output of your employer's automotive factory by 7.5%. As part of your approach to managing the engagement of your stakeholders, you are educating them on the benefits of Lean. What are the key benefits realized from applying Lean practices?
The correct answer is A.

> **A:** By applying the practices of Lean to your project or product, your processes will be more efficient. Efficient processes are free from waste. Waste slows progress and results in unnecessary costs.

> **B:** This answer is incorrect because reducing duration, not increasing it, is a key benefit of applying Lean practices.

> **C:** This answer is incorrect because both answers are the opposite of reducing duration and minimizing costs, which are key benefits realized from applying Lean practices.

> **D:** This answer is incorrect because maximized costs is not a key benefit from applying Lean practicies.

Question 32: Delays, duplication, over-production, and errors are all forms of what? **The correct answer is B.**

> **A:** WIP (work in progress) can be considered another form of waste, along with the examples listed in the question.

> **B:** Delays, duplication, over-production, and errors are considered forms of waste because they do not add value to the project or the client, and result in unnecessary spending.

> **C:** Risks can include the potential for waste activities to occur in a process, project, or product.
>
> **D:** The items listed could be considered issues, but waste is the more correct answer. Issues could include waste activities slowing progress, reducing efficiency, and increasing costs.

Project Integration Management

Question 33: You are in the process of developing your project closure checklist and selecting those items and actions that need to be completed to ensure your project is closed properly. A team member asks to help you do this work and asks how you know a project can be closed. A project can be considered finsihed under all of the following conditions except?

The correct answer is A.

> **A:** The project doesn't end simply because the project manager resigns. In this instance, a new project manager would be recruited and the project would continue.
>
> **B:** If the project objectives have been achieved, then the project would end because there is no longer a need to continue the project.
>
> **C:** If a project is terminated for any reason, it is considered as ended.
>
> **D:** If the need for the project no longer exists, then the project would end.

Question 34: During the preparation of the business case for your project you outline and document several different compelling reasons why your project should proceed. These reasons include the high ROI, delivering strategic value, and an increase in business value. What is the BEST definition of business value?

The correct answer is C.

> **A:** Business value is defined as the sum of both tangible and intangible elements.
>
> **B:** In addition to the value created by projects, business value also includes intangible elements.
>
> **C:** Business value is defined as the sum of all tangible and intangible elements including things such as monetary assets, fixtures, equity, good will, brand recognition, and trademarks.
>
> **D:** Business value is based on actual tangible and intangible value. Projects that are underway form a small part of this overall value.

CHAPTER 2 ▒ ANSWERS

Question 35: You are explaining to your team that all changes on your project must be documented and assessed in relation to any extra costs incurred. This is particularly important at what point in a project's timeline?

The correct answer is B.

> **A:** The cost of changes is lowest at the beginning of the project because very little commitment has been made at this point in terms of resources and executing the work.

> **B:** As you near the end of the project, the cost and impact of any requested change increases.

> **C:** There will be significant costs of changes during project execution but they won't be as much as towards the end of the project.

> **D:** The cost of changes increases the more you proceed through a project because greater commitment is made to the deliverable and the resources to produce the deliverable.

Question 36: While studying towards the PMP® examination, you memorize the processes in the PMBOK® Guide. How many processes are there in the Project Integration Management knowledge area in the PMBOK® Guide?

The correct answer is D because Project Integration Management has six processes in it. They are Develop Project Charter, Develop Project Management Plan, Direct and Manage Project Work, Monitor and Control Project Work, Perform Integrated Change Control, and Close Project or Phase. All the wrong answers contain the wrong number of processes.

Question 37: You are involved in making choices about resource allocation on your project, making trade-offs among competing objectives and alternatives, and managing the interdependencies among the different project management knowledge areas. Of which of the PMBOK® Guide knowledge areas will it be most useful to have an in-depth understanding?

The correct answer is B.

> **A:** Develop Project Management Plan is a specific process, not a knowledge area.

> **B:** Project integration management is the process of understanding the interaction and interdependencies between all of the different knowledge areas.

> **C:** Project risk management is related to anticipating and managing risk on the project, not trade-offs among competing objectives.

> **D:** Perform Integrated Change Control is a specific process, not a knowledge area.

Question 38: One of your team members has recently discovered the PMBOK®
Guide and is intent on doing a project using each and every process, tool, and technique.
You take this team member aside and explain to her that the knowledge and processes
described in the PMBOK® Guide should be applied in what way?
The correct answer is A.

> **A:** The PMBOK® Guide is a framework from which you select
> the appropriate knowledge, skills, and processes to apply a
> professional and rigorous project management approach
> appropriate to the size, industry, and complexity of your
> particular project.
>
> **B**: This answer is incorrect because the information in the
> PMBOK® Guide is not to be used rigorously and exactly as
> shown. It is stated several times in the guide that the information
> is to be tailored to your particular type of project.
>
> **C**: This answer is incorrect because even though the PMBOK®
> Guide is indeed a guide, you should make sure that you are able
> to use all the approriate parts and not be limited by applying
> only the parts you understand fully.
>
> **D**: This answer is incorrect because you do not have to apply all
> of the knowledge areas and processes to your project. You should
> only apply those that are useful and provide benefit.

Question 39: You are newly appointed to a project and are currently reading the
project charter to gain an understanding of what is known about the project at this point.
The project charter should contain enough information to do all of the following except?
The correct answer is A.

> **A:** The project charter is like the birth certificate for a project.
> You need it to prove that the project exists and to provide basic
> but extremely important information about the project. The
> information it contains is generally quite high level; it is the first
> document developed in an iterative process, so it won't contain
> enough information to complete a WBS.
>
> **B:** The project charter should always contain information about
> the project initiation.
>
> **C:** The project charter should contain a high-level description of
> the work to be done on the project.
>
> **D:** The project charter should be the document that appoints the
> project manager.

Question 40: You have been called in to evaluate a project that is experiencing some performance challenges. The team seems disorganized, and when you ask to meet the project sponsor, the project manager replies that she doesn't know who the sponsor is. She also shares with you that the planned value (PV) is $20,000, earned value (EV) is $14,500, and the actual cost (AC) is $36,000. You decide that you should really go back to the beginning and figure out how this project got started. What document should you request?
The correct answer is B.

> **A:** There are several issues outlined in this question but the root cause could be determined by examining a foundational document such as the project charter.

> **B:** The project charter is the document that formally authorizes a project. The project charter is the document issued by the sponsor that formally authorizes the project and provides the project manager with the authority to apply organizational resources to project activities.

> **C:** The cost performance analysis and report won't help deal with any underlying issues because it merely reports status.

> **D:** The project authorization memo is not a term referenced within the PMBOK® Guide.

Question 41: You and your team are currently developing the project charter and are looking for valuable inputs you can use to complete it. All of the following are inputs in the Develop Project Charter process except?
The correct answer is B.

> **A:** The business case can definitely be used as an input into the project charter because it contains information about the financial justification for the project.

> **B:** At the stage of developing the project charter you do not have a project management plan, so it can't be an input.

> **C:** Enterprise environmental factors like market conditions and industry regulations would definitely be considered part of the development of the project charter.

> **D:** The project statement work is a high-level narrative description of the work to be done on the project and as such would be part of the development of the project charter.

Question 42: You have completed a business case and project charter for your project and are presenting it to senior management for consideration and approval. Which of the following have you included in this document?

The correct answer is D.

> **A:** The project management plan is done after the development of the project charter and as such would not be included in the business case.

> **B:** There is no need for the project charter to have a copy of the stakeholder register, and the project charter is an input into the Identify Stakeholders process, which processes the stakeholder register.

> **C:** Blank templates are part of the development of the project charter but are not necessarily part of the business case.

> **D:** The business case contains information to enable the project sponsor to authorize the project from a business perspective and as such must contain information about expected market demand for the product.

Question 43: There are many ways to describe the work to be done on a project. What is the high-level, narrative description of products or services to be delivered by the project more commonly referred to as?

The correct answer is A.

> **A:** The project statement of work is a high-level document used as an input in the development of the project charter.

> **B:** The project scope statement is a detailed, not high-level, description of the work to be done.

> **C:** The project scope is another name for the project scope statement which is a detailed, not high-level, description of the work to be done.

> **D:** Product scope description is not a term referenced within the PMBOK® Guide.

Question 44: Which of the following is not a method you would expect to see used in a business case to justify a project on financial grounds?

The correct answer is A.

> **A:** External rate of investment (ERI) is not a term referenced within the PMBOK® Guide.

> **B:** You would expect to see return on investment (ROI) used to justify a project on financial grounds.

C: You would expect to see net present value (NPV) used to justify a project on financial grounds.

D: You would expect to see internal rate of return (IRR) used to justify a project on financial grounds.

Question 45: You are a project manager working for an organization and have been asked to help evaluate some potential projects and draft the statement of work (SOW) to be given to potential solution providers. One of the projects has an expected value of $50,000 in three years. Another project has an expected value of $60,000 in four years. The discount rate is 8.2%. You will want to make sure your statement of work indicates all the following except?
The correct answer is A.

A: The staffing plan is not part of the statement of work (SOW). Did you get confused by all the information in this question? You must be able to dissect a question and understand exactly what is it asking. In this instance, the question is in the last sentence.

B: The statement of work will include a description of the business need for the project.

C: The statement of work will include a high-level description of the project scope.

D: The statement of work will refer to the strategic plan and how the project delivers strategic goals.

Question 46: You are in the process of developing a project charter for your project. Which of the following is a tool or technique that you would find useful to complete this work?
The correct answer is B.

A: The Delphi technique is a specific type of information gathering technique, and it is not used in the Develop Project Charter process.

B: Expert judgment is used to assess the inputs used in the development of the project charter.

C: Analytical techniques are a tool or technique used in the Close Project or Phase process and the Monitor and Control Project Work process.

D: Although a business case may be part of the project charter, business case preparation is not one of the listed tools or techniques in the Develop Charter process.

125

Question 47: You have just taken over a project that has been underway for 10 months. The previous project manager left the project for health reasons. The project is performing well but you would like to become familiar with the way in which this particular project is being executed, monitored and controlled, and closed. What document will help you in this instance?

The correct answer is D.

> **A:** The quality management plan relates to project quality and will not be detailed enough to give you all of the information you require.

> **B:** The project statement of work will not be detailed enough to give you all of the information you require.

> **C:** The project charter will not be detailed enough to give you all of the information you require.

> **D:** The project management plan is a product of all of the different knowledge areas and contains the information required to execute, monitor, control, and close the project.

Question 48: You and your team are carrying out the development of the project management plan for your project. You are unsure about which inputs are best to use to develop it. All of the following may be of assistance to you except?

The correct answer is D.

> **A:** The communications management plan is an output from another process, specifically the Plan Communications Management process, and as such it is an input into the Develop Project Management Plan process.

> **B:** The project charter provides the authorization to begin the planning processes, which delivers the project management plan.

> **C:** The process improvement plan is an output from another process, specifically the Plan Quality Management process, and as such it is an input into the Develop Project Management Plan process.

> **D:** Work performance information is not a direct input into the development of the project management plan.

Question 49: After completing most of your project management plan, your project sponsor is so impressed that she comments, "With this level of planning and detail, we know exactly where the project will be nine months from now." What is the BEST response you should give to the sponsor?

The correct answer is A.

> **A:** Projects seldom run exactly according to the project management plan, which is why we have the integrated change control process. The project management plan and the project scope statement must be maintained by carefully and continuously managing changes.

B: Using the critical chain method will not completely eliminate any possible changes. Projects seldom run exactly according to the project management plan, which is why we have the integrated change control process. The project management plan and the project scope statement must be maintained by carefully and continuously managing changes.

C: Unfortunately, good planning does not give precise knowledge about how a project will perform; it gives an idea of how you plan for it to perform. Projects seldom run exactly according to the project management plan, which is why we have the integrated change control process. The project management plan and the project scope statement must be maintained by carefully and continuously managing changes.

D: The application of professional project management practices does not guarantee project success, but it does increase the chances of project success. Projects seldom run exactly according to the project management plan, which is why we have the integrated change control process. The project management plan and the project scope statement must be maintained by carefully and continuously managing changes.

Question 50: Which of the following would your project sponsor not expect to see in your project management plan?
The correct answer is B.

A: The project management plan can be either summary or detailed depending on the timing and complexity of the project and what is required to successfully plan it.

B: This description outlines the contents of a project charter, not the project management plan.

C: The project management plan contains the project scope and how the work will be executed to achieve this scope.

D: The project management plan is a collection of all of the other planning documents and subsidiary plans from the other planning processes.

Question 51: You and your project team are busy putting together a first iteration of your project management plan. One of your team members seems confused about what exactly a project management plan is. Which of the following answers would be your best response to this team member?
The correct answer is C.

A: It is the last part of this answer that makes it incorrect. Project management plans are always used in practice.

B: It is the last part of this answer that makes it incorrect. Project management plans are not similar, regardless of the complexity of the project.

127

C: While it may be your experience that a project management plan is rarely used, the best answer is that this document will vary depending on the application area and complexity of the project.

D: It is the last part of this answer that makes it incorrect. Project management plans are not an input into the project charter process.

Question 52: Which of the following tool or techniques would you find useful when developing your project management plan?
The correct answer is C.

A: Product scope analysis is not a term referenced within the PMBOK® Guide.

B: Project management information systems are not used during the Develop Project Management Plan process.

C: Expert judgment is used to assess the inputs used in the development of the project management plan.

D: Business case preparation is done as part of the Develop Project Charter process and is not used during the Develop Project Management Plan process.

Question 53: Your project management plan describes your performance measurement baseline against which you will measure project performance in several interrelated areas. This baseline is most commonly a combination of what other baselines?
The correct answer is D.

A: There is no procurement baseline.

B: There is no risk management baseline.

C: There is no communication baseline.

D: The performance measurement baseline is a combination of the scope, schedule, and cost baselines. Remember that you use the performance measurement baseline for your earned value measurements.

Question 54: You and your project team are implementing a variety of approved changes to your project. Which of the following would not be a type of approved change?
The correct answer is A.

A: Lessons learned are not part of the change control process itself. However, you may use the change requests you received in an analysis of what went well and not so well on the project.

B: Preventative action is not correct because the Direct and Manage Project Work process requires implementation of preventative actions, which are a type of approved change.

C: The Direct and Manage Project Work process requires implementation of corrective actions, which is a type of approved change.

D: The Direct and Manage Project Work process does require implementation of any identified defects needing repair.

Question 55: The activities involved in performing the work defined in the project management plan to achieve the project's objectives include all of the following except?
The correct answer is D.

A: Monitoring and controlling the work being done against what was planned is an essential part of the execution phase.

B: Managing identified risks is part of the work to be done because each risk response strategy represents project work.

C: Team members are essential for getting the planed work completed.

D: Development of the project charter is not part of the execution of the project management plan. It is part of project initiation.

Question 56: You are in the process of directing and managing the work to be done on the project. Which of the following would not be of use to you during this process?
The correct answer is B.

A: The project management plan is used as a key input into the Direct and Manage Project Work process because it outlines all of the work to be done.

B: Work performance data is an output of the Direct and Manage Project Work process.

C: Approved change requests are an input because they represent work to be done on the project.

D: Enterprise environmental factors such as market conditions and legislation are an important consideration and input into the Direct and Manage Project Work process.

Question 57: You are in the process of directing and managing the work to be done on the project. Which of the following would not be a useful type of Organizational Process Asset to use during this process?
The correct answer is C.

A: Issue and defect management procedures are examples of Organizational Process Assets used in the Direct and Manage Project Work process.

B: The process measurement database is an example of an Organizational Process Asset used in the Direct and Manage Project Work process.

C: This is a tough question that tests your knowledge of the difference between Organizational Process Assets and enterprise environmental factors. Stakeholder risk tolerances are an enterprise environmental factor because they are part of the environment in which the project operates.

D: Standardized guidelines and work instructions are an example of Organizational Process Assets used in the Direct and Manage Project Work process.

Question 58: You are the sponsor on a time-constrained project that must deliver the expected output by a defined date or your organization will face severe financial penalties. You meet with the project manager 20 days after the kick-off of the project and ask to have an update on schedule progress, schedule activities that have been started, and the extent to which quality standards are being met. The project manager looks at you somewhat uncomfortably and tells you that he doesn't have any of that information. What output from Direct and Manage Project Work process is the project manager missing?

The correct answer is D.

A: Change requests will not provide information about the schedule or quality standards.

B: Project management plan updates will not provide information about the schedule or quality standards.

C: The project deliverables will not provide information about the schedule or quality standards.

D: Work performance data provides information on the status of the project activities being performed to accomplish the project work.

Question 59: The process of tracking, reviewing, and regulating the progress of your project to meet the performance objectives defined in the project management plan is known as what?

The correct answer is C.

A: This answer is incorrect because the Perform Integrated Change Control process monitors, assesses, and controls change requests.

B: This answer is incorrect because the Direct and Manage Project Work process executes the project management plan.

C: The question is the PMBOK® Guide definition of the Monitor and Control Project Work process.

D: This answer is incorrect because the Develop Project Management Plan process produces the project management plan.

Question 60: You and your team are completing work to monitor and control project work. Which of the following tools or techniques would not be of use to you to complete this work?
The correct answer is B.

> **A:** Expert judgment is one of the tools and techniques used in the Monitor and Control Project Work process in the PMBOK® Guide.

> **B:** The Delphi technique is not a tool or technique used in the Monitor and Control Project Work process in the PMBOK® Guide. It is a powerful information gathering technique that can be used in many situations where you want expert opinion but you want to build consensus as well. Key elements are that it is iterative and anonymous, which eliminates peer pressure.

> **C:** Expert judgment is one of the tools and techniques used in the Monitor and Control Project Work process in the PMBOK® Guide.

> **D:** Meetings are one of the tools and techniques used in the Monitor and Control Project Work process in the PMBOK® Guide.

Question 61: You and your team are completing work to monitor and control project work. As part of this effort you are producing a variety of outputs. Which of the following is not one of these outputs?
The correct answer is B.

> **A:** Change requests, work performance reports, project management plan updates, and project documents updates are the four outputs from the Monitor and Control Project Work process.

> **B:** Work performance information is an input to, not an output from, the Monitor and Control Project Work process. During the process, it becomes the work performance reports.

> **C:** Change requests, work performance reports, project management plan updates, and project documents updates are the four outputs from the Monitor and Control Project Work process.

> **D:** Change requests, work performance reports, project management plan updates, and project documents updates are the four outputs from the Monitor and Control Project Work process.

Question 62: You and your team are considering making an early change to a part of the project management plan when one of your team members says that it is too early to be considering any changes. At what points in the project would you perform integrated change control?
The correct answer is B.

> **A:** Integrated change control is performed from project inception to completion and not just during project execution, so this is not the best possible answer of the choices given.
>
> **B:** Changes can affect a project at any point in the life cycle and therefore you must be ready to proactively influence, monitor, and control change requests.
>
> **C:** You perform integrated change control during the monitoring and controlling phase, and you perform it from inception to completion, so this answer is not the best of the possible answers presented to you.
>
> **D:** This answer is not correct because it does not acknowledge that integrated change control is also performed during the project initiation and project planning phases.

Question 63: Your client has requested a change to the project and as a result you are preparing a change request according to the approved change control process that your project management methodology prescribes. A project administrator on your project asks to assist in the preparation and assessment of the change request but seems confused about the key characteristics of a change request. You explain that all of the following are characteristics of a change request except?
The correct answer is B.

> **A:** All change requests must have a decision made about them.
>
> **B:** The word ALL in this answer makes it incorrect as the project manager can have a level of delegated authority to approve or decline requested changes so they don't all need to go to the change control board.
>
> **C:** A change request may be initiated verbally but should always be recorded in a document of some sort.
>
> **D:** A change request in one area, such as quality, may have impacts in other areas such as cost, time, and risk.

Question 64: You have developed a formal documented system and set of processes to assist with technical and administrative direction, control, and iteration management of project documents, records, accountability, physical characteristics, and required materials. What is this system called?
The correct answer is D.

> **A:** A work authorization system is not focused on consistently validating and improving the project by recording and considering the impact of each change.

B: A risk management system is not focused on consistently validating and improving the project by recording and considering the impact of each change. It is focused on identification, assessment, and responses to risk.

C: A project management information systems (PMIS) is not focused on consistently validating and improving the project by recording and considering the impact of each change. It is focused on storage and retrieval of project management information.

• **D:** Project-wide application of the configuration management system, including change control processes, accomplishes three main objectives: it establishes an evaluation method to consistently identify and request changes to established baselines; it provides opportunities to continuously validate and improve the project by considering the impact of each change; and it provides the mechanism for the project management team to consistently communicate all changes to stakeholders.

Question 65: You are carrying out project-wide application of the configuration management system in order to accomplish three main objectives. Which of the following is not one of these objectives?
The correct answer is B.

A: Establishing an evolutionary method to consistently identify and request changes to established baselines is an important objective of the configuration management system.

B: This answer describes part of the change control process, not the configuration management system, so it is the correct answer to the question.

C: Continuously validating and improving the project by considering the impact of each change is an important objective of the configuration management system.

D: Providing a mechanism for the project management team to consistently communicate all approved and rejected changes to the stakeholders is an important objective of the configuration management system.

Question 66: The configuration management system is a collection of formal documented procedures. Which of the following is not an objective of configuration management?
The correct answer is A.

A: The configuration management system controls and records changes, but it does not prevent them, so this is the correct answer.

B: Recording and reporting each change to the functional characteristics is an important attribute of the configuration management system.

C: Identifying and documenting the functional characteristics of a product is an important attribute of the configuration management system.

D: Supporting the audit of the products to verify conformance to requirements is an important attribute of the configuration management system.

Question 67: You are in the process of documenting, assessing, and making a decision on a requested change to your project. Which of the following configuration management activities would you not find useful at this time?
The correct answer is A.

A: Configuration control and assessment may sound like a correct answer but it is not a term referenced within the PMBOK® Guide.

B: Configuration identification is one the core activities of configuration management included in the Integrated Change Control process.

C: Configuration status accounting is one the core activities of configuration management included in the Integrated Change Control process.

D: Configuration validation and audit is one the core activities of configuration management included in the Integrated Change Control process.

Question 68: As an experienced project manager, you have been asked to review a project with an SPI of 0.86 and a CPI of 0.83. You quickly identify a number of changes that are required to fix defects and meet some critical customer needs. Which of the following PMBOK® Guide processes will you need to perform first?
The correct answer is A.

A: Project changes can require new or revised cost estimates, schedule dates, resource requirements, and other project deliverables. These changes can require adjustments to the project management plan project scope statement or other project deliverables. You have identified your changes and now need to put them in place.

B: The Direct and Manage Project Work process executes the planned work; it does not process change requests.

C: The Monitor and Control Project Work process identifies any variances from planned baselines and raises change requests but does not process change requests.

D: The Develop Project Management Plan process produces the project management plan; it does not process change requests.

Question 69: You are carrying out work to document and assess requested changes to your project. Which of the following would you find least helpful to you as an input as you complete this work?
The correct answer is C.

>**A:** Organizational Process Assets are an input into the Perform Integrated Change Control process in the PMBOK® Guide.

>**B:** Change request are an input into the Perform Integrated Change Control process in the PMBOK® Guide.

>**C:** Project document updates are an output of, not an input to, the Perform Integrated Change Control process in the PMBOK® Guide.

>**D:** Work performance reports are an input into the Perform Integrated Change Control process in the PMBOK® Guide.

Question 70: Your client has requested a change that is considered feasible but is outside of the already approved project scope, and your project is already significantly advanced. What should occur if the change is approved?
The correct answer is C.

>**A:** The project sponsor was either consulted or informed about the change as part of the normal integrated change control process, which will approve the change, so there is no special reason to inform them now.

>**B:** If the change request is feasible, it should definitely be considered and not just declined.

>**C:** Making changes to a project that are not part of the project scope is acceptable as long as the relevant process is followed and the relevant baseline is changed to reflect the new information. Remember that a baseline is the original baseline plus any approved changes.

>**D:** This answer is wrong because it is silly to think that there is conflict of interest simply because someone raises a change request.

Question 71: You and your project team are carrying out the work described in the Close Project or Phase process in the PMBOK® Guide. You want your team to understand the exact characteristics of this work, so you tell them that the process includes all of the following except?
The correct answer is C.

>**A:** Establishing the procedures to investigate and document the reasons for actions taken if a project is terminated before completion is an important characteristic of the Close Project or Phase process.

>**B:** Finalizing all activities across all of the project management process groups is an important characteristic of the Close Project or Phase process.

135

C: The process of closing and finalizing any contracts is done during the Close Procurements process in the PMBOK® Guide, so this is the correct answer.

D: Including all of the activities necessary for administrative closure of the project or phase is an important characteristic of the Close Project or Phase process.

Question 72: While carrying out the work to close the design phase of your project you are using a variety of useful inputs. Which of the following is not a useful input to you?
The correct answer is C.

A: Organizational Process Assets are an input in the Close Project or Phase process in the PMBOK® Guide, which is what the question is describing.

B: Accepted deliverables are an input in the Close Project or Phase process in the PMBOK® Guide, which is what the question is describing.

C: Work performance information is an input into several other processes but not the Close Project or Phase process in the PMBOK® Guide, which is what the question is describing, so this is the correct answer.

D: The project management plan is an input in the Close Project or Phase process in the PMBOK® Guide, which is what the question is describing.

Question 73: You are a project manager and you have just been informed that due to budget cuts your project has been cancelled and your team should cease work immediately. The project was doing very well and will likely be restarted at a later time when organizational finances are better. What is the BEST action to take next?
The correct answer is A.

A: If a project is terminated prior to completion, the formal documentation indicates why the project was terminated and formalizes the procedures for the transfer of the finished and unfinished deliverables of the project to others.

B: You cannot ignore a request like this because there is no funding to continue the project.

C: This answer is incorrect because it is entirely unprofessional to shred documents that could be used later when the project restarts.

D: The question clearly outlines that there is no budget for your project, so you must assume that this has already been done by those people responsible for funding projects.

Question 74: You are just about to complete administrative closure of your project and are updating the relevant Organizational Process Assets for your company. Which of the following is not an example of an Organizational Process Asset that you would update?

The correct answer is C.

> **A:** Project files, project closure documents, and historical information are all examples of Organizational Process Assets that would be updated.

> **B:** Project files, project closure documents, and historical information are all examples of Organizational Process Assets that would be updated.

> **C:** The stakeholder risk tolerance register is not be considered an Organizational Process Asset.

> **D:** Project files, project closure documents, and historical information are all examples of Organizational Process Assets that would be updated.

Question 75: Your project is reporting a CPI of 1.02 and a SPI of 1.1. The project you are delivering is for a customer who is notoriously difficult to please. Your team comes up with a way to deliver more functionality in the project than the customer is expecting, at a lower cost, and the change will result in improvements to the schedule. What is your BEST course of action?

The correct answer is B.

> **A:** This answer in incorrect because if you have the opportunity to deliver extra value you should investigate whether it can be done. You should also always expect and manage changes to a project.

> **B:** The necessary first step in the change control process in this instance is to contact the customer and explain the situation to them in order to get their approval, rather then risk gold plating.

> **C:** This answer is incorrect because you do not do the work without first checking with the customer.

> **D:** This answer is incorrect because without first checking with the customer you will not know if they will appreciate it or not.

Question 76: You are a project manager that is involved with the preparation of a business case to justify whether a particular project should go ahead. You are using net present value (NPV) as a key financial filter. Your project will spend $100,000 in the first year, and then it will generate revenue of $33,000 in the first year, $62,000 in the second year, and $85,000 in the third year. Assuming a discount rate of 10%, what is the net present value?

The correct answer is B.

> **A:** $100,000 represents the spend on the project in the first year, not the NPV.

> **B:** The formula to calculate NPV is -$100,000+($33,000 / (1+.1)^1)+($62,000 / (1+.1)^2)+($85,000 / (1+.1)^3) which equals $45,101.43.

> **C:** $80,000 represents the total revenue generated from the project with the cost of a project subtracted, not the NPV.

> **D:** You get $280,000 if you simply add the four figures in the question together, and they do not represent the NPV.

Question 77: You are choosing between two potential projects that your organization could undertake. The first project, Project Eagle, will cost $500,000 and will have a NPV of $50,000. The second project, Project Falcon, will cost $420,000 and will have a NPV of $48,000. Which of the two projects should you do?

The correct answer is C.

> **A:** The question presents enough information to enable you to compare NPV between the two projects, and you should choose the project with a higher NPV.

> **B:** The cost of Project Falcon has already been taken into account with the NPV calculation and therefore you should choose the project with a higher NPV, which is project Eagle.

> **C:** Between the two projects Project Eagle has the higher NPV and as such it should be preferred option.

> **D:** In order for a project to go ahead, it must have a positive NPV, and both projects do. You should choose the project with the highest NPV.

Question 78: After measuring expected project benefits, your project management office has four projects from which to choose. Project A has a NPV of $160,000 and will cost $10,000. Project B has a NPV of $470,000 and will cost $220,000. Project C has a NPV of $265,000 and will cost $33,000. Project D has a NPV of $335,000 and will cost $57,000. Which project would be BEST?

The correct answer is C.

> **A:** This answer is incorrect because Project C has an NPV of $265,000, which is not the highest NPV. Don't forget that the cost of the project has already been calculated in the NPV calculation so that information is not relevant.

B: This answer is incorrect because Project A has an NPV of $160,000, which is not the highest NPV. Don't forget that the cost of the project has already been calculated in the NPV calculation so that information is not relevant.

C: The question gives you lots of information about NPV and the cost of each project but the only relevant information is the NPV because it is recalculated the cost. Therefore, you should choose the project with the highest NPV, which is project B which is also the correct answer.

D: This answer is incorrect because Project D has an NPV of $335,000, which is not the highest NPV. Don't forget that the cost of the project has already been calculated in the NPV calculation so that information is not relevant. If you thought this was the correct choice, it is probably because you subtracted the cost from the NPV.

Question 79: You are assisting your portfolio manager in making a decision about which of two possible projects should be given approval to proceed. Project A would generate $75,000 in benefit. Project B would generate $225,000 in benefit. Unfortunately, due to limited resources, your company can only perform one project, and they choose Project B because of the higher benefit. What is the opportunity cost of performing Project B?
The correct answer is B.

A, C, and D: These answers are incorrect because when faced with a choice between two projects, the opportunity cost is the benefit that would be derived by doing the other project. In this case, the opportunity cost of performing project B is the benefit of project A, which is $75,000.

B: When faced with a choice between two projects, the opportunity cost is the benefit that would be derived by doing the other project. In this case, the opportunity cost of performing project B is the benefit of project A, which is $75,000.

Project Scope Management

Question 80: The processes that describe the work required to ensure that the project includes all the work and only the work required to complete the project successfully are collectively known as what?
The correct answer is A.

A: Project scope management makes it clear that at times you should ensure that you are delivering only what is documented. This allows for changes to occur but makes it clear that you should document all changes to the baseline and ensure you are delivering exactly what has been documented.

B: Project baseline delivery is incorrect because it is not a term referenced within the PMBOK® Guide.

C: Project specification delivery is incorrect because it is not a term referenced within the PMBOK® Guide.

D: Project management execution is incorrect because it is not a term referenced within the PMBOK® Guide.

Question 81: You are completing the work defined in the project scope statement of a new software development project when a team member points out that you have an opportunity to deliver enhanced capability to the client at no extra cost, time, or risk to the project. What should you do NEXT?
The correct answer is B.

A: If you are able to assess the request and approve it via your approved change control process, there is no reason to simply decline it. You should always look for ways to deliver more that what was expected as long as it is documented.

B: This is an issue about "gold plating," which means you are delivering more than what you were required to do. While this sounds like a good thing to do, it also means that you are not delivering what has been documented. There is no problem with seizing the opportunity to deliver more, but you must always be delivering what is agreed on and documented. In this case, you would formally assess the change; if it gets accepted by your change control process, you would then amend the necessary documents so that at all times you are delivering exactly what is documented.

C: The first step before doing this option is to assess the change via your change control process.

D: If you are able to assess the request and approve it via your approved change control process, there is no reason to simply decline it. You should always look for ways to deliver more that what was expected as long as it is documented.

Question 82: You are new to a project that has been underway for some time. One of your first jobs as project manager is to familiarize yourself with and understand the scope baseline. What documents will you require in order to do this?
The correct answer is A.

A: The scope baseline is made up of the detailed project scope statement (which will include all approved changes), the WBS, and the WBS dictionary, which provides additional information needed to fully understand the WBS.

B: The scope baseline is made up of the project scope statement, the WBS, and the WBS dictionary. It does not include the risk register.

C: The scope baseline is made up of the project scope statement, the WBS, and the WBS dictionary. It does not include the change register.

D: The scope baseline is made up of the project scope statement, the WBS, and the WBS dictionary. It does not include the either the project management plan or the change register.

Question 83: You are a project manager and you are working with your sponsor to define and plan a complex project. You plan to complete your initiation and planning documents sequentially to make sure the organization really understands and supports the project. What key deliverables will you produce in the correct order?
The correct answer is B.

A: The project charter comes before a project management plan and project scope statement.

B: First, you must always have the project charter; with it, you can determine the requirements documentation. Both of these are then inputs into the Define Scope process, which produces the project scope statement.

C: Requirements documentation must be completed before the scope statement.

D: The project charter is completed first, then the part of the project management plan that details the requirements gathering, and then requirements documentation.

Question 84: What is the name of the planning document that describes how requirements will be analyzed, documented, and managed?
The correct answer is C.

A: The requirements traceability matrix is an output from the Collect Requirements process and links product requirements from their origin to the deliverables that satisfy them.

B: The scope management plan is focused on the definition, documentation, and management of the entire project scope.

C: The requirements management plan is a part of the project management plan that describes how requirements will be analyzed, documented, and managed.

D: This answer is not correct because it is not a term referenced within the PMBOK® Guide.

Question 85: Completion of the project scope is measured against the scope management plan. What is completion of the product scope measured against?
The correct answer is D.

> **A:** Client expectations are captured in the requirements documentation of which a subset is the product requirements.

> **B:** The scope management plan is focused on the definition, documentation, and management of the entire project scope.

> **C:** The project management plan contains the project scope and how the work will be executed to achieve this scope, not just the product scope.

> **D:** The product scope is measured against the documented product requirements gathered during the Collect Requirements process.

Question 86: As part of your ongoing commitment to mentoring the next generation of professional project managers you have taken on an intern on your software development project. You are explaining to her the key differences between project requirements and product requirements. How would you best explain this to her?
The correct answer is D.

> **A:** This answer is incorrect because project requirements are much more than components of the project management plan and product requirements are more than just client specficiations and expectations.

> **B:** This answer is incorrect because it is simply incomplete, and and product requirments do not include the method of delivery.

> **C:** This answer is incorrect because project requirments are not just the detail included in the project management plan and product requirments are more than just the clients expectations.

> **D:** This is an important distinction that you must learn and look out for in the exam. Watch out for the use of PROJECT and PRODUCT when reading the questions because they are different things. Project requirements relate to the way the project is delivered while product requirements relate to the technical requirements of the product.

Question 87: You are carrying out the work to define and document the project stakeholders' needs to meet the project objectives. What PMBOK® Guide process describes this work best?
The correct answer is D.

> **A:** This answer is incorrect because it is not a PMBOK® Guide process.

> **B:** Project integration management is a PMBOK® Guide knowledge area, not a process.

C: Project scope management is a PMBOK® Guide knowledge area, not a process.

D: Collect Requirements defines and documents stakeholders' needs by producing the requirements documentation, requirements management plan, and the requirements traceability matrix.

Question 88: A team member on your project has questioned whether the project is delivering as per the original high-level requirements and narrative high-level product description, and is concerned that what you are doing has deviated from this. What is your BEST course of action?

The correct answer is C.

A: The project scope statement is not the best place to look for the original requirements and product description. The project charter is the best place to look for original descriptions.

B: The project management plan is not the best place to look for the original requirements and product description. The project charter is the best place to look for original descriptions.

C: The project charter is the founding document for the project. At the time it is developed, agreed on, and approved, generally only high-level information about the project requirements and product description is known but at all times the project should be aligned with the project charter. If the project changes significantly, then the project charter should also be amended. This can only be done with the consent of the project sponsor.

D: This answer is not correct because questioning should be encouraged among team members.

Question 89: You are carrying out the work to define and document the project stakeholders' needs to meet the project objectives. All of the following are tools or techniques that would be useful to you except?

The correct answer is B.

A: There are number of techniques for soliciting information about requirements from the relevant stakeholders. Focus groups are one of these techniques described in the Collect Requirements process in the PMBOK® Guide.

B: A requirements traceability matrix is an output of the Collect Requirements process in the PMBOK® Guide, not a tool or technique.

C: There are number of techniques for soliciting information about requirements from the relevant stakeholders. Group decision-making techniques are one of these techniques described in the Collect Requirements process in the PMBOK® Guide.

D: There are number of techniques for soliciting information about requirements from the relevant stakeholders. Interviews are one of these techniques described in the Collect Requirements process in the PMBOK® Guide.

Question 90: You have decided to use a technique to get a comprehensive set of project requirements that involves getting a group of experts to answer a series of questionnaires anonymously and provide feedback on information received in an iterative manner. What technique are you using?
The correct answer is D.

A: Mind mapping is incorrect because it is a graphical technique use to link ideas together.

B: The nominal group technique is an incorrect answer because it is a way to get a decisions from a group by considering all possible decisions and getting group members to rank their support for each one.

C: Brainstorming is incorrect because it is a method of getting a group to think laterally, or outside the square, and consider a wide range of ideas.

D: The Delphi technique is a powerful information gathering technique that can be used in many situations where you want expert opinion but want to build consensus as well. Key elements are that it is iterative and anonymous, which eliminates peer pressure and groupthink. It takes its name from the Oracle of Delphi.

Question 91: You have just completed the work of gathering, documenting, and prioritizing the project and product requirements, and mapping them back to original project objectives. Which PMBOK® Guide process best describes this work?
The correct answer is D.

A: Scope Definition is not a PMBOK® Guide process.

B: The Develop Project Charter process provides the project charter, not the requirements documentation.

C: The Project Scope Management knowledge area contains all the processes for planning, defining, and checking the project scope, and the requirements documentation is a small subset of this.

D: The Collect Requirements process produces your requirements documentation, requirements management plan, and the requirements traceability matrix.

Question 92: An experienced team member has taken responsibility for compiling the requirements documentation for the project. Which of the following components would you not expect to see included in this documentation?
The correct answer is D.

    A: Business rules stating the guiding principles of the organization are important components of the requirements documentation.

    B: The business need is an important component of the requirements documentation.

    C: Acceptance criteria are an important component of the requirements documentation.

    D: The requirements documentation describes how individual requirements meet the business need for the project. Configuration management activities are a component of the requirements management plan, not the requirements documentation.

Question 93: You are a project manager working on a complex construction project and have begun the process of planning your project. You have the project charter, which is guiding you in preparing your project management plan. Using your requirements documentation, you begin the process of developing a detailed description of the project and product. What process are you completing?
The correct answer is B.

    A: The Collect Requirements process identifies and documents the project and product requirements from stakeholders and does not relate to using the requirements documentation to begin the process of developing a detailed description of the project and product.

    B: Define Scope is the process of developing your detailed description of both the project and product. Having a detailed scope statement is critical to project success. Remember that this process will be iterative and can be fully developed as the project moves along.

    C: The Plan Scope Management process seeks to define the process for describing and controlling the project's scope and requirements, and does not relate to using the requirements documentation to begin the process of developing a detailed description of the project and product.

    D: The Define Activities process is part of the Project Time Management knowledge area and does not relate to using the requirements documentation to begin the process of developing a detailed description of the project and product.

Question 94: You are the project manager for a large project and have recently taken over the project from another project manager. On review of the project schedule, you learn that two major deliverables are missing. Your sponsor reminds you how important it is to complete this project on time and within budget. What part of scope management was likely not done properly and should be reviewed and perhaps even repeated?
The correct answer is D.

> **A:** Although decomposition is an important step in Scope Management and is necessary to generate the WBS, it is the subdivision of project deliverables into smaller, more manageable work components.

> **B:** Critical path analysis is not part of the Scope Management knowledge area. Critical path analysis is competed after the project schedule is done and is part of Time Management.

> **C:** The Integrated Change Control process receives, assess, and approves or declines change requests and is not part of the Scope Management processes. Integrated change control is done during the monitoring and controlling of a project.

> **D:** Stakeholder analysis is correct because it is likely that some of the stakeholders' requirements were not incorporated into the scope definition of the project, resulting in deliverables missing from the WBS and the project schedule.

Question 95: You are completing the work to define the scope of your project. This work is best performed with a certain variety of documents and processes already available to you. Which of the following is not a useful input for you to have in order to complete this work?
The correct answer is A.

> **A:** The project scope statement is an output from, not an input into, the Define Scope process.

> **B:** The project charter is one of the inputs into the Define Scope process in the PMBOK® Guide.

> **C:** Requirements documentation is one of the inputs into the Define Scope process in the PMBOK® Guide.

> **D:** Your organization's project management methodology is an example of an Organizational Process Asset, which is one of the inputs into the Define Scope process in the PMBOK® Guide.

Question 96: You have been assigned as a new project manager for a multi-phase project that is midway through phase 3 of 5 phases. While the overall work of the team seems pretty good, you feel that phase 3 is starting to drift from the original plan. You set up a meeting with the project sponsor to discuss your concerns. The sponsor is surprised and agrees that phase 3 includes work that was not documented in the original agreement. To prove this, the sponsor refers you to which document?

The correct answer is D.

> **A:** The requirements traceability matrix links the original requirements to the deliverables that are supposed to be met and would not be of assistance in this situation.

> **B:** The project management plan contains all the subsidiary plans for executing the project. But the project scope statement is the best answer for this question.

> **C:** The statement of work would not contain enough information to be useful in this situation.

> **D:** During subsequent phases of multi-phase projects, the project scope statement defines and validates (if necessary) the project scope.

Question 97: You and your project team have spent time decomposing the project scope statement using your organization's work breakdown structure template. What is the lowest level of the work breakdown structure called?

The correct answer is B.

> **A:** You may use the term tasks but it is not a standard term used in the PMBOK® Guide.

> **B:** When you undertake the process of decomposition to complete your WBS, you break down the deliverables into smaller, more manageable components. The smallest level in the WBS is the work package. A work package can be further divided into activities but this is beyond the WBS.

> **C:** Activities are work packages that are decomposed even further, but they are too detailed to be included as part of the WBS.

> **D:** Units is not a term referenced within the PMBOK® Guide.

Question 98: The PMBOK® Guide process of subdividing project deliverables and project work into smaller components is known as what?

The correct answer is D.

> **A:** The Collect Requirements process gathers stakeholder requirements for inclusion in the project scope but it does not subdivide project deliverables and project work into smaller components.

> **B:** The Define Activities process breaks down work packages even further than work packages and is not part of the Create WBS process, which is the best answer.

C: The Define Scope process does just what it sounds like. It defines the project and product scope, but does not break it down.

D: Developing a robust WBS is critical to the success of your project because it defines all the work packages that must be completed. The process of doing this is the Create WBS process.

Question 99: You have just completed a workshop with all of your senior project technicians to break the project work down into its component parts and produce the first iteration of your work breakdown structure. All of the following are true about the work breakdown structure except?
The correct answer is D.

A: Decomposition of the scope using the WBS does mean the planned work within the lowest levels can be scheduled, cost-estimated, monitored, and controlled.

B: The WBS is a deliverable-oriented hierarchical decomposition of the work to be executed by the project team.

C: Each descending level of the WBS does represent an increasingly detailed definition of the project work down to the work package level.

D: The work breakdown structure is an output of the Create WBS process, not Define Scope.

Question 100: The point in the decomposition of the WBS at which cost and activity durations for the work can be reliably estimated and managed is called what?
The correct answer is D.

A: Tasks is incorrect because it is not part of the standard terminology in the PMBOK® Guide.

B: Activities are work packages that are decomposed further for the purpose of building a project schedule.

C: Elements of the WBS dictionary provide additional information about each work package and not the point in the decomposition of the WBS at which cost and activity durations for the work can be reliably estimated and managed.

D: It is important that the WBS is decomposed down to the work package level. The appropriate level of decomposition means that the work package can be reliably estimated in relation to its cost and duration.

Question 101: You are consulting with senior technicians working on your project in order to decompose the project scope into its component parts to produce a work breakdown structure for your project. One team member with extensive experience and a focus on detail wishes to continue decomposing the project scope further but you advise him against doing this because excessive decomposition of the WBS can lead to all of the following except?

The correct answer is D.

> **A:** Going too far with decomposition means that the benefits derived from the additional work outweigh the costs incurred. This will result in non-productive management effort.

> **B:** Going too far with decomposition means that the benefits derived from the additional work outweigh the costs incurred. These costs will be generated by inefficient use of resources.

> **C:** Going too far with decomposition decrease the ability to get on with doing the actual work.

> **D:** A properly decomposed WBS has the work packages defined at a level where their cost and duration can be accurately estimated and managed. Going beyond this level does not add further benefit or value and may in fact create adverse results in relation to efficiency and effort.

Question 102: You have a new team member on board and she is new to the profession of project management. How would you explain the work breakdown structure to her?

The correct answer is D.

> **A:** The WBS does not describe project risks. It decomposes the scope statement into work packages.

> **B:** The WBS does not describe the resources by type. It decomposes the scope statement into work packages.

> **C:** The WBS does not define the scope of any contracts. It decomposes the scope statement into work packages.

> **D:** The work breakdown structure (WBS) organizes and defines the total scope of the project; subdivides the project work into smaller, more manageable pieces; and represents the work specified in the current approved project scope statement. A describes the risk breakdown structure, B describes the resource breakdown structure, and C describes the contract statement of work.

Question 103: Your project team has largely completed the creation of the WBS. However, some deliverables have not been decomposed because clarity is lacking. The project team decides to leave them and wait until more details are available. What is this an example of?

The correct answer is A.

> **A:** One important aspect of project management is acknowledging that project planning is iterative and subject to progressive elaborations; work such as decomposition of the WBS may not always be entirely possible because there may be a lack of clarity or a particular deliverable may rely on another deliverable to be complete before it can fully be defined. This process of leaving these uncertain deliverables until more detail is known is called rolling wave planning.

> **B:** This answer may seem correct at first glance but progressive decision making is not a term referenced within the PMBOK® Guide.

> **C:** This answer may seem correct at first glance but iterative expectation management is not a term referenced within the PMBOK® Guide.

> **D:** A fundamental attribute of project management planning is that it will be iterative and subject to rolling wave planning because you can not generally plan the entire project in detail, so this approach is not an example of poor project management planning.

Question 104: You are having trouble understanding some of the detail associated with your WBS work packages. To help you understand the components of your WBS in greater detail, which document would you use?

The correct answer is C.

> **A:** The project scope statement does not contain enough information to help you gain a more in-depth understanding of WBS components.

> **B:** The project charter does not contain enough information to help you gain a more in-depth understanding of WBS components.

> **C:** The WBS dictionary is a useful document that lists additional detail about the work packages. Both the project scope statement and the project charter are too high-level to provide further detail on work packages contained in the WBS.

> **D:** The activity list describes activities, not components of the WBS.

Question 105: A team member responsible for validating the scope of the project seems to be confusing this work with quality control work. How would you explain the difference between scope validation and quality control work on the project?
The correct answer is A.

> **A:** Scope validation differs from quality control because scope validation means making sure that the deliverables match the defined, detailed scope, whereas quality control is concerned with making sure the technical attributes of the product meet the specific quality requirements. Quality control is generally performed before scope validation.

> **B:** This answer is incorrect because scope validation is not just about checking the output from the project, nor is quality control only concerned with the output of the product.

> **C:** This answer is incorrect because scope validation is not primarily concerned with ensuring the scope management plan is being followed.

> **D:** This answer is incorrect because scope validation is not about checking that the requirements documentation reflects the project charter.

Question 106: You are currently completing work associated with the process called Validate Scope in the PMBOK® Guide. What is this process primarily focused on?
The correct answer is C.

> **A:** Performing variance analysis on the expected and actual deliverables is part of the Monitoring and Controlling process group not the Validate Scope process.

> **B:** Finalizing the project and product scope statement is in the Define Scope process, not the Validate Scope process.

> **C:** The Validate Scope process is the process where you formally check and accept completed project deliverables.

> **D:** Accepting approved change requests and amending the project scope baseline is not part of the Validate Scope process.

Question 107: You are using your project management plan, requirements documentation, and requirements traceability matrix, and you are undertaking inspection to validate the project and product. What PMBOK® Guide process group are you involved in?
The correct answer is B.

> **A, C, D:** These examples define the Validate Scope process, which is part of the Monitoring and Controlling process group, not work done as part of the Closing process group.

> **B:** You are completing the Validate Scope process, which is part of the Monitoring and Controlling process group.

Question 108: The customer has contacted you and has requested a change to the scope of your project, which is already well underway. They are in a hurry to get the change implemented and they tell you that they are prepared to pay whatever extra cost is associated with the change so you should just get on and do it. What is your BEST course of action?

The correct answer is B.

> **A:** You can not simply refuse to consider change requests, but you should always process each change according to your defined change control process.
>
> **B:** All requests for changes to the scope must be considered in light of your agreed integrated change control process. Additionally, as project manager, you should proactively influence any prospective change requests.
>
> **C:** You may do this, but only after referring to your change control process for controlling scope and submitting the request as detailed.
>
> **D:** You may do this, but only after referring to your change control process for controlling scope and submitting the request as detailed.

Question 109: Your team is receiving a large number of small change requests and some are being adopted without being fully documented and assessed. These uncontrolled scope changes are often referred to as what?

The correct answer is D.

> **A:** Scope amendment is not a term referenced within the PMBOK® Guide.
>
> **B:** Scope variance, if it was a real term, would refer to the difference between what your scope baseline is and what you are delivering.
>
> **C:** Scope change is part of the formal documented, not undocumented, change process.
>
> **D:** Uncontrolled change on a project is a big No. All changes must be recorded, documented, and assessed as per the integrated change control process. Any approved changes should be reflected in updated baselines.

Question 110: A team member is concerned that you have not documented how requirements activities will be planned, tracked, and changed. What document will you show this team member to show him how you did the work?

The correct answer is A.

> **A:** The requirements management plan documents all aspects of managing, reporting, and changing your project requirements.
>
> **B:** The change control plan shows how changes, not requirements, will be managed, assessed, and tracked.

C: The project management plan is the overall plan comprising all other sub-plans, including the requirements management plan, which is the best answer to this question.

D: The scope management plan sets out how the scope, not the requirements, will be planned, tracked, and changed.

Question 111: You are assessing the magnitude of variation of actual work performed from the original scope baseline. What technique are you utilizing?
The correct answer is C.

A: Scope baseline analysis is incorrect because it is not a term referenced within the PMBOK® Guide.

B: Change control assessment considers the impact of change requests received, not the magnitude of variation from the original scope baseline.

C: You use your project performance measurements to assess the difference between what the scope originally said and what it is now doing. This must always be reflected in the scope baseline.

D: Variation change analysis is incorrect because it is not a term referenced within the PMBOK® Guide.

Question 112: You are leading a PMP® study group within your organization. You are widely respected within the organization for your theoretical and practical knowledge, particularly in those areas required to pass the PMP®. Several of the students in the class are struggling with some of the concepts in the recommended study material, particularly the PMBOK® Guide. An area of concern to most of the class relates to the distinction between the focus of the Validate Scope and Quality Control processes. They look to you for clarification and a clear explanation. How do you best describe the difference between these two processes?
The correct answer is C.

A: This answer is incorrect because both Quality Control and Validate Scope are monitoring and controlling processes.

B: This answer is incorrect because while Quality Control is a quality management process concerned with the correctness and quality of the project deliverables, Validate Scope is concerned not with completeness of deliverables but with the acceptance of the deliverables against the customer requirements.

C: Quality Control is a quality management process concerned with the correctness and quality of the project deliverables; Validate Scope is concerned with the acceptance of the deliverables against the customer requirements.

D: This answer in incorrect because the project sponsor is not responsible for performing work in the Validate Scope process.

Project Time Management

Question 113: You are helping a colleague to study for the PMP® exam, and as part of his study plan he is using the PMBOK® Guide as one of his reference books. He is having difficulty understanding the Time Management knowledge area processes, particularly how inputs from one process are often outputs from other processes and as such there is an order in which the processes are generally performed. You offer some advice and describe the generally correct order of schedule development activities in the Time Management knowledge area in the PMBOK® Guide. What is your answer?
    The correct answer is A.

        A: If you read the sequence carefully, it becomes apparent that each one must precede the next because outputs from one become inputs into the other. You start by defining activities and end by developing the schedule. Along the way, you first put the defined activities in sequence; then, using this information, you estimate the activity resources; and then you can estimate the activity durations. Some smaller projects may do the activities concurrently.

        B: This answer is incorrect because if you read the sequence carefully, it becomes apparent that each one must precede the next because outputs from one become inputs into the other. For example, you must start, not end, with Define Activities.

        C: This answer is incorrect because if you read the sequence carefully, it becomes apparent that each one must precede the next because outputs from one become inputs into the other. For example, you generally sequence the activities immediately after defining the activities.

        D: This answer is incorrect because if you read the sequence carefully, it becomes apparent that each one must precede the next because outputs from one become inputs into the other. In this answer, you should define the activities before sequencing them.

    Question 114: You are using the work packages from your WBS to assist with creating your project schedule. You begin breaking the work packages down into the actual work necessary to complete the work package. What are you in the process of defining?
    The correct answer is C.

        A: WBS dictionary items provide more detailed information about each node of the WBS. They do not refer to any work below the level of work package.

        B: Project tasks is an informal term used by some project managers. For the purpose of the exam, the correct term to use is activities.

C: When you developed your WBS, your process of decomposition went down to a level where the element of the scope could be accurately estimated for duration and cost. The next step in the decomposition process is to break it down into activities that represent the actual work needed to complete the work package. This is essential to achieve a robust project schedule.

D: Work package assignments refer to the resources allocated to complete the work packages.

Question 115: You are the project manager on a project that is currently in the planning stage. You are working on your project schedule and beginning the process of defining your activity list. Involving your team members in this process would result in what outcome?
The correct answer is A.

A: Involving the people who will actually be responsible for completing the work will result in more accurate information. It is not certain that the involvement of team members will add extra cost to the project because you are not given enough information to decide this.

B: This answer is incorrect because involving the people who will actually be responsible for completing the work will result in more accurate information, leading to greater efficiencies.

C: This answer is incorrect because involving the people who will actually be responsible for completing the work will result in greater morale because people will feel valued.

D: This answer is incorrect because involving the people who will actually be responsible for completing the work will result in more accurate information. It is not certain the involvement of team members will add extra cost to the project because you are not given enough information to decide this.

Question 116: You have your activity list completed and are explaining to your team members what it contains. Which of the following is not contained on the activity list?
The correct answer is A.

A: The milestone list is found in your WBS dictionary.

B: The scope of work description is contained in the activity list.

C: All schedule activities required on the project are contained in the activity list.

D: Activity identifiers are contained in the activity list.

Question 117: You and your project management team are conducting the activity sequencing for a new project. The team has determined that Task A takes 3 days. Task B is dependent on Task A finishing and has a duration of 1 day. Task C takes 4 days. Task D is dependent on Task C starting and has a duration of 7 days. Task E is dependent on both Task C and Task D finishing and has a duration of 2 days. Task F is dependent on both Task E and Task B finishing and has a duration of 4 days. What is the duration of the project?
The correct answer is B.

> **A:** 10 days is incorrect. Did you read this question properly? Did you notice that there is a start-to-start relationship between Task D and Task C? Try recalculating with this information.

> **B:** 13 days is the correct answer. Well done for noticing that there is a start-to-start relationship between Task D and Task C.

> **C:** 17 days is incorrect. Did you read this question properly? Did you notice that there is a start-to-start relationship between Task D and Task C? Try recalculating with this information.

> **D:** 8 days is incorrect. Did you read this question properly? Did you notice that there is a start-to-start relationship between Task D and Task C? Try recalculating with this information.

Question 118: You are leading your team in the preparation of your project schedule and are currently sequencing the activities and determining which type of precedence relationship exists between them. Which of the following is the most commonly used type of precedence relationship that you will use?
The correct answer is D.

> **A:** Start-to-start is often used, but it is not the most common type of relationship.

> **B:** Very few activities have start-to-finish relationships, which means that the successor activity can't finish until its predecessor activity starts.

> **C:** Finish-to-finish is often used, but it is not the most common type of relationship.

> **D:** Finish-to-start means that the successor activity can't start until its predecessor activity is finished. Most activities have this sort of relationship. Very few have start-to-finish relationships, which means that the successor activity can't finish until its predecessor activity starts.

Question 119: You are using the precedence diagramming method to construct your project schedule network diagram. What other name is sometimes used to describe the precedence diagramming method?
The correct answer is A.

> **A:** The activity on node diagram is called this because the activity and information about the activity is shown on a node in the diagram represented by a square or rectangle. The relationship between nodes is shown by arrows.

B: Activity on arrow diagrams are referred to as arrow diagramming methods, not precedence diagramming methods.

C: Critical chain methodology refers to a process of including buffers throughout the schedule to deal with bottlenecks and uncertainty.

D: The precedence diagramming method can be used as part of the critical path methodology but the correct answer is activity on node.

Question 120: After talking with your team and the people responsible for completing the activity, you schedule two activities in your project so that the successor activity is able to start a week before the predecessor activity. What is this is an example of?
The correct answer is B.

A: Lag refers to the amount of time a successor activity must wait after the end of its predecessor before it can start.

B: A lead means that one activity can get a start before its predecessor finishes. Even through it has a finish-to-start relationship, it can start prior to the predecessor finishing. It would be shown on a network diagram as having a finish-to-start relationship with a week lead time.

C: Slack refers to the amount of time that an activity can be delayed before it impacts on successor activities start dates. It is one of the few instances in the PMBOK® Guide where two terms, slack and float, are interchangeable.

D: Float refers to the amount of time that an activity can be delayed before it impacts on successor activities' start dates. It is one of the few instances in the PMBOK® Guide where two terms, slack and float, are interchangeable.

Question 121: You are leading your project scheduling specialists in the completion of your project schedule and you wish to add leads and lags into your schedule to accurately reflect the total project duration. Some members of your team are confused about the two terms. How would you describe the difference between a lead and a lag to them?
The correct answer is A.

A: A lead means that one activity can get a start on its predecessor finishing. Even through it has a finish-to-start relationship, it can start prior to the predecessor finishing. It is shown on a network diagram as having a finish-to-start relationship with a certain lead time. A lag, on the other hand, is a delay between related activities.

B: This answer is incorrect because a lead does not mean both activities can start at the same time and a lag does not mean that neither can start until the other one starts.

CHAPTER 2 ▓ ANSWERS

C: This answer is incorrect because a lag does not mean the successor activity has a mandatory dependency and can not start until the predecessor activity is complete.

D: This answer is incorrect because a lead does not mean the amount of time free on the critical path between activities.

Question 122: You are completing the sequence of activities and note that one of your activities can not proceed until consent is granted by the local government agency. This is an example of what sort of dependency?
The correct answer is B.

A: A discretionary dependency is one where a successor should come after the predecessor but there is some discretion particularly if a schedule requires compression to shorten duration.

B: An external dependency means that you are waiting on work being done by people or organizations outside of the project.

C: There is no such term as environmental dependency in the PMBOK® Guide.

D: A mandatory dependency means that the successor must come after the predecessor. A mandatory dependency is also one which is internal, not external, to the project.

Question 123: You have successfully completed the first iteration of your project schedule network diagram. This indicates that you have completed the work in which PMBOK® Guide process?
The correct answer is D.

A: The Control Schedule process produces work performance information as its primary output.

B: The Define Activities process produces the activity list as its primary output.

C: The Develop Schedule process produces the schedule baseline as its primary output.

D: The first iteration of the project network schedule diagram is an output of the Sequence Activities process.

Question 124: Your project sponsor has asked to see your resource calendar. What sort of information is included in this document?
The correct answer is D.

A: The length of time the project will require input from external resources is not shown in the resource calendar. This is part of the information shown in the network schedule.

B: The dates of annual holidays for project team members is part of the information included in the resource calendar, but it is not the best answer available.

158

C: The resource calendar does not show the duration of each activity. This is shown in the network schedule.

D: Your resource calendar is a useful input into the Estimate Activity Resources process because it clearly shows when and where resources will be available to the project.

Question 125: You are estimating your activity resources and breaking down the work within each activity to its lowest level, and then aggregating these estimates to get a total quantity for each activity's resources. What tool or technique are you using?
The correct answer is B.

A: Published estimating data is a database of data about costs and quantities.

B: There are a number of ways to complete an estimating process. When an activity can not be estimated with a reasonable degree of confidence, the work within it is decomposed further down to its lowest level and the resource needs are then estimated. Aggregating these low-level estimates is called bottom-up estimating because you are working from the bottom level and going upwards.

C: Expert judgment is not the correct answer because it uses the experience of experts to help your estimating process.

D: Parametric estimating is a process that multiplies known quantities by known financial rates.

Question 126: You are about to begin the work to estimate activity durations on your project. Which of the following would not be an input you could use to complete this work?
The correct answer is B.

A: The Estimate Activity Durations process has many inputs, and activity attributes is one of them.

B: Activity duration estimates is an output, not an input, of the Estimate Activity Duration process, which is what the question is asking for.

C: The Estimate Activity Durations process has many inputs, and the project scope statement is one of them.

D: The Estimate Activity Durations process has many inputs, and the activity list is one of them.

Question 127: While estimating the activity durations on your project, you come across a similar project completed by your organization last year. To save time, you use information from this project to help estimate activity durations. This is an example of which tool or technique?
The correct answer is B.

> **A:** This is not an example of bottom-up estimating. Bottom-up estimating breaks down work packages and activities into the smallest possible piece of work and then adds up the time and cost for each to get a total project cost or duration.

> **B:** Analogous estimating involves using information from similar projects (i.e. an analogy) to estimate elements of your project, and it is generally less costly and time-consuming than other techniques.

> **C:** This is not an example of parametric estimating. Parametric estimating is a process that multiplies known quantities by known financial rates.

> **D:** This is not an example of three-point estimating. Three-point estimating uses the optimistic, realistic, and pessimistic estimates to calculate a weight average.

Question 128: As a result of a brainstorming session, your team determines that the most likely duration of an activity will be 8 days, the optimistic duration is 6 days, and the pessimistic duration is 16 days. What it the expected activity duration?
The correct answer is C.

> **A:** This answer is incorrect: it is arrived at by adding up the three duration estimates and dividing by 3, which is not the correct formula.

> **B:** This answer is incorrect: it is arrived at by adding up the three duration estimates and dividing by 6, which is not the correct formula.

> **C:** Using three-point estimating the expected duration is $(6+(8 \times 4)+16) / 6 = 9$ days.

> **D:** This answer is incorrect: it is arrived at simply by adding up the three duration estimates, which is not the correct formula.

Question 129: There is some uncertainty over the duration of a particular activity on your project. You call your team together, all of whom have experience in completing the activity. After a brainstorming session, they are able to determine a most likely duration, an optimistic duration, and a pessimistic duration. You then use these numbers to calculate the expected activity duration. This is an example of which sort of tool or technique?

The correct answer is B.

> **A:** This is not an example of bottom-up estimating. Bottom-up estimating breaks down work packages and activities into the smallest possible piece of work and then adds up the time and cost for each to get a total project cost or duration.

> **B:** Three-point estimating, or PERT analysis, uses a weighted average method with emphasis given to the most likely data in order to estimate a duration.

> **C:** This is not an example of analogous estimating. Analogous estimating involves using information from similar projects (i.e. an analogy) to estimate elements of your project, and it is generally less costly and time-consuming than other techniques.

> **D:** This is not an example of parametric estimating. Parametric estimating is a process that multiplies known quantities by known financial rates.

Question 130: To estimate the amount of time it will take to install 500 meters of cable on your project, you divide the number of meters required by how many meters an hour the person laying the cable can lay. This is an example of which sort of tool or technique?

The correct answer is D.

> **A:** This is not an example of three-point estimating. Three-point estimating uses the optimistic, realistic, and pessimistic estimates to calculate a weight average.

> **B:** This is not an example of bottom-up estimating. Bottom-up estimating breaks down work packages and activities into the smallest possible piece of work and then adds up the time and cost for each to get a total project cost or duration.

> **C:** This is not an example of analogous estimating. Analogous estimating involves using information from similar projects (i.e. an analogy) to estimate elements of your project, and it is generally less costly and time-consuming than other techniques.

> **D:** Parametric estimating uses numbers and quantifiable measures to estimate. Remember if you see the word "metric" it means number of measure.

Question 131: You are leading your team members in the development of your project schedule. You have just started the process and are checking that you have all the appropriate inputs required. Which of the following would not be an input into this process?
The correct answer is D.

> **A:** There are many inputs into the Develop Schedule process, and resource calendar is one of them.

> **B:** There are many inputs into the Develop Schedule process, and project schedule network diagrams is one of them.

> **C:** There are many inputs into the Develop Schedule process, and the activity list is one of them.

> **D:** The project schedule is an output from the Develop Schedule process.

Question 132: What is the PMBOK® Guide process of analyzing activity sequences, durations, resource requirements, and scheduled constraints to create the project schedule?
The correct answer is C.

> **A:** Project Schedule Development is not the name of a PMBOK® Guide process.

> **B:** Create Project Schedule is not the name of a PMBOK® Guide process.

> **C:** This is the final stage in the planning process group for the Time Management knowledge area. It takes all the previous information from the previous planning processes and makes the project schedule. This process will be quite iterative because at the start of the project the available information is less accurate.

> **D:** Schedule Management is not the name of a PMBOK® Guide process.

Question 133: You are completing a network diagram with the following information: Task A has a duration of 3 days and has the start as a predecessor; Task B has a duration of 5 days and also has the start as a predecessor; Task C has a duration of 4 days and has Task A as a predecessor; Task D has a duration of 4 days and has Task B as a predecessor; Task E has a duration of 6 days and has Tasks C and D as predecessors; Task F has a duration of 5 days and has Task D as a predecessor; the finish milestone has a duration of zero days and has Tasks E and F as predecessors. Using this data, what is the duration of the project?
The correct answer is D.

> **A:** 16 is not the correct answer. This question requires you to draw a network diagram. In this case, once you draw the network diagram correctly, you can see that the duration of the project is 15 days.

B: 14 is not the correct answer. In this case, once you draw the network diagram you can see that the duration of the project is 15 days.

C: 13 is not the correct answer. This question requires you to draw a network diagram. The duration of the project is represented by completing a forward pass over the network diagram. In this case, once you draw the network diagram you can see that the duration of the project is 15 days.

D: This question requires you to draw a network diagram. The duration of the project is represented by completing a forward pass over the network diagram. In this case, once you draw the network diagram you can see that the duration of the project is 15 days.

Question 134: You are completing a network diagram with the following information: Task A has a duration of 3 days and has the start as a predecessor; Task B has a duration of 5 days and also has the start as a predecessor; Task C has a duration of 4 days and has Task A as a predecessor; Task D has a duration of 4 days and has Task B as a predecessor; Task E has a duration of 6 days and has Tasks C and D as predecessors; Task F has a duration of 5 days and has Task D as a predecessor; the finish milestone has a duration of zero days and has Tasks E and F as predecessors. What is the critical path for this network diagram?

The correct answer is B.

A: Start-B-D-F-Finish is not a critical path. The critical path is obtained after you have completed both a forward pass and backward pass over the network diagram. In this instance, that forward pass reveals a duration of 15 days and the critical path is Start-B-D-E-Finish.

B: The critical path is obtained after you have completed both a forward pass and backward pass over the network diagram. In this instance, that forward pass reveals a duration of 15 days and the critical path is Start-B-D-E-Finish. Activities on the critical path have no float in them, thus any delays on the critical path directly impact the project duration.

C: Start-A-C-E-Finish is not a critical path. The critical path is obtained after you have completed both a forward pass and backward pass over the network diagram. In this instance, that forward pass reveals a duration of 15 days and the critical path is Start-B-D-E-Finish.

D: Start-A-C-F-Finish is not a critical path. The critical path is obtained after you have completed both a forward pass and backward pass over the network diagram. In this instance, that forward pass reveals a duration of 15 days and the critical path is Start-B-D-E-Finish.

Question 135: According to Goldratt's critical chain theory, what should you do in order to reduce risk in project schedules?
The correct answer is B.

> **A:** Starting activities in the feeder chains as late as possible would not reduce risk in the project schedule; it would add risk.

> **B:** In critical chain theory, the feeder chains are activities that are not on the critical path. These tasks are scheduled to be done as late as possible and then buffered so that they start earlier than the late schedule dates. Buffer is also added to the critical path of the schedule to improve the probability that the project will finish on time. Feeder chain activities as well as critical chain activities are not started as early as possible or as late as possible. They are started as late as possible minus their buffer.

> **C:** Starting activities in the critical chain as early as possible would not necessarily reduce risk, whereas the correct answer of adding a buffer would definitely reduce risk, making it the best answer.

> **D:** Starting activities in the feeder chains as early as possible would not necessarily reduce risk, whereas the correct answer of adding a buffer would definitely reduce risk, making it the best answer.

Question 136: During a discussion with a fellow project manager you realize that she is using the terms *critical path method* and *critical chain method* incorrectly. You offer some pieces of advice and insight into how the two methods are different. Which of these statements about the critical path method and the critical chain method is FALSE?
The correct answer is D.

> **A:** The critical chain method does not schedule only late start dates to planned activities, so this answer is incorrect.

> **B:** Both methods seek to use accurate estimates.

> **C:** The critical path method is not just focused on managing the total float of network paths, so this answer is incorrect.

> **D:** Both the critical path method and the critical chain method account for resource availability.

Question 137: You are adding duration buffers that are non-workable schedule activities to manage uncertainty in your project schedule. What tool or technique are you using?
The correct answer is D.

> **A:** Parametric estimating is a process that multiplies known quantities by known financial rates.

> **B:** The critical path method does not add in buffers between activities.

C: Three-point estimating uses the pessimistic, realistic, and optimistic estimates to get a weight average.

D: The critical chain method is a schedule network analysis technique that modifies a project schedule to account for limited resources by deliberately adding in non-working time buffers, which is intended to protect the target finish date from slippage along the critical chain.

Question 138: You are using a methodology that calculates the amount of float on various paths in the network diagram to determine the minimum project duration. What tool or technique are you using?
The correct answer is A.

A: Critical path methodology focuses on the amount of float in network paths to determine the critical path through a project. The critical path has no float associated with it and as such represents the greatest risk to the project duration.

B: The critical chain method is a schedule network analysis technique that modifies a project schedule to account for limited resources by deliberately adding in non-working time buffers, which is intended to protect the target finish date from slippage along the critical chain.

C: Parametric estimating is a process that multiplies known quantities by known financial rates.

D: Three-point estimating uses the pessimistic, realistic, and optimistic estimates to get a weight average.

Question 139: In the first attempt at resource leveling the project schedule, what would you expect to occur?
The correct answer is A.

A: The logical analysis of the schedule often produces a preliminary schedule that requires more resources during certain time periods than are available, or requires changes in resource levels that are not manageable. Heuristics such as "allocate scarce resources to critical path activities first" can be applied to develop a schedule that reflects such constraints. Resource leveling, because of the limited availability of the resources, often results in a project duration that is longer than the preliminary schedule.

B: The number of resources required does not generally decrease during a first attempt at resource leveling. It is more likely that the duration will increase.

C: The number of resources required does not generally increase during a first attempt at resource leveling. It is more likely that the duration will increase.

D: The first attempt at resource leveling generally increases, not decreases, the project duration due to the reallocation of resources and the consequences on the timing of the work being done.

Question 140: You are the project manager on a software project. While examining your schedule you see that there has been a delay in completing a task. The sensible choice seems to move a person, someone who is an expert on the work that is behind, from another task. There is a choice between two people who are working on different tasks. One person is working on a task that has 5 days of free float and the other is working on a task that has 8 days of total float and no free float. What is your BEST course of action?
The correct answer is D.

A: This answer is incorrect because you must choose the person with the least amount of float.

B: This answer is incorrect because the person working on the task that has total float of 8 days that can be used on the task that is in trouble, but since there is zero free float for this task, there will have to be a rescheduling of other tasks to allow this.

C: This answer is incorrect because you must choose the person with the least amount of float.

D: The person who is working on the task that has free float of 5 days can be used on the task that is in trouble for 5 days without affecting the other task schedules in the project. The person working on the task that has total float of 8 days can be used on the task that is in trouble, but since there is zero free float for this task, there will have to be a rescheduling of other tasks to allow this.

Question 141: You are using a computer-based modelling technique that examines possible outcomes based on a range of potential probabilities if a particular situation occurs. What is this technique called?
The correct answer is D.

A: This is not an example of parametric estimating. Parametric estimating is a process that multiplies known quantities by known financial rates.

B: Schedule compression involves using fast tracking or crashing to reduce the project duration.

C: The critical chain method is a schedule network analysis technique that modifies a project schedule to account for limited resources by deliberately adding in non-working time buffers, which is intended to protect the target finish date from slippage along the critical chain.

D: A what-if scenario analysis runs through all the different outcomes if a particular scenario occurs. This level of information can assist with many types of estimating to get the full range of possibilities. The most comprehensive type of what-if scenario analysis is a Monte Carlo analysis.

Question 142: Your project team is behind schedule and has decided to compress the schedule. They have requested extra budget to bring in the additional resources required. Which schedule compression technique are they seeking to use?
The correct answer is B.

A: Compressing is not the correct answer because it is a generic term for all schedule compression techniques.

B: Crashing a project schedule involves bringing in more resource to do the work. Extra resources usually cost more money. Fast tracking, on the other hand, involves completing activities in parallel that might normally be done in sequence. This does not always cost more money.

C: Fast tracking is a schedule compression technique but one that programs activities in parallel instead of in sequence. Crashing is the other main schedule compression technique and it uses extra budget to provide more resources.

D: Resource leveling is not the correct answer because it focuses on getting an optimal allocation of resources across the project.

Question 143: You have managed to bring forward the predicted completion date for your project by doing in parallel several of the activities that were scheduled to be done in sequence. What is this technique called?
The correct answer is C.

A: It may seem like you are accelerating the project schedule but the correct term to use is fast tracking.

B: Increasing priorities will not change the order in which work has to be done, nor the duration.

C: Fast tracking a schedule is finding activities that can be done in parallel that were originally scheduled to be done in sequence.

D: Crashing a project schedule involves bringing in more resources to do the work. Extra resources usually cost more money. Fast tracking, on the other hand, involves completing activities in parallel that might normally be done in sequence. This does not always cost more money.

Question 144: You are working on a project to build a new house. Usually you would wait until the concrete foundation dried, and then erect the wall on top of it. To speed up the project, you start putting the wall frame together off site while the concrete foundation is drying. This is an example of which schedule compression technique?
The correct answer is A.

> **A:** Fast tracking means running activities that might normally be run in sequence in parallel. It does not normally incur extra cost.

> **B:** Compressing is not the correct answer because it is a generic term for all schedule compression techniques.

> **C:** Crashing a project schedule involves bringing in more resources to do the work. Extra resources usually cost more money. Fast tracking, on the other hand, involves completing activities in parallel that might normally be done in sequence. This does not always cost more money.

> **D:** Resource leveling is not the correct answer because it focuses on getting an optimal allocation of resources across the project.

Question 145: Your project sponsor asks you to attend a senior management meeting and present a brief update on your project progress. Which of the following would be best to use in the presentation?
The correct answer is A.

> **A:** The question sets out that it is senior management and you only have a short amount of time, therefore you want to present only high-level information about the project. A bar chart, such as a Gantt chart, does this very well.

> **B:** The project management plan would not be the best answer because it contains far too much detail to communicate effectively in this situation.

> **C:** Work performance information would not be the best answer because it contains far too much detail to communicate effectively in this situation.

> **D:** The schedule network diagram would not be the best answer because it contains far too much detail to communicate effectively in this situation.

Question 146: What is the name of the process in the PMBOK® Guide that monitors the status of the project to update project progress and manage changes to the schedule baseline?
The correct answer is D.

> **A:** The Develop Schedule process produces the project schedule and schedule baseline.

> **B:** Monitoring and Controlling is a process group, not an individual process.

C: This answer is not correct because it is a made-up process name.

D: Control Schedule is the only Time Management knowledge area process that appears in the Monitoring and Controlling process group.

Question 147: Your project is underway and you are measuring the forecast schedule against the actual schedule, checking for variances between the two and initiating corrective actions if required. To successfully complete this work you require a range of inputs. Which of the following is not one of these inputs?
The correct answer is B.

A: The Control Schedule process has several inputs, and the project management plan is one of them.

B: This is a tricky question that requires you to know the difference between inputs and outputs. Work performance information, such as the calculated SV and SPI values for WBS components, are outputs of the Control Schedule process.

C: The Control Schedule process has several inputs, and the project schedule is one of them.

D: The Control Schedule process has several inputs, and work performance data is one of them.

Question 148: While using the earned value management technique to measure project schedule progress on your project, you discover that your project's schedule performance index (SPI) is 0.9. What does this mean?
The correct answer is C.

A: This calculation does not immediately tell you if your amount of buffer is less than optimal.

B: This calculation does not immediately tell you if your network diagram was incorrectly put together.

C: An SPI of 1 means the project is on schedule, less that 1 means behind schedule, and greater than 1 means ahead of schedule.

D: This answer is incorrect because an SPI of 1 means the project is on schedule, less that 1 means behind schedule, and greater than 1 means ahead of schedule.

Question 149: You are a project manager on a project where your SPI has been calculated at .95. Your earned value (EV) has been calculated at $10,000, and your actual cost (AC) is $10,400, so what is your planned value (PV)?
The correct answer is B.

> **A:** $10,000 is not the correct answer. To get this answer, you need to work backward from the normal equation for calculating SPI. In this case, the value equals $10,000 divided by .95, which is $10,526.

> **B:** To get this answer you need to work backward from the normal equation for calculating SPI. In this case, the value equals $10,000 divided by .95, which is $10,526.

> **C:** $9,500 is not the correct answer. To get this answer, you need to work backward from the normal equation for calculating SPI. In this case, the value equals $10,000 divided by .95, which is $10,526.

> **D:** $10,947 is not the correct answer. To get this answer, you need to work backward from the normal equation for calculating SPI. In this case, the value equals $10,000 divided by .95, which is $10,526.

Question 150: As part of the development of your project schedule you are informed that a particular activity has an estimated optimistic duration of 7 days, an estimated pessimistic duration of 15 days, and will most likely take 10 days to complete. Using PERT analysis, what is the standard deviation?
The correct answer is D.

> **A:** 0.5 is incorrect, and for the PMP® exam you will need to know how to calculate standard deviation and variance by simple means. In this case, Standard Deviation = (P - O) / 6.

> **B:** 10.33 is incorrect, and for the PMP® exam you will need to know how to calculate standard deviation and variance by simple means. In this case, Standard Deviation = (P - O) / 6.

> **C:** 1.76 is incorrect, and for the PMP® exam you will need to know how to calculate standard deviation and variance by simple means. In this case, Standard Deviation = (P - O) / 6.

> **D:** For the PMP® exam you will need to know how to calculate standard deviation and variance by simple means. In this case, Standard Deviation = (P - O) / 6.

Question 151: As part of development of your project schedule, you are informed that a particular activity has an estimated optimistic duration of 7 days, an estimated pessimistic duration of 15 days, and will most likely take 10 days to complete. Your sponsor asks you the activity duration range in which you are 95% confident that the activity will be delivered. What is your response?

The correct answer is B.

> **A:** 8-12 days is incorrect because the question is asking you to calculate 2 standard deviations on either side of the expected mean of 10 days. The 95% confidence interval is two standard deviations on either side of the mean. We know the mean equals 10.33 and the standard deviation equals 1.33, so the duration range that we are 95% confident about is 10.33±(2 x 1.33).

> **B:** The 95% confidence interval is two standard deviations on either side of the mean. We know the mean equals 10.33 and the standard deviation equals 1.33, so the duration range that we are 95% confident about is 10.33±(2 x 1.33).

> **C:** 9-11.66 days is incorrect because the question is asking you to calculate 2 standard deviations on either side of the expected mean of 10 days. The 95% confidence interval is two standard deviations on either side of the mean. We know the mean equals 10.33 and the standard deviation equals 1.33, so the duration range that we are 95% confident about is 10.33±(2 x 1.33).

> **D:** 10 days is incorrect because the question is asking you to calculate 2 standard deviations on either side of the expected mean of 10 days. The 95% confidence interval is two standard deviations on either side of the mean. We know the mean equals 10.33 and the standard deviation equals 1.33, so the duration range that we are 95% confident about is 10.33±(2 x 1.33).

Question 152: Yvette is the project manager for a software project. She and her team are determining the activity duration estimates for the project. She has requested that each team member determine the estimates by multiplying the quantity of work to be performed by the known historical productivity rate of the individual department. Yvette has asked her team to generate the estimates using what technique?

The correct answer is A.

> **A:** Parametric estimating is an estimating technique that uses a statistical relationship between historical data and other variables to calculate an estimate for activity parameters.

> **B:** Analogous estimate use an analogy from a previous project and extrapolates from that an estimate for a current project. The question presents an example of parametric estimating.

> **C:** Three-point estimating uses the pessimistic, realistic, and optimistic estimates to get a weight average.

> **D:** Expert judgment uses the experience of experts to assist in preparing estimates.

Question 153: Consider the following information. What is the critical path? Task A has a duration of 3 days and is a starting activity. Task B has a duration of 6 days and has Task A as a predecessor. Task C has a duration of 5 days and has Tasks A and B as predecessors. Task D has a duration of 4 days, and has Task B as a predecessor. Task E has a duration of 1 day and has Task C as the predecessor. Task F has a duration of 6 days and has Tasks D and E as predecessors. Task G has a duration of 4 days, and has Tasks E and F as predecessors.

The correct answer is A.

Once you have compiled information in the question into a table that lists task ID, duration, and predecessors, you need to map out a network diagram. This will show that the critical path is A-B-C-E-F-G. This question may have taken you quite a while to work out; if you get a question such as this in the exam, you must remember that every question is worth one point. In the time taken to answer this question you could have answered several other questions.

Question 154: Consider the following information. How many tasks have a slack of 2 days? Task A has a duration of 3 days and is a starting activity. Task B has a duration of 6 days and has Task A as a predecessor. Task C has a duration of 5 days and has Tasks A and B as predecessors. Task D has a duration of 4 days and has Task B as a predecessor. Task E has a duration of 1 day and has Task C as a predecessor. Task F has a duration of 6 days and has Tasks D and E as predecessors. Task G has a duration of 4 days and has Tasks E and F as predecessors.

The correct answer is D.

Once you have compiled information in the question into a table that lists task ID, duration, and predecessors, you need to map out a network diagram. This will show that the critical path is A-B-C-E-F-G and that only Task D has slack of 2 days. This question may have taken you quite a while to work out; if you get a question such as this in the exam, you must remember that every question is worth one point. In the time taken to answer this question you could have answered several other questions.

Project Cost Management

Question 155: You have finished putting together your project budget and notice that there is a point at which cost and staffing levels are highest. At which point in the project would this generally be?

The correct answer is C.

> **A:** There are costs associated with the start of the project part of the project life cycle but they are not as high as carrying out the project work, which has the greatest assignment of resources and activities.

> **B:** There are costs associated with the organizing and preparing part of the project life cycle but they are not as high as carrying out the project work, which has the greatest assignment of resources and activities.

C: Generally speaking, cost and staffing levels are highest during the phase in the project life cycle where work is being carried out.

D: There are costs associated with the closure part of the project life cycle but they are not as high as carrying out the project work, which has the greatest assignment of resources and activities.

Question 156: You are completing the work of aggregating the estimated costs of individual activities or work packages to establish an authorized cost baseline. What PMBOK® Guide process are you completing?

The correct answer is D.

A: The cost performance baseline is an output, not a process.

B: The Estimate Costs process does not aggregate individual cost estimates.

C: The Control Costs process monitors and controls change to the costs estimates and project budget and does not aggregate individual cost estimates.

D: This description matches the PMBOK® Guide description of the Determine Budget process.

Question 157: You have completed the work required to develop your cost management plan and are introducing it to your team members so that they are aware of its purpose and limitations. The cost management plan can establish all of the following except?

The correct answer is C.

A: The cost management plan establishes several things relating to costs on the project, and the units of measure is one of them.

B: The cost management plan establishes several things relating to costs on the project, and the level of accuracy is one of them.

C: Activity definition is performed during the project schedule management processes.

D: The cost management plan establishes several things relating to costs on the project, and the control thresholds is one of them.

Question 158: Costs that cannot be directly traced to a specific project and are accumulated and allocated equitably over multiple projects are known as what?

The correct answer is A.

A: This answer is correct because costs such as organization overheads that are spread over several projects are known as indirect costs.

B: This answer is incorrect because costs that are directly attributable to a project are known as direct costs.

C: This answer, allocatable costs, is not correct because it is not a term referenced within the PMBOK® Guide.

D: This answer, non-projectized costs, is not correct because it is not a term referenced within the PMBOK® Guide.

Question 159: While completing the processes required to develop an approved project budget, you have started the work required to estimate costs on your project. In order to do this successfully, you should have access to several important inputs. Which of the following is not an input you would find useful to complete this work?
The correct answer is A.

A: Activity cost estimates is the output from the Estimate Costs process, which is what the question is referring to.

B: The question is asking about inputs into the Estimate Costs process in the PMBOK® Guide. This process has several inputs, and the project schedule is one of them.

C: The question is asking about inputs into the Estimate Costs process in the PMBOK® Guide. This process has several inputs, and the risk register is one of them.

D: The question is asking about inputs into the Estimate Costs process in the PMBOK® Guide. This process has several inputs, and the scope baseline is one of them.

Question 160: Which of the following is not an Organizational Process Asset you would consider when estimating costs on your project?
The correct answer is C.

A: There are many Organizational Process Assets you could use when estimating costs, and any historical information your organization has would be one of them.

B: There are many Organizational Process Assets you could use when estimating costs, and any cost estimating templates your organization has would be one of them.

C: Market considerations are an example of an enterprise environmental factor, not an Organizational Process Asset.

D: There are many Organizational Process Assets you could use when estimating costs, and any lessons learned database your organization has would be one of them.

Question 161: You are estimating the costs in your project and are using information from a previous, similar project as the basis for estimating in your current project. What technique are you using?

The correct answer is B.

> **A:** Parametric estimating is a process that multiplies known quantities by known financial rates.
>
> **B:** Analogous estimating is used several times as a tool and technique in different estimating areas throughout the PMBOK® Guide.
>
> **C:** Three-point estimating uses the pessimistic, realistic, and optimistic estimates to get a weight average.
>
> **D:** Published estimating data is a database of data about costs and quantities.

Question 162: You and your team are currently breaking down all the project deliverables into the smallest useful unit so that you can then estimate costs for each of these units and then aggregate these estimates into a total project cost estimate. What is the name of the technique you are using to estimate costs?

The correct answer is B.

> **A:** Parametric estimating is an estimating technique that uses a statistical relationship between historical data and other variables to calculate an estimate for activity parameters.
>
> **B:** Bottom-up estimating is a technique for estimating the cost of individual work packages with the lowest level of detail.
>
> **C:** Low-level estimating may sound correct but it is not a term referenced within the PMBOK® Guide.
>
> **D:** Project management software may be useful for developing cost estimates but it is a tool, not a technique.

Question 163: While developing individual costs estimates for work packages on your project, you use a technique that requires you to use a statistical relationship between historical data and other variables to calculate a cost estimate for a schedule activity resource. What is this estimating technique more commonly referred to as?

The correct answer is C.

> **A:** This answer is incorrect because it is not a term referenced within the PMBOK® Guide.
>
> **B:** Bottom-up estimating is a technique for estimating the cost of individual work packages with the lowest level of detail.
>
> **C:** Parametric estimating is a technique that uses a statistical relationship between historical data and other variables to calculate a cost estimate for a schedule activity resource.
>
> **D:** Top-down estimating is a macro estimating technique that assigns costs to particular deliverables and work packages.

Question 164: Your project sponsor has asked you to provide a cost estimate quickly to give the project steering group an idea of what the costs for a particular work package will be. Which of the following estimating techniques would you choose to use?
The correct answer is A.

> **A:** Analogous estimating can be done faster than the other techniques. It is generally less costly than other estimating techniques but it is also generally less accurate.

> **B:** Parametric estimating requires access to estimating databases and as such is generally more costly that analogous estimating.

> **C:** Resource rate estimating is not correct because it is a made-up term.

> **D:** Bottom-up estimating is not correct because the time and cost involved in decomposing the WBS means that it is more costly than analogous estimating.

Question 165: While completing the cost estimating process for a particular activity in your project, several members of your team disagree over the estimate to do the work. After a discussion with the team, you determine that the most likely cost of the activity will be $25, the optimistic cost of the activity will be $15, and the pessimistic cost will be $70. Using the three-point estimating technique what is the expected cost of the activity?
The correct answer is C.

> **A:** $110 is not the correct answer. The three point-estimating technique, or PERT analysis, uses a weighted average method to arrive at what should be a more accurate estimate. In this case, the correct answer is $(15+(4 \times 25)+70) / 6 = \$30.83$.

> **B:** $36.66. is not the correct answer. The three-point estimating technique, or PERT analysis, uses a weighted average method to arrive at what should be a more accurate estimate. In this case, the correct answer is $(15+(4 \times 25)+70) / 6 = \$30.83$.

> **C:** The three-point estimating technique, or PERT analysis, uses a weighted average method to arrive at what should be a more accurate estimate. In this case, the correct answer is $(15+(4 \times 25)+70) / 6 = \$30.83$.

> **D:** $25.83 is not the correct answer. The three-point estimating technique, or PERT analysis, uses a weighted average method to arrive at what should be a more accurate estimate. In this case, the correct answer is $(15+(4 \times 25)+70) / 6 = \$30.83$.

Question 166: While completing the cost estimating for a particular activity in your project, several members of your team disagree over the estimate to do the work. After a discussion with the team, you determine that the most likely cost of the activity will be $50, the optimistic cost of the activity will be $30, and the pessimistic cost will be $70. Using the three-point estimating technique, what is the expected cost of the activity?
The correct answer is D.

> **A:** $150 is not the correct answer. The three-point estimating technique, or PERT analysis, uses a weighted average method to arrive at what should be a more accurate estimate. In this case, the correct answer is $(30+(4 \times 50)+70) / 6 = \$50$.

> **B:** $25 is not the correct answer. The three-point estimating technique, or PERT analysis, uses a weighted average method to arrive at what should be a more accurate estimate. In this case, the correct answer is $(30+(4 \times 50)+70) / 6 = \$50$.

> **C:** $70 is not the correct answer. The three-point estimating technique, or PERT analysis, uses a weighted average method to arrive at what should be a more accurate estimate. In this case, the correct answer is $(30+(4 \times 50)+70) / 6 = 50$.

> **D:** The three-point estimating technique, or PERT analysis, uses a weighted average method to arrive at what should be a more accurate estimate. In this case, the correct answer is $(30+(4 \times 50)+70) / 6 = 50$.

Question 167: During your cost estimating you include a figure for cost uncertainty on your project, and the project sponsor agrees to give you delegated authority to manage this reserve. What is this figure generally known as?
The correct answer is B.

> **A:** Reserve analysis is the process of deciding what sort of reserve you need and once agreed on, reexamining it to make sure it is still appropriate.

> **B:** When you are preparing estimates, generally there are still a few unknowns in the project and it is wise to include a contingency reserve as part of your project budget. This can be reduced or given up as the project progresses and more information is known.

> **C:** Management reserve is a fund held by management for unforeseen risks that emerge on projects. It is not generally calculated for individual projects.

> **D:** Slush fund is an informal name sometimes given to management reserves.

Question 168: You are using the three-point estimating method of scheduling for a project. The variance for the project is found to be 16 days and the duration of the project is found to be 90 days. What is the range of values for the project duration such that there will be at least a 95% probability that the actual project completion will fall between the high and low value of the range of values?
The correct answer is C.

> **A:** 58-122 days is not the correct answer because the question is asking you to calculate 2 standard deviations on either side of the mean of 90, where the standard deviation is 4, which is the square root of the variance.

> **B:** 74-106 days is not the correct answer because the question is asking you to calculate 2 standard deviations on either side of the mean of 90, where the standard deviation is 4, which is the square root of the variance.

> **C:** The question is asking for two standard deviations on either side of the mean of 90. So to get the answer you first get the square root of 16, which is 4. You multiply this by 2 to get 8, and then add 8, and then subtract 8 from the mean of 90.

> **D:** 86-94 is not the correct answer because the question is asking you to calculate 2 standard deviations on either side of the mean of 90, where the standard deviation is 4, which is the square root of the variance.

Question 169: You are aggregating the cost estimates of individual activities and work packages to establish an authorized cost baseline. Which PMBOK® Guide process are you engaged in?
The correct answer is B.

> **A:** Budget preparation is not a PMBOK® Guide process.

> **B:** Once you have done all your costs estimating, you can add them all together to get a cost baseline; this is known as the Determine Budget process. Although represented as sequential processes, they may be done concurrently.

> **C:** The Estimate Costs process develops individual cost estimates, which are then aggregating over time in the Determine Budget process to establish an authorized cost baseline.

> **D:** The cost performance baseline is not a PMBOK® Guide process.

Question 170: You have spent time with your team developing individual cost estimates and are now using the project schedule to determine your project budget. Which of the following inputs would you not find helpful to complete this work?

The correct answer is A.

> **A:** The cost baseline is an output, not an input of the Determine Budget process in the PMBOK® Guide, so this is the correct answer.

> **B:** The basis of estimates is an input into the Determine Budget process in the PMBOK® Guide, which is helpful.

> **C:** Activity cost estimates are an input into the Determine Budget process in the PMBOK® Guide, which is helpful.

> **D:** The scope baseline is an input into the Determine Budget process in the PMBOK® Guide, which is helpful.

Question 171: What is the authorized time-phased budget at completion used to measure, monitor, and control overall cost performance on the project more commonly known as?

The correct answer is B.

> **A:** The approved project budget may sound like a correct term but it is not one that is in the PMBOK® Guide.

> **B:** The cost baseline is the aggregation of your Estimate Cost and Determine Budget processes.

> **C:** Activity cost estimates are an input into the Determine Budget process and they become the cost baseline once amalgamated with elements of the schedule.

> **D:** Total funding requirements may sound like a correct term but it is not one that is in the PMBOK® Guide.

Question 172: You are monitoring the status of the project to update the project budget and manage changes to the cost baseline. Which PMBOK® Guide process best describes the work are you carrying out?

The correct answer is B.

> **A:** Determine Budget develops the project cost baseline, which is then monitored during the Control Costs process.

> **B:** The process of controlling costs is one of the more technical processes to understand for the PMP® exam because it includes the earned value tools and techniques.

> **C:** Earned value management is not a process but a tool that can be used during the Control Costs process.

> **D:** Cost aggregation is when you add all your individual cost estimates together. It is not a Monitoring and Controlling process.

Question 173: While using a technique that gathers a number of key metrics to assess, track, and forecast variances in both project cost and time, you discover that the tool is being used without all of the required inputs. Which of the following inputs would you not require to use this particular technique?

The correct answer is A.

> **A:** Work performance information is an input to the Control Cost process. The other three are key dimensions of the Earned Value Management tool.
>
> **B:** Earned value is the value of the work actually performed and is a key element in earned value management.
>
> **C:** Planned value is the planned value of work performed and is a key element in earned value management.
>
> **D:** Actual cost is the cost to do the work performed and is a key element in earned value management.

Question 174: After measuring your project performance you note that your schedule variance is $75,000. What would your BEST course of action be?

The correct answer is C.

> **A:** You don't need to fast track the schedule because a positive schedule variance means you are ahead of time.
>
> **B:** You don't need to crash the schedule because a positive schedule variance means you are ahead of time.
>
> **C:** A positive schedule variance means you are achieving ahead of your baseline, so feel free to congratulate your team. Remember that you must always be delivering to the agreed documentation, including the relevant baseline documents. As such, you will need to take the information that informed you of your positive schedule variance and, after properly considering it through your Change Control process, update your baseline documents.
>
> **D:** You are doing well but you must process the variance through your agreed Change Control process.

Question 175: The earned value on your project is $15,000, the planned value is $20,000 and the actual cost is $18,000. What is your schedule variance?

The correct answer is D.

> **A-C:** These answers are not correct. If you arrived at one of these values, remember that schedule variance = earned value - planned value, so SV = 15,000 - 20,000 = -5,000.
>
> **D:** Schedule variance = earned value - planned value, so SV = 15,000 - 20,000 = -5,000.

Question 176: The earned value on your project is $18,000, the planned value is $20,000, and the actual cost is $15,000. What is your cost variance?
The correct answer is A.

> **A:** Cost variance = earned value - actual costs, so
> CV = 18,000 - 15,000 = 3,000.

> **B-D:** These answers are not correct. If you arrived at one of these answers, remember that cost variance = earned value - actual costs (AC), so CV = 18,000 - 15,000 = 3,000.

Question 177: The earned value on your project is $26,000, the planned value is $20,000, and the actual cost is $18,000. What is your schedule variance?
The correct answer is A.

> **A:** Schedule variance = earned value - planned value, so
> SV = 26,000 - 20,000 = 6,000.

> **B-D:** These answers are not correct. If you arrived at one of these answers, remember that schedule variance = earned value - planned value, so SV = 26,000 - 20,000 = 6,000.

Question 178: The earned value on your project is $52,000, the planned value is $51,000 and the actual cost is $49,000. What is your cost variance?
The correct answer is A.

> **A:** Cost variance = earned value - actual costs, so CV = 52,000 - 49,000 = 3,000.

> **B-D:** These answers are not correct. If you arrived at one of these answers, remember that cost variance = earned value - actual costs, so CV = 52,000 - 49,000 = 3,000.

Question 179: A new junior project manager seems to be having some difficulty understanding key terms used in the reports being prepared for the project. He is particularly confused by the earned value management system and the approved project budget. You explain to him that there are easy ways to understand what each element means and demonstrate this by point out that the total planned value of the project is better known as what?
The correct answer is D.

> **A:** The approved project budget is more correctly called the cost baseline.

> **B:** The cost baseline represents the approved budget for the project.

> **C:** Actual cost is the cost to do the work performed and is a key element in earned value management.

> **D:** Budget at completion (BAC) is the total planned value for the project.

Question 180: What is the term for the measurement of the authorized work that has been completed and the authorized budget for such completed work?
The correct answer is B.

> **A:** The cost baseline represents the approved budget for the project.

> **B:** Earned value measures what work you have actually completed and compares this to the actual costs of completing the work. When compared to the planned value of the project at a given point in time, you can see if the project is on track or not.

> **C:** Actual cost is the cost to do the work performed and is a key element in earned value management.

> **D:** Budget at completion is the total planned value for the project.

Question 181: You are a project manager on a large software project using the earned value reporting system to manage your project. At this point in time the EV is $24,000, the BAC is $97,000, the PV is $29,000, and the AC is $45,000. What is the percent complete?
The correct answer is B.

> **A:** 30% is incorrect. The percent complete is the work completed, or the earned value, divided by the total work to be done. EV / BAC = 24 / 97 = 25%.

> **B:** The percent complete is the work completed, or the earned value, divided by the total work to be done. EV / BAC = 24 / 97 = 25%.

> **C:** 46% is incorrect. The percent complete is the work completed, or the earned value, divided by the total work to be done. EV / BAC = 24 / 97 = 25%.

> **D:** 53% is incorrect. The percent complete is the work completed, or the earned value, divided by the total work to be done. EV / BAC = 24 / 97 = 25%.

Question 182: You are working on a large project and have determined that your CV is $50,000 and that your EV is $125,000. What is your AC?
The correct answer is A.

> **A:** The formula for cost variance is CV = EV - AC. Therefore, if CV = $50,000 and EV = $125,000, then AC must equal $75,000.

> **B-D:** These answers are not correct. If you arrived at one of these anwers, remember that the formula for cost variance is CV = EV - AC. Therefore, if CV = $50,000 and EV = $125,000, then AC must equal $75,000.

Question 183: The earned value on your project is $20,000, the actual cost is $18,000, and the planned value is $25,000. What is your schedule performance index (SPI)?
The correct answer is C.

> **A, B, and D:** These answers are not correct. If you arrived at one of them, remember that the SPI = EV / PV, so SPI = 20000 / 25000 = 0.8.
>
> **C:** Schedule performance index (SPI) = EV / PV, so SPI = 20000 / 25000 = 0.8.

Question 184: The earned value on your project is $25,000, the actual cost is $20,000, and the planned value is $20,000. What is your SPI?
The correct answer is B.

> **A, C, and D:** These answers are not correct. If you arrived at one of them, remember that the SPI = EV / PV, so SPI = 25,000 / 20,000 = 1.25.
>
> **B:** SP) = EV / PV, so SPI = 25,000 / 20,000 = 1.25.

Question 185: The planned value on your project is $120,000, the earned value is $100,000, the actual cost is $90,000, and your cost variance is $10,000. What is your cost performance index (CPI)?
The correct answer is D.

> **A-C:** These answers are not correct. If you arrived at one of them, remember that the CPI = EV / AC, so CPI = 100,000 / 90,000 = 1.11.
>
> **D:** CPI = EV / AC, so CPI = 100,000 / 90,000 = 1.11.

Question 186: The planned value on your project is $9,000, the earned value is $9,000, the actual cost is $8,000, and your cost variance is $1,000. What is your cost performance index?
The correct answer is B.

> **A, C, and D:** These answers are not correct. If you arrived at one of them, remember that the CPI = EV / AC, so CPI = 9,000 / 8,000 = 1.125.
>
> **B:** CPI = EV / AC, so CPI = 9,000 / 8,000 = 1.125.

Question 187: You are working on a large project and have determined that your cost variance is $50,000 and that your earned value is $125,000. What is your cost performance index?
The correct answer is D.

> **A-C:** These answers are not correct. If you arrived at one of them, remember that the formula for cost variance is CV = EV - AC. Therefore, if CV = $50,000 and EV = $125,000, then AC must equal $75,000. The formula for CPI is CPI = EV / AC. Therefore, CPI = $125,000 / $75,000 or 1.66.
>
> **D:** The formula for cost variance is CV = EV - AC. Therefore, if CV = $50,000 and EV = $125,000, then AC must equal $75,000. The formula for CPI is CPI = EV / AC. Therefore, CPI = $125,000 / $75,000 or 1.66.

Question 188: Your project control measurements show a CPI of 0.89. What does this show about your project?
The correct answer is B.

> **A:** A CPI of 0.89 means that for every dollar you are spending you are getting 89 cents of value.

> **B:** A CPI below 1 tells you that you are experiencing a cost overrun on the project. This is true for the SPI measurement as well.

> **C:** A CPI below 1 tells you that you are experiencing a cost overrun on the project. This is true for the SPI measurement as well.

> **D:** The CPI tells you about cost performance only and can't tell you anything about schedule performance.

Question 189: Your project has a CPI of 1.1 and a SPI of .9. What does this mean?
The correct answer is C.

> **A:** This answer is incorrect because while a CPI above 1 does mean a cost underrun, an SPI below 1 means you are not achieving all the work you had planned within the timeframe you are measuring.

> **B:** This answer is incorrect because a CPI above 1 means a cost underrun, not and overrun. An SPI below 1 means you are not achieving all the work you had planned within the timeframe you are measuring and are behind schedule.

> **C:** A CPI above 1 means a cost underrun, while an SPI below 1 means you are not achieving all the work you had planned within the timeframe you are measuring.

> **D:** This answer is incorrect because while a CPI above 1 means a cost underrun, an SPI below 1 means you are not achieving all the work you had planned within the timeframe you are measuring and are behind, not ahead of, schedule.

Question 190: You are forecasting your estimate to complete your project and are incurring extra costs to do this work. What sort of estimating technique are you using?
The correct answer is B.

> **A:** Earned value management is a valuable technique for assessing any cost and schedule variance.

> **B:** Bottom-up estimating is a technique for estimating the cost of individual work packages with the lowest level of detail, and as such it incurs extra cost because of the effort involved.

> **C:** The estimate to complete (ETC) forecast does not require as much effort or incur as many costs as the bottom-up estimating technique.

> **D:** The To Complete Performance Index (TCPI) measures the rate at which you must work to achieve either the EAC or BAC.

Question 191: Your actual costs on your project are $75,000, the budget at completion is $100,000 and the earned value is $85,000. Your project has experienced some atypical variances to date which have affected its financial performance but from this point forward you expect it to perform at the originally budgeted rate. What is your estimate at completion?
The correct answer is A.

> **A:** In this instance, with the information provided, you are being lead to use EAC = AC+BAC - EV to calculate EAC. So, EAC = 75,000+100,000 - 85,000 = 90,000.

> **B-D:** These answers are incorrect. In this instance, with the information provided, you are being lead to use EAC = AC+BAC - EV to calculate EAC. So, EAC = 75,000+100,000 - 85,000 = 90,000.

Question 192: Your budget at completion is $50,000, your earned value is $40,000, and your actual cost is $45,000. Using an estimate at completion forecast for ETC work performed at the present CPI, what is your estimate at completion?
The correct answer is C.

> **A, B, and D:** These answers are not correct. This question requires you to first work out the CPI, which is EV / AC = 40,000 / 45,000 = 0.88. Then use this number in the equation EAC = BAC / cumulative CPI = 50,000 / .88 = 56,818.

> **C:** This question requires you to first work out the CPI, which is EV / AC = 40,000 / 45,000 = 0.88. Then use this number in the equation EAC = BAC / cumulative CPI = 50,000 / .88 = 56,818.

Question 193: The calculated projection of cost performance that must be achieved on the remaining work to meet a specified management goal such as the BAC or the EAC is known as what?
The correct answer is D.

> **A:** Earned value is the value of work performed.

> **B:** The estimate to complete is the estimate of the amount of funds required to complete the project and is the difference between your EAC and AC.

> **C:** The cost baseline is the approved project budget.

> **D:** The To Complete Performance Index (TCPI) is a useful tool for assessing the actual financial performance of the project baseline against actual performance and the amount of cost-based work required to finish the project.

Question 194: Your actual cost on the project is $10,000, the budget at completion is $20,000, the earned value is $8,000, the cumulative CPI is 0.8, and the cumulative SPI is 0.9. Using both your CPI and SPI factors, what is your estimate at completion forecast?
The correct answer is D.

> **A-C:** These answers are incorrect. If you arrived at one of them, remember that the EAC using both SPI and CPI factors = AC + [(BAC - EV) / (cumulative CPI x cumulative SPI)] = 10,000+[(20,000 - 8,000) / (0.8 x 0.9)] = 10,000+[(12,000 / .72)] = 26,666.

> **D:** EAC using both SPI and CPI factors = AC + [(BAC - EV) / (cumulative CPI x cumulative SPI)] = 10,000+[(20,000 - 8,000)/ (0.8 x 0.9)] = 10,000+[(12,000 / .72)] = 26,666.

Question 195: You are approximately half way through a complex construction project and are presenting the data from earned value management analysis of the project to your team. You have a BAC of $500,000, an EV of $2,800,000, an AC of $260,000, and a PV of $250,000. The team members are happy with these figures and want to know the rate at which they have to work to achieve the revised estimate at completion. What is your answer?
The correct answer is C.

> **A:** 1.0 is incorrect and I suspect you guessed the answer. The question is asking for your TCPI to achieve your EAC. The formula for this is TCPI = (BAC - EV) / (EAC - AC). So first you must calculate EAC with the figures provided, and the easiest way to do this is to first calculate CPI, which is EV / AC. Then use these figures in the formula to get TCPI = (500000 - 280000) / (462963 - 260000) = 1.08. You may get a slightly different answer depending on how you rounded up the numbers but it should be very close to 1.08.

> **B:** If you got this answer, you probably used the wrong formula to calculate TCPI. You may have used TCPI = (BAC - EV) / (BAC - AC), which is the formula for calculating TCPI for the BAC. This question is asking you to calculate TCPI for the EAC so try again and start by using the numbers given to calculate EAC = BAC / CPI.

> **C:** This is quite a lengthy calculation so well done for getting it right. The question is asking for your TCPI to achieve your EAC. The formula for this is TCPI = (BAC - EV) / (EAC - AC). So first you must calculate EAC with the figures provided and the easiest way to do this is to first calculate CPI, which is EV / AC. Then use these figures in the formula to get TCPI = (500000 - 280000) / (462963 - 260000) = 1.08. You may get a slightly different answer depending on how you rounded up the numbers but it should be very close to 1.08.

D: 0.5 is incorrect and I suspect you guessed the answer. The question is asking for your TCPI to achieve your EAC. The formula for this is TCPI = (BAC - EV) / (EAC - AC). So first you must calculate EAC with the figures provided, and the easiest way to do this is to first calculate CPI, which is EV / AC. Then use these figures in the formula to get TCPI = (500000 - 280000) / (462963 - 260000) = 1.08. You may get a slightly different answer depending on how you rounded up the numbers but it should be very close to 1.08.

Question 196: As part of the work to check if you are achieving your expected and approved spend on the project, you are completing a process of controlling project costs. Which of the following is not an output from this process?
The correct answer is B.

A: Work performance information is an output from the Control Costs process in the PMBOK® Guide.

B: Variance analysis is a tool that examines the difference between where you thought you should be in the project and where you actually are. It is used as a tool and technique in several of the Monitoring and Controlling processes.

C: Cost forecasts are an output from the Control Costs process in the PMBOK® Guide.

D: Change requests are an output from the Control Costs process in the PMBOK® Guide.

Question 197: You are managing a project and the original scope baseline of the project was budgeted at $100,000. Since work on the project started there have been 13 authorized and approved changes to the project. The changes have a value of $12,000 and the cost of investigating them prior to their approval was $1,500. What is the current budget for the project?
The correct answer is A.

A: The current budget of the project contains all of the authorized funding for the project including additions to the project since the setting of the original baselines. This includes any and all authorized work done on the project, including the investigation of work that may be done to investigate the feasibility of changes.

B-D: These answers are incorrect because the current budget of the project contains all of the authorized funding for the project including additions to the project since the setting of the original baselines. This includes any and all authorized work done on the project, including work that may be done to investigate the feasibility of changes, so in order to arrive at the correct answer you simply add all of the numbers up.

Question 198: The project you are managing is going well and you are using the earned value management system to assess historical information and forecast a likely future financial state of the project. You have a budget at completion of $120,000, earned value of $50,000, planned value of $55,000, and an actual cost of $45,000. What is your To Complete Performance Index to achieve the budget at completion?
The correct answer is C.

> **A, B, and D:** These answers are incorrect. If you arrived at one of them, remember that in order to calculate the TCPI you need to use the formula (BAC - EV) / (BAC - AC), which gives an answer of 0.93.

> **C:** In order to calculate the TCPI you need to use the formula (BAC - EV) / (BAC - AC), which gives an answer of 0.93.

Question 199: You are nearing the end of a residential remodeling project and are presenting the data from earned value management analysis of the project to your team. You have a BAC of $300,000, an EV of $2,500,000, an AC of $260,000, and a PV of $250,000. The team members are happy with these figures and want to know the rate at which they have to work to achieve the budget at completion. What is your answer?
The correct answer is A.

> **A:** The question is asking you to calculate TCPI for the BAC. The formula for this is TCPI = (BAC - EV) / (BAC - AC). This gives you (300000 - 250000) / (300000 - 260000), which equals 50000 / 40000, which equals a TCPI of 1.25.

> **B:** If you got this answer you probably used the wrong formula to calculate TCPI. You probably used the formula to calculate TCPI for EAC when the question is asking you to calculate TCPI for the BAC, and the formula for this is TCPI = (BAC - EV) / (BAC - AC).

> **C:** 1.1 is incorrect. If you thought this was the answer, you probably guessed rather than tried to work it out. The questions is asking you to calculate TCPI for the BAC, and the formula for this is TCPI = (BAC - EV) / (BAC - AC), which is 1.25.

> **D:** 0.85 is incorrect. If you thought this was the answer, you probably guessed rather than tried to work it out. The questions is asking you to calculate TCPI for the BAC, and the formula for this is TCPI = (BAC - EV) / (BAC - AC), which is 1.25.

Project Quality Management

Question 200: Customer satisfaction means that customer requirements are met. Meeting customer requirements requires a combination of what two factors?
The correct answer is D.

> **A:** This answer is incorrect because both continuous improvement, or Kaizen, and prevention over inspection are a fundamental concepts underlying quality management but they do not directly link to customer satisfaction.

> **B:** This answer is incorrect because prevention over inspection is a fundamental concept underlying quality management but it does not directly link to customer satisfaction.

> **C:** This answer is incorrect because continuous improvement, or Kaizen, is a fundamental concept underlying quality management but it does not directly link to customer satisfaction.

> **D:** The product's conformance to the customer's requirements and the fitness of use of the product are both factors in achieving customer satisfaction and defining quality of product.

Question 201: You are successful using the FMEA approach to assess implications of quality decisions on your project. Your client asks you what FMEA stands for. What is your answer?
The correct answer is D.

> **A-C:** These answers are all made-up terms. The correct answer is failure mode and effects analysis.

> **D:** Failure mode and effects analysis (FMEA) is one of several non-proprietary approaches to quality management.

Question 202: Modern quality management complements project management very highly, with both disciplines recognizing the importance of all the following characteristics except?
The correct answer is D.

> **A:** Customer satisfaction is one of four characteristics shared by quality management and project management.

> **B:** Prevention over inspection is one of four characteristics shared by quality management and project management.

> **C:** Continuous inspection is one of four characteristics shared by quality management and project management.

> **D:** Total quality management is an approach to quality. The other three answers are all characteristics shared by quality management and project management. The fourth characteristic is management responsibility.

Question 203: Quality is planned, designed, and built into your project instead of being inspected in. What is the main reason that prevention of mistakes in quality is preferred over finding the mistakes via inspection?

The correct answer is C.

> **A:** This answer is incorrect; you should not try to avoid inspection because it is a necessary part of quality management.

> **B:** This answer is incorrect; carrying out preventive work does not mean you will be able to avoid inspection.

> **C:** Building in the quality systems to minimize the amount of defects found via inspection is generally cheaper in the long run than having to perform rework to fix defects found by inspection.

> **D:** This answer is incorrect; your quality management plan focuses on more than just prevention.

Question 204: How would you best describe to your client the difference between precision and accuracy?

The correct answer is B.

> **A:** This answer is incorrect. Precision means the values of the repeated measurements are clustered and have little scatter. Accuracy means that the measured value is very close to the true value.

> **B:** This answer is correct, and you need to know that there is a difference between precision and accuracy. For the exam, you need to know how and when to use the two terms.

> **C:** This answer is incorrect. Precision means the values of the repeated measurements are clustered and have little scatter. Accuracy means that the measured value is very close to the true value.

> **D:** This answer is incorrect. Precision means the values of the repeated measurements are clustered and have little scatter. Accuracy means that the measured value is very close to the true value.

Question 205: A member of your project team seems confused about the differences between quality approaches to the project and product. How would you best explain these differences?

The correct answer is A.

> **A:** Quality of the project relates to the degree to which the project is run according to the agreed project management plan. Quality of the product relates to the ability of the product to meet customer requirements.

B: This answer is incorrect because there is a distinct difference between the two concepts. Quality of the project relates to the degree to which the project is run according to the agreed project management plan. Quality of the product relates to the ability of the product to meet customer requirements.

C: This answer is incorrect because quality of the project relates to the degree to which the project is run according to the agreed project management plan. Quality of the product relates to the ability of the product to meet customer requirements.

D: Quality of the project relates to the degree to which the project is run according to the agreed project management plan. Quality of the product relates to the ability of the product to meet customer requirements.

Question 206: Your project is behind schedule and you have asked your project team to work longer hours to make up the time so that the customer's needs are met as planned. As project manager, you should monitor your quality management plan for what reason?
The correct answer is A.

A: Quality on a project can be adversely affected in a number of ways. Overworking staff can cause human errors to creep into the process and should be recognized within the quality management plan.

B: This answer is incorrect because the fact that customer requirements and specifications can change rapidly during periods of rework is not directly connected to the issue at hand: asking staff to work longer hours.

C: This answer is incorrect because the primary issue here is the potential errors caused by tired staff, and the issue is about not achieving customer needs.

D: This answer is incorrect because the primary and most pressing issue is the potential adverse impact on quality by tired staff. A subsequent issue may be overtime cost but it is not a quality issue.

Question 207: Your project team has completed a check of the project and the product you are managing. They discover that although you are meeting the quality requirements, the product is of a low grade. What should you do FIRST?
The correct answer is A.

A: Quality and grade are different. You can manufacture a high- or low-grade product depending on what the customer specified, so finding a low-grade product is probably exactly in line with the customer specifications.

B-D: Did you read this question properly? There isn't any problem with the scenario so there is no need to act. Quality and grade are different. You can manufacture a high- or low-grade product depending on what the customer specified, so finding a low-grade product is probably exactly in line with the customer specifications.

191

Question 208: What is the method of modern quality management that relies on continuing small improvements involving everyone from the top management to the lowest-level worker in the organization more most commonly known as?
The correct answer is D.

> **A:** Kampai is not correct. It is a Japanese term used when making a toast usually when drinking alcohol.
>
> **B:** Kanban is not correct. It is a Japanese term for visual card-based system for inventory or work control.
>
> **C:** Kawasaki is not the correct term. Kawasaki is a Japanese manufacturer of motorized vehicles.
>
> **D:** Kaizen means improvement in Japanese. It means continuing improvement involving everyone, including managers and workers alike, from the top to the bottom of the organization.

Question 209: The PMBOK® Guide process groups of initiating, planning, executing, monitoring, and controlling a project are based on the work of Shewhart and Deming. What is their quality improvement model known as?
The correct answer is C.

> **A:** Six Sigma is a proprietary quality management tool focused on eliminating errors.
>
> **B:** The Organizational Project Management Maturity Model (OPM3) is a tool for measuring the level of project management maturity within an organization.
>
> **C:** There are several important proprietary and non-proprietary quality management models that you should be aware of. The work by Shewhart and Deming produced the plan-do-check-act cycle for quality management.
>
> **D:** Total quality management is a quality system that holds all parties involved in quality management accountable for ensuring quality.

Question 210: You are explaining to your project sponsor that the decision made to lower the quality of deliverables on the project to save money will have long-lasting cost impacts beyond the project. The project sponsor does not seem convinced so you refer to the concept of cost of quality to make your point. How would you best describe cost of quality to your sponsor?
The correct answer is C.

> **A:** Cost of quality is not the total cost of the quality effort throughout just the project life cycle. The cost of quality refers to the whole of the product life cycle, which includes not only the cost of quality during manufacture but also the cost of product returns, warranty claims, and recall campaigns over the life of the product.

B: Cost of quality is not related to the amount of money required to complete your project quality management plan. The cost of quality refers to the whole of the product life cycle, which includes not only the cost of quality during manufacture but also the cost of product returns, warranty claims, and recall campaigns over the life of the product.

C: The cost of quality refers to the whole of the product life cycle, which includes not only the cost of quality during manufacture but also the cost of product returns, warranty claims, and recall campaigns over the life of the product.

D: Cost of quality is not best described as the total cost of implementing a prevention and inspection regime. The cost of quality refers to the whole of the product life cycle, which includes not only the cost of quality during manufacture but also the cost of product returns, warranty claims, and recall campaigns over the life of the product.

Question 211: The PMBOK® Guide process that is focused on identifying quality requirements and standards for the project and product is known as what?
The correct answer is C.

A: Control Quality is the process of monitoring and recording results of executing quality activities.

B: The cost of quality refers to the whole of the product life cycle, which includes not only the cost of quality during manufacture but also the cost of product returns, warranty claims, and recall campaigns over the life of the product.

C: Plan Quality Management is the process of identifying quality requirements and standards for both the project and product.

D: Perform Quality Assurance is the process of auditing quality requirements and processes.

Question 212: You are completing the work to identify and document quality requirements and standards for your project. Which of the following would you not use as an input into this process?
The correct answer is D.

A: The requirements documentation is one of the inputs into the Plan Quality Management process in the PMBOK® Guide, so you would use it.

B: The stakeholder register is one of the inputs into the Plan Quality Management process in the PMBOK® Guide, so you would use it.

C: The risk register is one of the inputs into the Plan Quality Management process in the PMBOK® Guide, so you would use it.

D: Quality checklists are an output, not an input, from the Plan Quality Management process in the PMBOK® Guide, so you could not use them, making this the correct answer.

Question 213: When considering the cost of quality on your project you should consider all of the following characteristics except?
The correct answer is A.

A: Destructive testing loss is a specific cost of conformance, not a general characteristic of cost of quality.

B: Cost of quality does include investment in preventing non-conformance to requirements.

C: Cost of quality does include appraising the product or service for conformance to requirements.

D: Cost of quality does include consideration of the impact of failing to meet requirements.

Question 214: Which of the following is not an example of a cost of conformance?
The correct answer is D.

A: Equipment is part of appraisal costs of conformance to assess the quality.

B: Equipment is part of prevention costs of conformance to build a quality product.

C: Training is part of prevention costs of conformance to build a quality product.

D: Rework is a cost of non-conformance in that it is incurred when you do not conform with the quality plan.

Question 215: You and your team are checking data that has been gathered and presented in a control chart to determine whether the product you are producing is meeting the required quality objectives. What is your main objective in completing this work and representing it in this way?
The correct answer is D.

A: This answer is incorrect because it is refering to cost benefit analysis, not a control chart.

B: This answer is incorrect becaue it is refering to quality assurance activities, not a control chart.

C: This answer is incorrect becaue it is refering to quality control activities, not a control chart.

D: A control chart measures and tracks quality data and assesses it within predetermined upper and lower control limits.

Question 216: Control limits for the production rates for the machines your project is building are set at 3 and 9, with a mean value of 6 units per hour. The results this week are as follows: 4, 7, 10, 5, and 6. What should you do first?
The correct answer is A.

> **A:** The third result is outside the control limits and should be investigated.
>
> **B:** You should not just continue working because the third result is outside the control limits and should be investigated.
>
> **C:** The question does not give you the tenth result.
>
> **D:** The first result is within the control limits so it does not need investigating.

Question 217: You have received the results of statistical sampling performed on the product of your project. The control chart shows nine data points in a row just under the mean. What should you do first?
The correct answer is B.

> **A:** You should not simply change the control limits. This scenario indicates the rule of seven; it requires investigation and for you to find the cause.
>
> **B:** This is an example of the rule of seven where there are seven or more consecutive points either above or below the mean, which indicates the process is moving out of acceptable limits, so the team needs to investigate and determine the assignable cause.
>
> **C:** This answer is not correct because the data is indicating that there is a potential problem, and doing nothing is not an option.
>
> **D:** Firing the quality assurance team will not solve the problem. This scenario indicates the rule of seven, and requires investigation and for you to find the cause.

Question 218: Upper and lower control limits on a control chart are generally set at how many standard deviations above and below the acceptable mean?
The correct answer is C.

> **A, B, and D:** These answers are not correct. Control limits are generally set at three standard deviations above and below the acceptable mean of data.
>
> **C:** Control limits are generally set at three standard deviations above and below the acceptable mean of data.

Question 219: Your project data, as shown on the control chart, indicates the latest seven consecutive points are above the mean but within the upper control limit. What is your BEST course of action?

The correct answer is C.

> **A:** This is a good option but not the best option. You should first refer to your quality management plan, which may direct you to stop work immediately and investigate the root cause of the problem.

> **B:** This is an example of the rule of seven where there are seven or more consecutive points either above or below the mean, which indicates the process is moving out of acceptable limits so the team needs to investigate and determine the assignable cause.

> **C:** Data outside the upper or lower control limits, or seven consecutive points above or below the mean, indicates the process is out of control and requires corrective action.

> **D:** You should not simply change the control limits. This scenario indicates the rule of seven, and requires investigation and for you to find the cause.

Question 220: Your project is generating useful data for your control chart. The latest data indicates that the process of manufacturing the product has produced units below the lower control limit but above the lower specification limit. What is your BEST course of action?

The correct answer is A.

> **A:** Data that is beneath the lower control limit but above the lower specification limit indicates that the product is still within the customer specification but may be in need of corrective action to ensure it stays there.

> **B:** You should not do nothing because data that is beneath the lower control limit but above the lower specification limit indicates that the product is still within the customer specification but may be in need of corrective action to ensure it stays there.

> **C:** This is a good option but not the best option. You should first refer to your quality management plan, which may direct you to stop work immediately and investigate the root cause of the problem. Data that is beneath the lower control limit but above the lower specification limit indicates that the product is still within the customer specification but may be in need of corrective action to ensure it stays there.

> **D:** You should not simply change the control limits. Data that is beneath the lower control limit but above the lower specification limit indicates that the product is still within the customer specification but may be in need of corrective action to ensure it stays there.

Question 221: While working on the project to assess and measure quality, you are determining the number and type of tests and their impact on cost of quality. What technique are you using?
The correct answer is A.

> **A:** Design of experiments is a statistical method for identifying which factors may influence specific variables or a product or a process under development.

> **B:** Analogous estimating is used for estimating time or cost.

> **C:** Benchmarking is the technique of comparing your quality activities to another project or organization.

> **D:** Cost of quality considers the cost of quality decision you make over the life of the product.

Question 222: You are comparing actual or planned project practices to those of comparable projects to identify best practices and generate ideas for improvement for your project. What quality technique are you using?
The correct answer is D.

> **A:** Cost of quality considers the cost of quality decision you make over the life of the product.

> **B:** Analogous estimating is used for estimating time or cost.

> **C:** Design of experiments is a statistical method for identifying which factors may influence specific variables or a product or a process under development.

> **D:** Benchmarking is a process of comparing your projects to others in relation to quality management.

Question 223: A quality technique that chooses only a part of a population of interest for studying, and is often used to reduce cost, is called what?
The correct answer is C.

> **A:** Inspection is physically inspecting a product for defects.

> **B:** Flowcharting is a technique for graphically mapping a quality process.

> **C:** It is less expensive to examine only a part of the population.

> **D:** This answer is incorrect because it is not a term referenced within the PMBOK® Guide.

Question 224: Your project team is working on a software project with over two million lines of code and has just randomly selected a number of lines of code for inspection. What quality technique are they using?
The correct answer is C.

> **A:** Benchmarking is the technique of comparing your quality activities to another project or organization.

> **B:** Design of experiments is a statistical method for identifying which factors may influence specific variables or a product or a process under development.

> **C:** When you have a large amount of data to check, it can be too time consuming and cost too much to examine every product. In this case, taking a relevant sample and extrapolating the quality of this sample to the whole data range is much more efficient.

> **D:** This answer is incorrect because it is a made-up quality term.

Question 225: During a project to deliver a complex set of requirements for a wide range of stakeholders, you and your team have placed a great deal of importance on the quality of the project. You have decided to use a wide variety of tools and techniques to help you achieve the desired quality standards. Which of the following is not an example of a quality planning tool that you would find useful in this endeavor?
The correct answer is D.

> **A:** An affinity diagram is a quality management tool and provides a graphical method of structuring and displaying a large number of discrete pieces of information.

> **B:** A force field diagram is a quality planning tool that is used to weigh the points for and against a potential decision or action.

> **C:** Matrix diagrams are a quality management tool and are used to compare information between two or more lists.

> **D:** Quality checklists are an output, not a tool, from the Plan Quality Management process in the PMBOK® Guide, making this the correct answer.

Question 226: While completing work associated with ensuring quality in a project, it is important that you know the difference between several different quality-related terms. Several of your team members regularly get confused about the difference between the different terms, particularly understanding exactly what a quality metric is. To demonstrate to your team the difference, you point out that one of the following is not a quality metric. Which one do you point out?
The correct answer is D.

> **A:** Failure rate is a quality metric that records the number of failures and their impact.

> **B:** Budget control is a quality metric used to align quality decisions with the project budget.

C: Defect frequency is a quality metric that measures the frequency of defects discovered and is used for root cause analysis.

D: The upper control limit is part of the control chart tool; it is not a quality metric.

Question 227: You have completed the work to plan and document your particular approach to quality on your project. Which of the following is not an output you would expect to produce as a result of this work?
The correct answer is B.

A: Quality metrics are an output from the Plan Quality Management process in the PMBOK® Guide.

B: Flowcharting is not an output; it is a technique used in the Plan Quality Management process in the PMBOK® Guide, so this is the correct answer.

C: The process improvement plan is an output from the Plan Quality Management process in the PMBOK® Guide.

D: The quality management plan is the primary output from the Plan Quality Management process in the PMBOK® Guide.

Question 228: The process of continuous process improvements to reduce waste and eliminate activities that do not add value to a project is known as what?
The correct answer is D.

A: Progressive elaboration is a form of iterative planning.

B: Plan Quality Management is the process that produces the quality management plan.

C: Control Quality is the process of monitoring and recording results of executing quality activities.

D: Perform Quality Assurance is an executing process that is focused on constantly improving the quality processes on the project.

Question 229: You are using your quality management plan to guide the work being done to ensure that project quality assurance expectations are being met. Which of the following would not be a useful input to you?
The correct answer is B.

A: The process improvement plan is an important input into the Perform Quality Assurance process because it outlines how processes will be improved.

B: Quality audits are a technique used in the Perform Quality Assurance process, not an input.

C: Quality metrics are an input into the Perform Quality Assurance process because they guide the assessment of quality assurance activities.

199

D: Quality control measurements are an input into the Perform Quality Assurance process because they are used to determine if processes are being performed as planned.

Question 230: A project administrator has asked for guidance on completing a project audit as per the approved quality management plan for your project. They are seeking your guidance on what exactly a quality audit is. How is a quality audit best defined?
The correct answer is B.

A: This answer is incorrect because it refers to product specifications and the audit is focused on processes.

B: The quality audit focuses on the quality processes of the project and is not generally focused on the quality of the product of the project.

C: This anser is incorrect because it is focussed on product specifications, which is not a focus of a project audit.

D: This answer is incorrect because the quality audit will look at more than just whether the project management plan contains an appropriate quality management plan.

Question 231: You are completing the work to ensure the required quality assurance levels are met on your project. Which of the following is an output of this work?
The correct answer is C.

A: Quality audits are a technique used in the Perform Quality Assurance process, not an output.

B: Quality metrics are an input into the Perform Quality Assurance process because they guide the assessment of quality assurance activities.

C: Change requests are an important output from the Perform Quality Assurance process as a result of your constant examination of the quality processes and procedures of your project.

D: Process analysis is a technique used in the Perform Quality Assurance process, not an output.

Question 232: What is the process of monitoring and recording results of executing the quality activities to assess performance and recommend necessary changes known as?
The correct answer is B.

A: The Perform Quality Assurance process examines the process of the project.

B: Control Quality is the correct answer and it is part of the Monitoring and Controlling process group.

C: The Plan Quality Management process produces the quality management plan.

D: Statistical sampling is a tool for taking a small sample from a large population and extrapolating the results of the sample to the entire population.

Question 233: During a workshop to define quality control processes on your project, you sense that team members are confused abut the difference between prevention and inspection. What is the BEST description of the difference between prevention and inspection?
The correct answer is A.

A: Prevention and inspection are two different concepts in the quality management area. Prevention is designed to keep errors out of the process while inspection is about discovering the errors prior to handover.

B-D: These answers are incorrect because prevention and inspection are two different concepts in the quality management area. Prevention is designed to keep errors out of the process while inspection is about discovering the errors prior to handover.

Question 234: What is the BEST description of the difference between tolerances and control limits?
The correct answer is C.

A, B, and D: These answers are incorrect because tolerances specify the acceptable range of specifications while control limits indicate that a process may be out of control.

C: Tolerances specify the acceptable range of specifications while control limits indicate that a process may be out of control.

Question 235: All of the following are an example of one of Ishikawa's seven tools of quality except?
The correct answer is B.

A, C, and D: The seven tools of quality according to Ishikawa are the following: cause and effect diagrams, control charts, flowcharts, histograms, Pareto charts, run charts, and scatter diagrams.

B: Inspection is not one of Ishikawa's seven tools of quality. The seven tools of quality according to Ishikawa are cause and effect diagrams, control charts, flowcharts, histograms, Pareto charts, run charts, and scatter diagrams.

Question 236: You are the project manager for a project where quality is an important constraint, and you are trying to correct a problem with a machine that makes parts that are used in complex medical imaging equipment. As a result of carrying our your Control Quality process, you discover that unfortunately these parts are frequently made with defects. You have decided to hold a meeting to discuss the process of making the parts. You create a diagram that has branches that show the possible causes of the problems. Each of the branches breaks the cause down into more and more detail. What is this diagram called?

The correct answer is B.

> **A:** This answer is not correct because it is not a term referenced within the PMBOK® Guide.

> **B:** The diagram is a cause and effect diagram, also known as a fishbone or Ishikawa diagram.

> **C:** A Pareto diagram or chart determines frequency of defects and arranges them in hierarchical order so you can determine which defects are causing the most problems. This is often called the 80:20 rule.

> **D:** A scatter diagram plots the results of two variables on an x and y axis diagram.

Question 237: You are trying to find the cause of an identified problem on your project by examining the various factors that might be linked to potential problems. What technique are you using?

The correct answer is A.

> **A:** A cause and effect diagram, also known as an Ishikawa or fishbone (on account of its shape) diagram, tries to determine the root cause of a problem so the cause and not the symptom is identified.

> **B:** Control charts identify when a process may be going out of control. They do not help find the cause of the problem.

> **C:** A Pareto diagram or chart determines frequency of defects and arranges them in hierarchical order so you can determine which defects are causing the most problems. This is often called the 80:20 rule.

> **D:** A run chart plots a particular variable over a period of time.

Question 238: The quality manager on your project wishes to analyze the data that is being received in the form of a list of defects that have occurred in the manufacturing department. The report comes with defects listed chronologically as they occurred, the cost of the repair necessary to correct each defect, the person involved, and a description of the defect. The quality manager would like to determine which of the defects should be corrected first according to the frequency of the defect occurring. Which of the following tools should she use?

The correct answer is A.

> **A:** A Pareto diagram is a histogram, ordered by frequency of occurrence, that shows how many results were generated by type or category of identified cause. By using this tool the manager can identify the defects that occurred most often.

> **B:** This answer is not correct. It is a combination of two familiar words but it is a made-up term.

> **C:** A cause and effect diagram, also known as an Ishikawa or fishbone (on account of its shape) diagram, tries to determine the root cause of a problem so the cause and not the symptom is identified.

> **D:** This answer is not correct because it is not a term referenced within the PMBOK® Guide.

Question 239: You are explaining to your project team the ranking of causes for defects on your project to enable them to focus their corrective actions on those causes that are responsible for the greatest defects. What sort of diagram would you use for this?

The correct answer is A.

> **A:** A Pareto chart is a type of histogram that shows the rank ordering of defects by type of category so that corrective action can be focused in the correct place.

> **B:** A scatter diagram plots the results of two variables on an x and y axis diagram.

> **C:** Control charts identify when a process may be going out of control; they do not help find the cause of the problem.

> **D:** A histogram, or bar chart, can be used for graphically representing the frequency of events.

Question 240: While performing quality control inspections you note down relevant data and use a vertical bar chart to show how often a particular variable state occurred. What is this sort of bar chart more commonly called?

The correct answer is A.

> **A:** A histogram or bar chart is one of the most commonly used and easiest to understand visual representations of information, especially to show relationships between different areas.

> **B:** A Pareto diagram is a histogram, ordered by frequency of occurrence, that shows how many results were generated by type or category of identified cause. However, in this question you should see a Pareto chart as a subset of histograms, which is the best answer.

C: Control charts identify when a process may be going out of control; they do not help find the cause of the problem.

D: A scatter diagram plots the results of two variables on an x and y axis diagram.

Question 241: While performing quality control inspections, you note down relevant data and use a chart similar to a control chart without displayed limits, which shows the history and pattern of a variation. What sort of chart are you using?
The correct answer is D.

A: A cause and effect diagram, also known as an Ishikawa or fishbone (on account of its shape) diagram, tries to determine the root cause of a problem so the cause and not the symptom is identified.

B: Control charts identify when a process may be going out of control; they do not help find the cause of the problem.

C: A Pareto diagram is a histogram, ordered by frequency of occurrence, that shows how many results were generated by type or category of identified cause. By using this tool the manager can identify the defects that occurred most often.

D: A run chart is a simplified control chart without the displayed limits that can indicate a trend over time and forecast future outcomes based on historical results using such techniques as linear regression.

Question 242: A visual presentation of quality data gathered showing the relationship between a dependent and independent variable is known as what?
The correct answer is D.

A: A run chart is a simplified control chart without the displayed limits that can indicate a trend over time and forecast future outcomes based on historical results using such techniques as linear regression.

B: A Pareto diagram is a histogram, ordered by frequency of occurrence, that shows how many results were generated by type or category of identified cause. By using this tool the manager can identify the defects that occurred most often.

C: Control charts identify when a process may be going out of control; they do not help find the cause of the problem.

D: A scatter diagram plots the relationship between two variables, one on the x axis and one on the y axis.

Question 243: Your team members have completed work to perform quality control on the project. Which of the following outputs would you not expect them to produce as a result of doing this work?
The correct answer is A.

> **A:** Quality metrics is an input, not an output, into the Control Quality process in the PMBOK® Guide, so this is the correct answer.

> **B:** Validated changes are an output; they are work required by an approved change request that has been checked for quality.

> **C:** As a result of carrying out this monitoring and controlling process, it may be necessary to generate change requests as an output as a result of variances discovered.

> **D:** Quality control measurements are the primary output from the Control Quality process.

Question 244: You and your team are working hard to produce a quality wireless headphone product capable of high-quality audio transmission. You are discussing an approach with your Quality Assurance Team Leader that will aim to reduce the variation the team is experiencing with the prototype headsets being produced. What technique are you discussing?
The correct answer is A.

> **A:** Six Sigma is a quality improvement method that seeks to improve the quality of the output of a process. It does this by identifying and addressing the factors that cause defects and variability.

> **B:** Lean is a process that focuses on eliminating waste and improving value, not reducing variation.

> **C:** Scrum is an Agile methodology that is focused on delivering features in small iterations via the use of empowered teams.

> **D:** Kanban is an Agile methodology that emphasizes the visualization of activities and limitations of a work in progress.

Question 245: If a process is considered to have only 3.4 defects per million opportunities, which sigma class is this defined as?
The correct answer is C.

> **A:** Two Sigma indicates that 69.15% of the products manufactured meet all quality specifications and are free from defects. This means that 308,500 products, for every 1 million manufactured, do not meet the desired level of quality.

> **B:** Three Sigma indicates that 93.32% of the products manufactured meet all quality specifications and are free from defects. This means that 66,800 products, for every 1 million manufactured, do not meet the desired level of quality.

C: Six Sigma indicates that 99.99966% of the products manufactured meet all quality specifications and are free from defects. This means that only 3.4 products, for every 1 million manufactured, do not meet the desired level of quality.

D: Twelve Sigma is a made-up term. This would be considered beyond the possibility of perfection.

Question 246: The terms Yellow Belt, Green Belt, and Black Belt are terms given to individuals that practice which methodology?
The correct answer is B.

A: Rapid Application Development (RAD) is a software development methodology that focuses on prototyping software quickly and iteratively. It does not use colored belts to class its practitioners.

B: The varying belt colors represent the level of expertise an individual has in the application of the Six Sigma methodology.

C: Scrum is an Agile methodology that is focused on delivering features in small iterations via the use of empowered teams. It does not use colored belts to class its practitioners.

D: Kanban is an Agile methodology that emphasizes the visualization of activities and limitations of a work in progress. It does not use colored belts to class its practitioners.

Question 247: You have been asked by senior management to focus on eliminating any bottlenecks that exist in your project's processes. What methodology will be most effective in highlighting bottlenecks?
The correct answer is D.

A: Prince2 is a project management methodology, but it is not specifically aimed at reducing bottlenecks.

B: MPMM is a project management methodology, but it is not specifically aimed at reducing bottlenecks.

C: Lean is a project management methodology, but it is not specifically aimed at reducing bottlenecks.

D: Kanban is a project management methodology used to identify bottlenecks through the visualization of all tasks/activities and the application of work in progress limits.

Question 248: Your Quality Assurance Manager has requested that you assist her in mapping the value stream for the assembly of a new combustion engine. Value stream mapping is part of which methodology?
The correct answer is C.

A: Waterfall and Scrum are development methodologies that can be applied to the development of a combustion engine, but they do not include the concept of value stream mapping.

B: Waterfall and Scrum are development methodologies that can be applied to the development of a combustion engine, but they do not include the concept of value stream mapping.

C: Value stream mapping is a principle of Lean. This activity involves formally documenting a process and assessing each component to understand which provides value and which does not.

D: Kaizen is a Japanese word, meaning continuous improvement. This method also does not include the concept of value stream mapping.

Project Human Resource Management

Question 249: The PMBOK® Guide processes that organize, recruit, reward, manage, and lead the project team are collectively known as what?
The correct answer is A.

A: This is the correct collective term for all of the processes that make up the Human Resource Management knowledge area.

B: This may seem like a sensible answer but managing the project team is only one part of Project Human Resource Management, which is the best answer.

C: Project management covers the entire profession and all the knowledge areas. Project Human Resource Management is the specific area that organizes, recruits, rewards, manages, and leads the project team.

D: This may seem like a sensible answer but team building and development is only one part of Project Human Resource Management, which is the best answer.

Question 250: The project sponsor has several responsibilities while working with the project management team. Which of the following is not a responsibility of the project sponsor?
The correct answer is B.

> **A:** The project sponsor has the responsibility of influencing high-level stakeholders to provide political and financial support for the project.

> **B:** The project sponsor performs a high-level role and is responsible for ensuring the project has the funding it requires, monitoring progress, acting as project champion, influencing others in support of the project, and, when required, clarifying high-level scope questions. They are not responsible for detailed work such as completing the WBS.

> **C:** The project sponsor has the responsibility of monitoring the progress of the project at a high level. They are not responsible for low-level monitoring; that is the responsibility of the project manager.

> **D:** The project sponsor is responsible for securing financial support and funding for the project.

Question 251: A team member is studying towards obtaining the PMP® credential and has asked for your assistance with her study. She is having difficulty remembering the generally correct order of activities in the PMBOK® Guide Project Human Resource Management knowledge area. What is your answer to this question?
The correct answer is A.

> **A:** This process generally takes the following sequence: first plan, then do what you planned, and then check that what you are doing is correct. So, first plan your approach to getting, developing, and managing your human resources. Next, using the plan, acquire your project team, then develop them, and finally monitor or manage them.

> **B-D:** These answers are incorrect because the process generally follows the sequence of plan first, then do what you planned, and then check that what you are doing is correct. So first plan your approach to getting, developing, and managing your human resources. Next, using the plan, acquire your project team, then develop them, and finally monitor or manage them.

Question 252: You have completed your human resource management plan for your project. You recognize that the profession of project management features a lot of interdependencies, and you want to make sure that the human resource plan is used in other appropriate parts of your project work. This plan is used as an input into all of the following processes except?

The correct answer is C.

> **A:** The Identify Risks process uses information from the human resource management plan to identify risks associated with human resources.

> **B:** The Estimate Costs process using the human resource management plan to assist in estimating costs associated with human resources on the project.

> **C:** The outputs from the Estimate Activity Resources process are used as inputs into the Plan Human Resource Management process.

> **D:** The Acquire Project Team process uses the human resource management plan to recruit the team members.

Question 253: While completing initial planning work on your project, you begin to develop your human resource plan. Which of the following inputs would not be of use to you to complete this plan?

The correct answer is B.

> **A:** You need the activity resource requirements to know what work you need people to complete and how much work is needed to be done.

> **B:** You don't need the WBS to prepare your human resource management plan but any changes to the WBS may mean changes to your human resource plan.

> **C:** Enterprise environmental factors such as external market conditions for salaries and employment law are an input into the Plan Human Resource Management process.

> **D:** Organizational process assets such as existing recruitment policies are an input into the Plan Human Resource Management process.

Question 254: You are showing your project team members the organizational structure, and you point out where in the structure their role is located. What tool would be useful to you in preparing this information?

The correct answer is D.

> **A:** The responsibility assignment matrix (RAM) does not show any information about the organizational structure; it shows who is responsibility for individual work packages and activities.

> **B:** The work breakdown structure (WBS) does not show any information about the organizational structure; it decomposes deliverables down into work packages.

C: The resource breakdown structure (RBS) does not show any information about the organizational structure; it breaks down the resources required for the project.

D: The organizational breakdown structure (OBS) is arranged according to an organizations existing departments, units, or teams with the project activities or work packages listed under each department.

Question 255: You are using a matrix-based chart to give a clear indication of the connection between work packages and team members. Additionally, the chart shows who is responsible, accountable, consulted, and informed about the work. What is the common name of this type of chart?
The correct answer is A.

A: A RACI chart is a specific type of responsibility assignment matrix that lists additional information about who is responsible or accountable, and who should be consulted and informed in relation to project activities.

B: The organizational breakdown structure is arranged according to an organization's existing departments, units, or teams with the project activities or work packages listed under each department. It does not show who is responsible, accountable, consulted, and informed about the work.

C: The work breakdown structure does not show any information about who is responsible, accountable, consulted, and informed about the work; it decomposes deliverables down into work packages.

D: A RACI chart is a specific type of responsibility assignment matrix, and as such it is the best answer.

Question 256: As a competent project manager you should be aware of the leading and foundational theories relating to the management of human resources and their practical application. Which of the following is not one of these theories?
The correct answer is A.

A: This answer is not correct because it is not a term referenced within the PMBOK® Guide.

B: Maslow's Hierarchy of Needs specifies a set of needs an individual will seek to fulfill, with the current need being the strongest motivator.

C: McGregor's Theory X and Theory Y summarizes management views of employees as either naturally unmotivated and untrustworthy (Theory X) or naturally motivated and trustworthy (Theory Y).

D: Herzberg's Motivation-Hygiene Theory says that employees requires hygiene factors to be present before motivation factors will work.

Question 257: As a competent project manager you should be aware of the leading and foundational theories relating to the management of human resources and their practical application. Which of the following is not one of these theories?
The correct answer is C.

> **A:** Vroom's Expectancy Theory states that the expectation of receiving a reward for a certain accomplishment will motivate people to work harder but this will only work if the accomplishment is perceived to be achievable.
>
> **B:** Ouchi's Theory Z says that organizations should seek to fulfill a large role in an employee's life beyond just an employment agreement.
>
> **C:** This answer is not correct because it is not a term referenced within the PMBOK® Guide.
>
> **D:** McClelland's Human Motivation, Achievement, or Three Needs Theory states that people are motivated to work by the need for achievement, power, and affiliation.

Question 258: While completing initial planning work on your project, you begin to develop your human resource management plan. The human resource management plan can include all the following information except?
The correct answer is C.

> **A:** The human resource management plan may have project organization charts so team members can see reporting lines and relationships within the organization.
>
> **B:** The human resource management plan includes the staffing management plan, which specifies how and when project team members will be required on the project.
>
> **C:** Cost estimates for staff time will be included in your cost management plan.
>
> **D:** The human resource management plan has a description of team member's roles and responsibilities.

Question 259: What does a resource calendar show?
The correct answer is C.

> **A:** Annual leave may be a small part of the resource calendar but it is not the best answer to this question. The resource calendar will clearly show what resources you need, when you need them, and how much commitment they need to have when you need them as well as any constraints on the time they can give to the project such as other work commitments, working hours, and holidays.

> **B:** The resource calendar does not show the cost of staff members over time. This will be in your project cost baseline. The resource calendar will clearly show what resources you need, when you need them, and how much commitment they need to have when you need them as well as any constraints on the time they can give to the project such as other work commitments, working hours, and holidays.

> **C:** The resource calendar will clearly show what resources you need, when you need them, and how much commitment they need to have when you need them as well as any constraints on the time they can give to the project such as other work commitments, working hours, and holidays.

> **D:** Programmed team building activities throughout the project will not be shown on the resource calendar. The resource calendar will clearly show what resources you need, when you need them, and how much commitment they need to have when you need them as well as any constraints on the time they can give to the project such as other work commitments, working hours, and holidays.

Question 260: You are currently attempting to acquire project team members on a project that is just about to start. You are meeting resistance from the functional managers of the staff you want to use on your project, and it appears that you may have to seek help from external consultants. Your project sponsor is concerned about the impact this process is having on the project. All of following are potential adverse effects of not acquiring your project team except?
The correct answer is C.

> **A:** Reduced quality is a potential adverse effect caused by delays and by less experienced people working on the project.

> **B:** Decreased customer satisfaction is a very real potential outcome because the work may not start on time or be produced to the expected quality.

> **C:** It is very doubtful that failure to acquire your project team would result in reduced project costs because there will most likely be delays associated with getting alternate team members.

> **D:** Failing to acquire the staff you need when you need them will result in delays to the project schedule.

Question 261: Your construction manager approaches you about a particular team member that has just been assigned to the project. She thinks that he does not have the required skills to complete the work expected of him and suggests that this team member be assigned to a different project. What is your BEST course of action?
The correct answer is A.

> **A:** You have a responsibility, where possible, to provide training for your team members to ensure they have the appropriate skills to complete the work asked of them.

> **B:** Firing the team member would not solve the problem, which is a lack of training.

> **C:** Learning on the job is not the safest or most efficient way to get team members trained.

> **D:** Assigning the team member to another project does not deal with the real issue, which is a lack of training.

Question 262: You are in the process of obtaining the staff members you require on your project from other functional areas within your organization. You have made a request to a particular functional manager to have one of her staff members assigned part time to your project. The functional manager is concerned about the effect this will have on her operational goals and suggests instead that the staff member be assigned to your project for 30% of her time instead of 50%. What technique are you engaged in?
The correct answer is A.

> **A:** This is an example of a negotiation within a matrix organization for a human resource.

> **B:** Pre-assignment of staff does not involve negotiations such as outlined in the question.

> **C:** Acquisition is the procedure of searching outside the organization for team members.

> **D:** Acquire Project Team is the process that includes negotiation, which is the best answer to this question.

Question 263: The software project you are working on is using developers from different geographic areas around the world because the high level of experience required for this project could not be obtained locally. With the different time zones you are having difficulty organizing regular meetings between all the project team members. What would be the BEST thing you could do to improve communication between your virtual team?
The correct answer is D.

> **A:** Acquire Project Team is the process that includes negotiation, which is the best answer to this question.

> **B:** This will only cause problems in the long term as 10 AM your time may be 3 AM for someone else. Use of virtual teams is increasingly common and provides many potential benefits.

There are additional risks associated with managing team members who you may never meet face to face but the use of electronic video conferencing is a great way to overcome some of the communication problems.

C: Running multiple meetings on the same topic is not an efficient way to deal with this issue. Use of virtual teams is increasingly common and provides many potential benefits. There are additional risks associated with managing team members who you may never meet face to face but the use of electronic video conferencing is a great way to overcome some of the communication problems.

D: Use of virtual teams is increasingly common and provides many potential benefits. There are additional risks associated with managing team members who you may never meet face to face but the use of electronic video conferencing is a great way to overcome some of the communication problems.

Question 264: What is the PMBOK® Guide process of improving the competencies, team interaction, and the overall team environment to enhance project performance known as?
The correct answer is C.

A: Acquire Project Team is the process of obtaining your project team members as outlined in your human resource management plan.

B: Plan Human Resource Management is the process of producing the human resource management plan.

C: Develop Project Team is the executing process of making sure your team is capable of performing the work expected of it.

D: Manage Project Team is the process of ensuring your team is performing optimally and of improving the performance of the team.

Question 265: You are holding a weekly project meeting when a disagreement between two members of the project team begins. The disagreement is over a technical detail of the project. It is important that the conflicting opinions of the two team members be resolved as quickly as possible. It is even more important that the difference of opinion be resolved correctly. What is your BEST course of action?
The correct answer is C.

A: This answer suggests forcing as a method to resolve the conflict. There are several methods for resolving conflict: forcing, withdrawal, smoothing, compromise, and problem solving. Of these, problem solving is the best because the new facts allow the two disagreeing parties to resolve their differences with factual information and not opinion.

B: This answer proposes withdrawing from addressing the conflict. There are several methods for resolving conflict: forcing, withdrawal, smoothing, compromise, and problem solving. Of these, problem solving is the best because the new facts allow the two disagreeing parties to resolve their differences with factual information and not opinion.

C: There are several methods for resolving conflict: forcing, withdrawal, smoothing, compromise, and problem solving. Of these, problem solving is the best because the new facts allow the two disagreeing parties to resolve their differences with factual information and not opinion.

D: Compromise does not deal with the root cause of the problem. There are several methods for resolving conflict: forcing, withdrawal, smoothing, compromise, and problem solving. Of these, problem solving is the best because the new facts allow the two disagreeing parties to resolve their differences with factual information and not opinion.

Question 266: Which of the following is not an objective of developing your project team?
The correct answer is B.

A: A key objective of the Develop Project Team process is to improving team members' knowledge and skills.

B: As project manager, you must recognize that when working on a project with people from different cultures, it is important to not try to assimilate everyone to one particular culture.

C: Improving trust and agreement between team members is a key objective of the Develop Project Team process.

D: Creating a dynamic and cohesive team culture is a key objective of the Develop Project Team process.

Question 267: The Tuckman theory of team development states that team development generally follows a sequence of stages. Which is the correct order of those stages?
The correct answer is B.

A: This answer is not correct because a team will first go through the forming stage, then storming, then norming, then performing, and finally adjourning. A team can also drop back several stages in the model when an existing team member leaves or a new team members joins.

B: The Tuckman five-stage model of team development outlines the stages a group of people will go through. A team will first go through the forming stage, then storming, then norming, then performing, and finally adjourning. A team can also drop back several stages in the model when an existing team member leaves or a new team members joins.

C: This answer is not correct because a team will first go through the forming stage, then storming, then norming, then performing, and finally adjourning. A team can also drop back several stages in the model when an existing team member leaves or a new team members joins.

D: This answer is not correct because a team will first go through the forming stage, then storming, then norming, then performing, and finally adjourning. A team can also drop back several stages in the model when an existing team member leaves or a new team members joins.

Question 268: You have offered everyone on your team an individual financial bonus if they are the first to complete a particular piece of work. Instead of motivating the team, your offer has caused unhealthy competition in some staff and apathy in others. What could be the problem with your offer?
The correct answer is D.

A: Whether or not your project team respect you as a project manager, it is more likely that this scenario is because your team culture does not support individualism.

B: The amount of money offered is probably not the problem; you will find that other motivations such as power, achievement, and affiliation are better.

C: The amount of money offered is probably not the problem; you will find that other motivations such as power, achievement, and affiliation are better.

D: Deciding the appropriate recognition and rewards requires the project manager to know exactly what motivates people. People generally only want rewards that they value, and recent research has shown that money is not generally the highest motivator for people. Praise and opportunity for advancement is often more highly sought after.

Question 269: Your have decided that all of you project team members must move into their own space within the organization's main headquarters to improve efficiency and team building. What is this commonly called?
The correct answer is C.

A: Assignment generally refers to assigning team members to specific roles and responsibilities.

B: This answer is incorrect because it is not a term referenced within the PMBOK® Guide.

C: Co-locating team members where possible improves team performance.

D: A war room is a specific meeting room for project team members to be co-located and focus on doing the project work. The best answer to this question is co-location.

Question 270: After completing some work required to develop your project team members, you have noted several outputs that have been produced. Which of the following is an output that you would expect to produce?
The correct answer is A.

> **A:** The Develop Project Team process is focused on ensuring the team has the necessary skills to complete the work required of them. To ensure that this is effectively done, you need to have team performance assessments.

> **B:** Team building activities may sound like the correct answer, but they are a tool or technique used during the Develop Project Team process.

> **C:** Project staff assignments are an output from the Acquire Project Team process.

> **D:** WBS dictionary elements are part of the WBS dictionary, which is created during the Create WBS process.

Question 271: As a project manager, your greatest challenge has been managing your project team. You have decided to gain extra skills to help you in this task. All of the following are areas you should focus on except?
The correct answer is C.

> **A, B, and D:** Team management involves a combination of skills with special emphasis on communication, conflict management, negotiation, and leadership.

> **C:** Effective management of your project team is critical to the success of the project. Team management involves a combination of skills with special emphasis on communication, conflict management, negotiation, and leadership. Remuneration is not one of these key skills.

Question 272: Your project is more than halfway through and you have a CPI of 1.08 and an SPI of 1.03. You attribute a lot of the success so far to the work being done by the team and the way in which they are working together. This has been as a result of the work you have done as project manager in managing the project team. In order to complete the work associated with managing the project team successfully you have used a variety of inputs to help your efforts. Which of the following is not an input that you would have used?
The correct answer is D.

> **A:** Team performance assessments are a useful input into the Manage Project Team process because they get information about how well the team is performing.

> **B:** Project staff assignments are an input into the Manage Project Team process in the PMBOK® Guide.

C: The project management plan is an input into the Manage Project Team process in the PMBOK® Guide.

D: Project performance appraisals are a tool or technique used in the Manage Project Team process in the PMBOK® Guide, so this is the correct answer.

Question 273: In his theory of motivation of employees, Herzberg divided motivation factors into two classes: satisfiers and dissatisfiers. Which of the following are examples of satisfiers according to Herzberg?
The correct answer is D.

A: Vacation time and assignment of a personal staff assistant are factors that are classified as satisfiers in Hertzberg's theory of motivation.

B: Work satisfaction and fringe benefits are classified as satisfiers in Hertzberg's theory of motivation.

C: Plush office space and performance-based salary raises are classified as satisfiers in Hertzberg's theory of motivation.

D: This is an example of a question that the PMBOK® Guide does not answer. It requires you to have additional knowledge about leading theories of managing people.

Question 274: As a project manager, you understand how important effective management of your team is to the success of the project. Which of the following is not a key interpersonal skill that you should have as a project manager to help you manage your team?
The correct answer is C.

A: Strong and well-developed leadership skills that can operate in a variety of scenarios are an essential interpersonal skill for a project manager.

B: Having the ability to persuade people and having mature listening skills are key interpersonal skills for a project manager to have.

C: A focus on prevention over inspection and an eye for detail when reporting your project status reports is a strong technical, not interpersonal skill. Having good interpersonal skills is absolutely critical to the success of your project because it directly influences how well you manage your project team.

D: A project manager must have effective decision-making skills as part of their suite of interpersonal skills.

Question 275: Your project has been underway for 18 months and currently has a CPI of 1.02 and an SPI of 1.07. During the project two of your project team members have disagreed constantly over non-technical issues and on occasion have shown open hostility towards each other, often in front of other team members. Lately the situation has escalated, and during your last project team status meeting they openly shouted at each other. As project manager, you decide to call both team members into your office and explain to them that the best way to resolve this conflict is a give-and-take attitude and open dialogue. What conflict resolution technique are you using?

The correct answer is B.

> **A:** Forcing a solution on participants in a conflict is not a long-lasting solution; the conflict will eventually resurface.

> **B:** Confronting a problem and looking for a clear and permanent solution is the best way to resolve conflict. Your own personal conflict resolution style and any that you choose to adopt will dictate how successful you are in resolving conflict. Remember that conflict is not necessarily a bad thing but it can lead to poor performance if not managed well.

> **C:** Smoothing over a conflict situation in the hope that it will go away will not result in a permanent solution to the conflict.

> **D:** Withdrawing from and avoiding dealing with conflict does not resolve the issue in a proactive manner, and eventually the conflict will have an adverse effect on team performance and ultimately the chances of project success.

Question 276: As part of your own professional development plan, you have approval from your senior manager to undertake leadership training. As part of your training, you have asked your team members for their opinion on what constitutes the key elements and characteristics of an effective leader. What are the key elements of effective leadership?

The correct answer is D.

> **A:** Fear and submission are not good elements of effective leadership. Leadership is an important facet of the interpersonal skills you must be aware of and develop throughout your career as a project manager. Central to effective leadership are soft skills, including the ability to generate respect and trust for yourself from your team members, and also to give respect and trust to your team members.

> **B:** Friendship and admiration may arise from your effective leadership, but they are based on the key elements of respect and trust. Leadership is an important facet of the interpersonal skills you must be aware of and develop throughout your career as a project manager. Central to effective leadership are soft skills, including the ability to generate respect and trust for yourself from your team members, and also to give respect and trust to your team members.

C: Vision and humor are important elements of effective leadership but not as important as respect and trust. Leadership is an important facet of the interpersonal skills you must be aware of and develop throughout your career as a project manager. Central to effective leadership are soft skills, including the ability to generate respect and trust for yourself from your team members, and also to give respect and trust to your team members.

D: Leadership is an important facet of the interpersonal skills you must be aware of and develop throughout your career as a project manager. Central to effective leadership are soft skills, including the ability to generate respect and trust for yourself from your team members, and also to give respect and trust to your team members.

Question 277: Which of the following is not one of the four basic decision-making styles normally used by project managers?
The correct answer is A.

A: Ideas to action is not one of the four basic decision styles normally used by project managers. The four basic decision styles are command, consultation, consensus, and coin flip or random.

B-D: These answers are incorrect because the four basic decision styles are command, consultation, consensus, and coin flip or random.

Question 278: You are faced with a large decision to make on your project. After fully defining the problem, you call in your team to brainstorm multiple solutions. You then define the evaluation criteria and rate the pros and cons of different options. Prior to making a decision, you go through a process of problem definition, solution generation, ideas to action, solution action planning, solution evaluation planning, and evaluation of the outcome and process. What process are you using?
The correct answer is C.

A: Kouzes and Posner are names generally associated with leadership development, not decision making. This answer is not a term referenced within the PMBOK® Guide.

B: Shewhart and Deming's plan-do-check-act cycle is the basis of modern project management and modern quality management. It is not used to make decisions.

C: The six-phase model is outlined in Appendix X3 on interpersonal skills of the PMBOK® Guide as an important interpersonal skill for managing your team.

D: This answer is incorrect because it is made-up term.

Project Communications Management

Question 279: It is commonly acknowledged that one of the most important sets of skills a project manager should develop is their communication skills. All of the following are examples of communication skills except?

The correct answer is A.

> **A:** Reviewing the work breakdown structure is a technical, not a communication, skill. We can not stress enough the role that effective communications plays in project success. Many people seem to think that technical, financial, risk, quality, and scope management skills are more important contributors to project success. But without effective communication they are all useless.

> **B:** Setting and managing the expectations of stakeholders is achieved through the effective use of communication skills.

> **C:** In order to persuade a person or organization to form an action, you will need to display very strong and well-developed communication skills.

> **D:** Communication is a two-way process and therefore listening actively and effectively is a key communication skill.

Question 280: Your project is experiencing a range of variations that require one of the contracts you are using to engage an external vendor to be amended. What sort of communication is most appropriate when dealing with changes to a contract?

The correct answer is B.

> **A:** Informal written forms of communication are best used for memos and internal notes. When dealing with changes to a contract, formal written forms of communication are best.

> **B:** A contract is a legally binding document and as such all communication about contracts should be formal and in writing.

> **C:** Formal verbal forms of communication are presentations and speeches. When dealing with changes to a contract, formal written forms of communication are best.

> **D:** Electronic forms of communication include e-mails and the Internet. When dealing with changes to a contract, formal written forms of communication are best.

Question 281: After conducting your stakeholder analysis you determine that there are, excluding you, 7 stakeholders on the project. How many communication channels are there?
The correct answer is C.

> **A:** 7 is not the correct answer. Did you get this one wrong because you forgot to count yourself? There are 7 stakeholders and you, as the project manager, so that is 8 people, therefore the calculation is $8 (8 - 1) / 2 = 56 / 2 = 28$.

> **B:** 21 is not the correct answer. Did you get this one wrong because you forgot to count yourself? There are 7 stakeholders and you, as the project manager, so that is 8 people, therefore the calculation is $8 (8 - 1) / 2 = 56 / 2 = 28$.

> **C:** There are 7 stakeholders and you as the project manager so that is 8 people, therefore the calculation is $8 (8 - 1) / 2 = 56 / 2 = 28$.

> **D:** 35 is not the correct answer. Did you get this one wrong because you forgot to count yourself? There are 7 stakeholders and you as the project manager so that is 8 people, therefore the calculation is $8 (8 - 1) / 2 = 56 / 2 = 28$.

Question 282: There are 12 stakeholders including yourself on the project, so how many communication channels are there?
The correct answer is A.

> **A:** The question makes it clear that including you there are 12 stakeholders, so the formula is $12 (12 - 1) / 2 = 132 / 2 = 66$.

> **B-D:** These answers are not correct. The question makes it clear that including you there are 12 stakeholders, so the formula is $12 (12 - 1) / 2 = 132 / 2 = 66$.

Question 283: All of the following are factors that influence the method of communication disbursement between team members except?
The correct answer is C.

> **A:** The type and availability of technology will influence the method of communications on your project. You must always select an appropriate method of communication to ensure it is effective.

> **B:** The duration of the project will influence what style of communication you choose because you will have to keep stakeholders effectively engaged over longer periods of time. You must always select an appropriate method of communication to ensure it is effective.

> **C:** Local government regulations are related to building and town planning matters and may effect your project in other ways, but will not effect the communication distribution method.

D: The urgency of the information will influence the choice of communication method. You must always select an appropriate method of communication to ensure it is effective.

Question 284: You are leading a team on a complex project that requires constant communication with influential stakeholders. Despite your best efforts, the message that you send to the stakeholders is disrupted and misunderstood. Communication between the sender and the receiver is often affected by communication barriers or noise. These include all of the following except?
The correct answer is C.

A: Educational differences can present problems in communication, particularly in the languages and the medium chosen to communicate.

B: If one party is motivated to be part of the conversation occurring and one isn't, there will be a disruption to the communication.

C: Communication involves at least two people who may have very different backgrounds, experience, and education. Many times these individuals come from different cultures, speak different languages, and certainly have different drivers.

D: Cultural differences represent noise because many misunderstandings can arise due to different cultural expectations around appropriate forms of communication.

Question 285: You are having difficulty concentrating on what a stakeholder is saying during a business meeting and you feel you are not fully understanding them. What technique could help you to understand them better?
The correct answer is A.

A: Part of effective communication is ensuring that the message from the sender to the receiver is decoded properly. An effective way to do this is to repeat the key points back to get clarity.

B: Asking somebody to write down the message won't improve your ability to understand it. The solution to this problem is actively engaging in effective listening.

C: It is your responsibility to ensure that you are actively engaged in effective listening to a conversation; postponing the meeting will only complicate communication matters.

D: The problem is not the speed at which the speaking; the problem is your ability to concentrate. To help you concentrate, you could simply repeat the message back to the stakeholder.

Question 286: Your project team is scattered over three countries in three different time zones. Each project office has a different language as its first language, so to improve communication you have asked that all correspondence be conducted in English. In doing this, what are you trying to minimize in your team's communication?

223

The correct answer is C.

> **A:** By asking your project team to use English as a standardized language, you are not trying to minimize environmental constraints; you are trying to minimize noise and communications.

> **B:** You are trying to minimize noise that may corrupt communications, not minimize cold references.

> **C:** Noise is the term used to describe anything that gets in the way of the message between sender and receiver. Using English as a common language is an attempt to avoid the noise of different languages.

> **D:** Simply asking your team to use English as a first language does not minimize the use of foreign accents.

Question 287: The skill of listening involves more than just hearing the sounds. Which of the following is a characteristic of a good listener?
The correct answer is B.

> **A:** Taking good notes is an example of a good note taker, not a good listener.

> **B:** Good listening is an important skill for any manager. One of the ways that you can become a skilled listener is by repeating some of the things that are said. Summarizing gives yourself and others a repeat of important points and makes the speaker feel more relaxed and in a friendly atmosphere.

> **C:** Finishing the speaker's sentences is often considered quite rude and is not the sign of a good listener.

> **D:** Simply agreeing with the speaker for no good reason is not a sign of a good listener.

Question 288: You are in the process of sending out your weekly project update to a wide range of stakeholders. This is an example of what sort of communication method?
The correct answer is D.

> **A:** The stakeholder management strategy may guide some of your communications, particularly those in relation to stakeholder expectation management, but it is not a type of communication method.

> **B:** Pull communication occurs when the recipient must go to the source to get the communication.

C: Interactive communication occurs when both sender and recipient engage in mutual exchange of information concurrently.

D: In this instance, you are pushing the information out to stakeholders. Push communication occurs when the sender pushes the information to the recipient.

Question 289: You are using your intranet site to post large amounts of information that team members can log into to read. This is an example of what sort of communication method?
The correct answer is D.

A: Encoding and decoding is what senders and receivers do in the standard communications model.

B: Push communication occurs when the sender pushes the information to the recipient.

C: Interactive communication occurs when both sender and recipient engage in mutual exchange of information concurrently.

D: It is called pull communication because recipients pull it down at their leisure, rather than having it pushed to them.

Question 290: Your project team has spent a considerable amount of time and energy completing the stakeholder analysis and putting together the communications management plan but is now disagreeing what, how, and when different communication methods are to be used. Who should take responsibility for determining this?
The correct answer is D.

A: The responsibility does not lie with any representative or stakeholder; that could refer to anybody at all. The responsibility lies with the project manager.

B: The project team should not be left make this decision; the project manager must take responsibility.

C: This issue does not need to be escalated to the project sponsor because it is the responsibility of the project manager to make this decision.

D: It is the responsibility of the project manager to decide what communication methods are to be used how and when in the project.

Question 291: You are regularly referring to your communications management plan to help guide your project communications. Which of the following would you not expect to find in your communications management plan?
The correct answer is B.

> **A:** The communications management plan will refer to the person who has responsibility for authorizing the release of confidential information to stakeholders.

> **B:** You wouldn't normally find information as specific as team member addresses and phone numbers in the communications management plan.

> **C:** For ease of use and standardization, it is common for the communications management plan to have a glossary of common terminology.

> **D:** At the core of the communication management plan is the stakeholder communication requirements.

Question 292: As part of your project, you regularly hold status meetings with project team members and influential stakeholders. You endeavor at all times to ensure that these meetings are productive and contribute to successful communication on the project. All of the following are techniques to ensure your project meetings are more productive except?
The correct answer is A.

> **A:** Meetings need to have structure around them, and setting an agenda, ground rules, and a set time for the meeting to run are good ways of improving efficiency. Teleconferencing is not a standardized way to make them more productive; the preference is for participants to be face-to-face.

> **B:** Establishing ground rules for attendance, conduct, and follow-up at a meeting will make it more productive.

> **C:** Setting clear start and finish times for a meeting so that participants know when they should be there and when they can return to work is a way to make meetings more productive.

> **D:** Following a clear and defined agenda will make meetings more efficient and productive.

Question 293: While carrying out the work described in your project communications plan you go to great lengths to ensure that relevant information is disseminated to the correct stakeholders in the right way at the right time. As a senior project manager you know that effective information distribution is a key factor in project success. This is because effective information distribution includes all of the following techniques except?

The correct answer is C.

> **A:** Selecting the appropriate writing style to match stakeholder needs is an effective information distribution technique.
>
> **B:** Presentation techniques are a very effective way of distributing information to stakeholders.
>
> **C:** The issue log can be used as a communications tool to let stakeholders know the issues are being monitored, but it is not a means of information distribution itself.
>
> **D:** Selecting the correct and appropriate choice of media is an effective information distribution technique.

Question 294: You have decided to study for the PMP® credential and are currently learning the way in which the project life cycle can be described in terms of process groups associated with initiating, planning, executing, monitoring and controlling, and closing activities. You then move on to studying the ways in which successful communication occurs in a project. In order to demonstrate how much you have learned, you are able to describe to a colleague how some aspect of project communication occurs in different process groups. The Manage Communications process occurs within which PMBOK® Guide process group?

The correct answer is C.

> **A, B, and D:** These answers are incorrect because Manage Communications is part of the Executing process group.
>
> **C:** Manage Communications is part of the Executing process group.

Question 295: You and your project team have been in negotiations with a potential supplier for several hours over an important contract that will deliver a large part of the one product required to complete your project. You and your team are getting frustrated at the slow rate of progress on the negotiations but know it is important that they are done thoroughly. How important is non-verbal communication to the negotiations?

The correct answer is A.

> **A:** Humans are complex communicators and the non-verbal communications we make are always very important, often more so than the verbal communications we make.
>
> **B-D** These answers are incorrect because humans are complex communicators and the non-verbal communications we make are always very important, often more so than the verbal communications we make.

Question 296: You have called a team member into your office to deal with unacceptable behavior towards other project team members. After the meeting you decide to follow up to make clear what was discussed. What is the best form of communication to use in this instance?

The correct answer is A.

> **A:** Since this situation is a serious one that needs to be documented for future reference, it is best to use formal written forms of communication.

> **B:** Using formal verbal or any verbal form of communication could mean that the message was understood and forgotten. In this instance, a formal written form of communication is best.

> **C:** Since this situation is a serious one that needs to be documented for future reference, it is best to use formal, rather than informal, written forms of communication.

> **D:** Using informal verbal or any verbal form of communication could mean that the message was understood and forgotten. In this instance, a formal written form of communication is best.

Question 297: Your project sponsor has asked you to present a detailed project update to some high-level stakeholders who are concerned that the project is not meeting its agreed timeframes, its agreed budget, nor delivering the quality the customer is expecting. What information and method would be BEST to use in this situation?

The correct answer is D.

> **A:** A verbal presentation given casually during a 10-minute meeting will not contain the detailed information desired by the stakeholders.

> **B:** A summary milestone report will not contain the detailed information desired by the stakeholders.

> **C:** A PowerPoint presentation outlining the major issues will not contain the detailed information desired by the stakeholders.

> **D:** Choosing the most appropriate information and the way in which you deliver it is an important decision to ensure the efficacy of your project reporting.

Question 298: You are attempting to communicate with various project stakeholders, and despite your best efforts you find that the information that you send to them is misunderstood. Cultural differences and using unfamiliar technology are the main problems contributing to this lack of understanding. What is the best term to describe these characteristics?

The correct answer is C.

> **A:** Decoding is the process that the receiver of the message does once the message has been received.

> **B:** Feedback is a process where the receiver provides feedback to the sender of the message to facilitate more effective listening.

> **C:** In the standard communications model, noise refers to any obstacle in the selected medium between sender and receiver that can impact the communication.

> **D:** Transmission is the process of communicating the message via a selected medium.

Question 299: You are actively monitoring and controlling the project communications according to your approved communications management plan and are seeking to generate work performance information about the effectiveness of your project communications. Which of the following would be least useful to you?
The correct answer is D.

> **A:** The question is asking about the inputs into the Control Communications process, and the project communications are an input in this process.

> **B:** The questions is asking about the inputs into the Control Communications process, and the issue log is an input in this process.

> **C:** The questions is asking about the inputs into the Control Communications process, and work performance data is an input in this process.

> **D:** The questions is asking about the inputs into the Control Communications process and change requests are an output from, not an input into, this process.

Question 300: You are using historical data about your project to forecast an estimated future outcome in your project performance reporting. This is an example of what forecasting method?
The correct answer is D.

> **A:** Budget forecasts are part of earned management, which is an example of time series methods, which is the best answer.

> **B:** The judgmental forecasting method uses methods from experts such as the Delphi method.

> **C:** Econometric methods use tools such as linear regression.

> **D:** Earned value is one example of time series method.

Question 301: Your project team has just finished the first round of soliciting information from experts about what they think the forecasted future performance on your project will be using information supplied to them. You are currently assessing the information supplied anonymously by the respondents and plan to request a second round of opinions to use in your project forecasts. What forecasting method are you using?
The correct answer is A.

> **A:** This is an example of using the Delphi technique, which is an example of a judgmental forecasting method.

> **B:** Causal is another name for econometric methods, which use tools such as linear regression.

> **C:** Earned value is one example of a time series method.

> **D:** Econometric methods use tools such as linear regression.

Question 302: Which of the following would you not expect to see in a detailed project performance report?
The correct answer is B.

> **A:** Current status of risks and issues would definitely be included in a detailed project performance report.

> **B:** Staff performance review information would not generally be included in project performance reports. This information would be included team assessments.

> **C:** The forecasted project completion would definitely be included in a detailed project performance report.

> **D:** A clear summary of changes approved since the last report would definitely be included in a detailed project performance report.

Question 303: Several of your stakeholders are raising issues with you, and you are documenting their issues in an issue log and providing feedback to the stakeholders about the status and any resolution of the issues. Furthermore, you are using the issue log as an input into a process because it provides a repository for what has already happened in the project and a platform for subsequent communication to be delivered. Which process are you involved in?
The correct answer is A.

> **A:** The issue log is an important input into the Control Communications process because it does identify and document what has already happened in the project and provides an effective platform for the subsequent communications to be delivered to stakeholders.

> **B-D:** These answers are incorrect because the issue log is an important input into the Control Communications process.

Question 304: A project manager should spend approximately how much of their time communicating to team members and stakeholders to effectively contribute to project success?
The correct answer is C.

> **A:** 50% is not correct. It is commonly accepted that communication is key to project success, and that a project manager should always be undertaking communication, and that 90% of a project manager's time should be spent on communication, with 50% of this time spent communicating with the project team.

> **B:** 5% is simply not enough time allocated to communications. It is commonly accepted that communication is key to project success, and that a project manager should always be undertaking communication, and that 90% of a project manager's time should be spent on communication, with 50% of this time spent communicating with the project team.

> **C:** It is commonly accepted that communication is key to project success, and that a project manager should always be undertaking communication, and that 90% of a project manager's time should be spent on communication, with 50% of this time spent communicating with the project team.

> **D:** 70% is not correct. It is commonly accepted that communication is key to project success, and that a project manager should always be undertaking communication, and that 90% of a project manager's time should be spent on communication, with 50% of this time spent communicating with the project team.

Question 305: Which of the following has been identified as one of the single biggest reasons for project success or failure?
The correct answer is C.

> **A:** There are many enterprise environmental factors that can positively and adversely affect the project but appropriate communication is the single biggest reason for project success or failure.

> **B:** Financial accountability and accuracy will contribute to project failure but a lack of appropriate communication is a larger reason.

> **C:** Communication is the essential element of project success. People need to communicate to be effective. It is true that most project problems can be traced back to the lack of appropriate communication. A project manager should spend 90% of their time communicating, and 50% of this time should be communicating with members of the project team.

> **D:** Is important that the project sponsor and the project manager have a professional relationship but one of the single biggest reasons for project success or failure is appropriate communication.

Question 306: There are 36 communications channels on a project. How many stakeholders are there in the project?
The correct answer is D.

> **A-C:** These answers are not correct. This question requires you to take the normal formula for calculating communications channels and use it backward. The formula is $(n (n - 1)) / 2$. So working backward, the answer is $((36 \times 2) / 9)+1 = 9$.

> **D:** This question requires you to take the normal formula for calculating communications channels and use it backward. The formula is $(n (n - 1)) / 2$. So working backward, the answer is $((36 \times 2) / 9)+1 = 9$. If pressed for time in the exam you could quickly work out all four answers.

Project Risk Management

Question 307: What is the best description of the objectives of the risk management work you will undertake on your project?
The correct answer is A.

> **A:** Risks can be both positive and negative. If they are positive, you want them to happen; if they are negative, you don't want them to happen.

> **B:** This answer is incorrect because it describes your risk management objectives the wrong way. Risks can be both positive and negative. If they are positive, you want them to happen; if they are negative, you don't want them to happen.

> **C:** This answer is incorrect because you will aim to increase the probability and impact of positive risks. Risks can be both positive and negative. If they are positive, you want them to happen; if they are negative, you don't want them to happen.

> **D:** This answer is not the best answer because it does not describe all the work you will do in relation to positive risks. Risks can be both positive and negative. If they are positive, you want them to happen; if they are negative, you don't want them to happen.

Question 308: All of the following are characteristics of risks except?
The correct answer is D.

> **A:** Risk is always in the future because once the timeframe for a risk has passed, it is no longer worth assessing.

> **B:** Risk is an uncertain event or condition, and the point of risk management activities is to anticipate this uncertainty and the resulting impact on the project.

C: Is a risk occurs, it will have an effect on at least one project objective because if it didn't, you wouldn't be interested in it.

D: One of the risk strategies available to you is avoidance.

Question 309: When completing your risk management plan you also decide to create a contingency plan. What is the main reason for creating a risk contingency plan? **The correct answer is A.**

A: Unknown risks cannot be managed proactively; contingency plans are for unknown risks.

B: Risk contingency plans deal with all unknown risks, no matter if they are large or small.

C: Risk contingency plans deal with risks that haven't been identified in the risk management plan.

D: Risk contingency plans deal with unknown risks, not known risks.

Question 310: While completing your risk management plan you also decide to create a fallback plan. What is the main reason for creating a fallback plan? **The correct answer is B.**

A: Risk fallback, or contingency, plans deal with all unknown risks, no matter if they are large or small.

B: Unknown risks are risks that cannot be managed proactively, and fallback, or contingency, plans are for unknown risks.

C: Risk fallback, or contingency, plans deal with risks that haven't been identified in the risk management plan.

D: Risk fallback, or contingency, plans deal with unknown risks, not known risks.

Question 311: The willingness to accept varying degrees of risk is called what? **The correct answer is A.**

A: Risk tolerance is the degree to which you will or will not accept risk on your project.

B: Risk acceptance is a strategy for dealing with risk. It does not refer to the willingness to accept varying degrees of risk.

C: Risk planning is the process you undertake order to proactively manage uncertainty of a project.

D: Risk analysis is one of the tools that you can use to analyze the probability and impact of identified risks.

Question 312: When should you begin risk management on a project?
The correct answer is D.

> **A-C:** These answers are incorrect because risks can occur at any stage in the project. You should begin risk management planning as soon as the project is initiated or conceived.
>
> **D:** Risk can affect a project as soon as it is conceived, and you need to be aware, even at a basic level, of the potential impacts of these risks. Risk management occurs throughout the life of the project.

Question 313: During a meeting to develop your risk management plan, a senior team member questions whether you have all the required inputs to develop a robust risk management plan that is appropriate for your project. Which of the following is not an input that you could use to complete this work successfully?
The correct answer is A.

> **A:** The risk management plan is the output from, not an input to, the Plan Risk Management process in the PMBOK® Guide, so this is the correct answer.
>
> **B-D:** The inputs into the Plan Risk Management process include the project management plan, project charter, stakeholder register, enterprise environmental factors, and organizational process assets.

Question 314: You and your project team are currently involved in the process to plan your particular approach to risk management on your project and are using a variety of tools and techniques to assist you in producing the risk management plan. Which of the following is not a tool or technique used during the Plan Risk Management process?
The correct answer is A.

> **A:** Risk probability and impact assessment is a tool and technique used during the Perform Qualitative Risk Analysis process.
>
> **B:** Analytical techniques are one of the three tools and techniques used during the Plan Risk Management process, the other two being expert judgment and meetings.
>
> **C:** Expert judgment is one of the three tools used in the Plan Risk Management process, the other two being analytical techniques and meetings.
>
> **D:** Meetings are one of the three tools and techniques used in the Plan Risk Management process, the other two being analytical techniques and expert judgment.

Question 315: As part of your risk management planning you develop a diagram showing the hierarchy of project risks arranged by risk category and subcategory. What is this diagram commonly called?
The correct answer is B.

> **A:** The risk assessment register is merely a list of known risks and their assessments. It does not break risks down into categories and subcategories; this is the job of the risk breakdown structure.

> **B:** Your risk breakdown structure does what the other breakdown structures do (i.e. WBS and OBS): it takes a high-level items and breaks them down into easier-to-understand-and-manage subcomponents arranged by category.

> **C:** The probability and impact matrix shows the combined probability and impact of identified risks should they occur on the project. The risk breakdown structure shows the hierarchy of project risks arranged by risk category and subcategory.

> **D:** The risk register contains information about risk categories, risk events, qualitative risk analysis, quantitative risk analysis, and plan risk responses. The risk breakdown structure shows the hierarchy of project risks arrange by risk category and subcategory.

Question 316: Your risk management planning session has produced definitions of risk probability and impact. These are used during which PMBOK® Guide process?
The correct answer is C.

> **A:** The purpose of the standardized definitions of risk probability and impact is to assist with the Perform Qualitative Risk Analysis Process, not the Perform Quantitative Risk Analysis process.

> **B:** The purpose of the standardized definitions of risk probability and impact is to assist with the Perform Qualitative Risk Analysis Process, not the Identify Risks process.

> **C:** Before qualitatively assessing risks, you must have a predetermined and pre-agreed definition of the different categories to make sure the subjective nature of qualitative analysis is standardized.

> **D:** The purpose of the standardized definitions of risk probability and impact is to assist with the Perform Qualitative Risk Analysis Process, not the Plan Risk Management process.

Question 317: Your team is carrying out the process of determining which risks may affect the project and documenting their characteristics. You are using a variety of tools and techniques, including documentation, reviews, information gathering techniques, checklist analysis, and SWOT analysis. What is the name of this process?

The correct answer is B.

> **A:** The Perform Qualitative Risk analysis process is performed after the individual risks have been identified in the Identify Risks process.
>
> **B:** Identify Risks is the first stage in the risk management process after you have completed your risk management plan and it uses these tools and techniques to prepare the first iteration of the risk register.
>
> **C:** The Perform Quantitative Risk analysis process is performed after the individual risks have been identified in the Identify Risks process.
>
> **D:** The Plan Risk Management process is the first process completed, and it produces the risk management plan. It is the Identify Risks process that uses these particular tools and techniques to produce the first iteration of the risk register.

Question 318: You are congratulating your team for the time and effort taken to develop the first iteration of your project risk register. You are now contemplating the many uses that your risk register will have in your project and the many different areas in which it can be used as an input into the work being done. Which of the following PMBOK® Guide processes does not use the risk register as an input?

The correct answer is B.

> **A:** The Control Risks process does use the risk register as an input so it knows what risks it is intending to monitor and control.
>
> **B:** The risk register is not used as an input into this process.
>
> **C:** The Plan Procurement Management process does use a risk register as an input so it can take into account contract-related risks that have been identified.
>
> **D:** The Perform Qualitative Risk Analysis process does use a risk register as an input so it knows which risks to perform qualitative risk analysis on.

Question 319: You and your team are in the process of identifying all potential uncertainty and risk on your project. You wish to ensure that your risk register is as comprehensive as possible; as such you are looking for as many relevant inputs as possible to assist you in this process. Which of the following is not an input into this process?

The correct answer is B.

> **A:** Activity duration estimates are a useful input when identifying risks because they allow you to focus on specific time allowances that may be required.

> **B:** Assumptions analysis is a tool and technique, not an input, used in the Identify Risks process in the PMBOK® Guide so this is the correct answer.

> **C:** The stakeholder register is a useful input because it identifies stakeholders, and they can then be asked for input to assist with the identified risks.

> **D:** Activity cost estimates are useful in identifying risks because they provide a quantitative assessment of the risk.

Question 320: You are using your risk management plan to guide the work needed to identify both positive and negative risks on your project. Which of the following is not a tool or technique you would find useful to complete this work?

The correct answer is C.

> **A:** Assumptions analysis allows you to document any and all assumptions made as part of the risk of unification process.

> **B:** Risk registers are typically built up using a variety of information-gathering techniques in order to solicit information from people with experience in your type of project.

> **C:** Risk urgency assessment is a tool and technique from the Perform Qualitative Risk Analysis process, not the Identify Risks process in the PMBOK® Guide.

> **D:** Diagramming techniques are useful tools to use to identify risks and their root causes.

Question 321: You and your team are completing the process of identifying risks on your project, and you wish to use a particular type of diagram to represent risk characteristics. All of the following are diagramming techniques used during the Identify Risks process except?

The correct answer is C.

> **A:** The process flowchart can be used to identify points in a process where risk or uncertainty is greatest.

> **B:** The cause and effect diagram can be used to get to the root cause of any identified risks.

> **C:** A Pareto chart is a type of histogram that shows the rank ordering of quality defects by type of category so that corrective action can be focused in the correct place.

> **D:** An influence diagram can show how one risk may impact on the probability or impact of another risk occurring.

Question 322: Your team has successfully identified many categories of risks, and within each category they have identified specific risk events that may impact your project. You have documented all of this information in an initial list of identified risks as part of the iterative development of your risk register. At this early stage, this document will generally have all of the following information on it except?

The correct answer is D.

> **A:** Your initial list of identified risks may describe the known causes of individual risk events.

> **B:** Your initial list of identified risks will describe individual risk events.

> **C:** Your initial list of identified risks will describe the consequences of individual risk events should they occur.

> **D:** You don't determine probability of risks until completing qualitative and quantitative risk analysis, so the first iterations of your list of identified risks may not have probability information on it.

Question 323: Your team is carrying out the process to identify the risks to the project and is identifying strengths and weaknesses of the organization by looking at the way these strengths offset threats and opportunities that may serve to overcome weaknesses. What technique are they using?

The correct answer is A.

> **A:** SWOT stands for strengths, weaknesses, opportunities, and threats.

> **B:** Expert judgment relates to soliciting people's opinion and experience.

> **C:** PERT analysis is used in other parts of project management, particularly the critical path method and three-point estimating.

> **D:** PEST analysis describes political, economic, social, and technological analysis of a particular event or organization.

Question 324: As project manager on a project, you have begun the process of qualitatively assessing the probability and impact to risks that have been identified on your project. Which of the following is not an input you would find useful in completing this work?

The correct answer is A.

> **A:** The project charter is used as an input into several processes, but not the Perform Qualitative Risk Analysis process in the PMBOK® Guide, so this is the correct answer.

> **B:** The risk management plan is an essential input into this the Perform Qualitative Risk Analysis process in the PMBOK® Guide.

C: The risk register is an essential input into the Perform Qualitative Risk Analysis process in the PMBOK® Guide.

D: The scope baseline is used as an input into the Perform Qualitative Risk Analysis process in the PMBOK® Guide.

Question 325: Your team is using the project risk register and has started a quantitative assessment of the risks. You tell your team that it is better to start with qualitative analysis first. What reasons do you give your team for this decision?
The correct answer is D.

A: This answer is incorrect because quantitative analysis does not use any form of intiuitve interpretation of risks.

B: This answer is incorrect because qualitative analysis is subjective and does not assign quantifiable and accurate numerical values.

C: This answer is incorrect because qualitative risk analysis is generally done first to prioritize risks quickly and to indicate which risks can and should be subject to the more accurate quantitative analysis.

D: Qualitative risk analysis is done first to prioritize risks quickly and indicate which risks can and should be subject to the more accurate quantitative analysis.

Question 326: Your team is using your risk register to prioritize risks for further analysis by assessing their probability of occurrence and impact. What PMBOK® Guide process best describes the work they are carrying out?
The correct answer is D.

A: The Plan Risk Management process is the process that outlines how your risk management activities will be executed on the project.

B: Quantitative risk analysis uses numerical data of probability and impact to get an assessment of time or dollars.

C: The Identify Risks process is the first of the risk processes that identifies individual risks but does not carry out any assessment of probability or impact.

D: Assessing probability and impact to determine priorities is a characteristic of the Qualitative Risk Analysis process.

Question 327: While completing your assessment of the risks on your project, you begin to examine the ones with the greatest potential threat to your project. You are using a diagram to help you complete this task, and you are currently looking at the high priority risks for further analysis. What diagram would best help you?
The correct answer is A.

> **A:** The probability and impact matrix shows the low, medium, and high risks on the project.
>
> **B:** A scatter diagram is generally used during quality management, and it plots two variables on the X and Y axis.
>
> **C:** A Pareto chart lists the hierarchical order of the frequency of known events or defects to allow you to assess which 20% of events or defects are causing 80% of the problems.
>
> **D:** The risk register contains information about risk categories, risk events, qualitative risk analysis, quantitative risk analysis, and plan risk responses. It is the risk breakdown structure. It shows the hierarchy of project risks by risk category.

Question 328: An important aspect of your qualitative risk analysis is determining the validity of the information you are using. What is this technique commonly called?
The correct answer is A.

> **A:** Since qualitative analysis contains a high degree of subjectivity, it is important that you determine the quality of the data you are using.
>
> **B:** Assumptions analysis documents the assumptions made during the risk management processes.
>
> **C:** Risk urgency assessment looks at the timeframe for risks occurring, with those risks in the near future deemed to be more urgent than those that may occur further off.
>
> **D:** Risk categorization is one of the tools that is used to create the risk breakdown structure.

Question 329: Your team is completing the process of numerically analyzing the effect of identified risks on your project objectives. Which PMBOK® Guide process best describes the work they are carrying out?
The correct answer is C.

> **A:** The Plan Risk Responses process develops potential responses to identified risks.
>
> **B:** Qualitative risk analysis does not use objective numerical data.
>
> **C:** The key word here is *numerical*, which clearly indicates a quantitative approach.
>
> **D:** The Identify Risks process is the process where risk and uncertainty are identified and the risk register is created.

Question 330: After completing work to perform qualitative risk analysis on identified risks in your risk register, you have produced several updates to your risk register. Which of the following processes described in the PMBOK® Guide indirectly uses these updates?

The correct answer is A.

> **A:** The risk register update is indirectly used as an input into the Identify Risks process because the risk register is refined and subject to iterations.
>
> **B:** The Project Integration Management knowledge area of the PMBOK® Guide contains six processes, none of which uses risk register updates as an input.
>
> **C:** The Project Time Management knowledge area of the PMBOK® Guide contains seven processes, none of which uses risk register updates as an input.
>
> **D:** The Plan Risk Responses process does not utilize risk register updates.

Question 331: Three-point estimating is a commonly used technique for gathering and analyzing data. It is used in all of the following project areas except?

The correct answer is C.

> **A:** Three-point estimating is useful for quantifying the impacts of risks using an optimistic, realistic, and pessimistic assessment of the risk probability or impact.
>
> **B:** Three-point estimating is used in project time management for getting a weighted average of optimistic, realistic, and pessimistic time estimates.
>
> **C:** Any time you are using numbers such as dollar values, length of time, or quantifying the impact of risks, the three-point estimating technique will come in handy.
>
> **D:** Three-point estimating is used in project cost management for getting a weighted average of optimistic, realistic, and pessimistic cost estimates.

Question 332: If a project has a 40% chance of achieving a $17,000 profit and a 60% chance of achieving a $20,000 loss, what is the expected monetary value of the project?

The correct answer is D.

> **A-C:** These answers are incorrect. Remember that EMV = total probability x impact = (.4 x $17,000)+(.6 x -$20,000) = $6,800 - $12,000 = -$5,200.
>
> **D:** EMV = total probability x impact = (.4 x $17,000)+ (.6 x -$20,000) = $6,800 - $12,000 = -$5,200.

Question 333: If a project has a 65% chance of a $200,000 profit and a 35% chance of a $100,000 loss, what is the expected monetary value for the project?
The correct answer is D.

> **A-C:** These answers are incorrect. Remember that EMV = total probability x impact = (.65 x $200,000)+(.35 x -$100,000) = $130,000 - $35,000 = $95,000.
>
> **D:** EMV = total probability x impact = (.65 x $200,000)+ (.35 x -$100,000) = $130,000 - $35,000 = $95,000.

Question 334: If a risk event has a 80% chance of occurring, and if it does occur, the consequence will be a $10,000 cost to the project, what does -$8,000 represent to the project?
The correct answer is D.

> **A:** This may look like the correct answer in the sense that the -$8000 does represent a quantified risk, but the correct answer is the expected monetary value.
>
> **B:** This answer is incorrect because it is not a term referenced within the PMBOK® Guide.
>
> **C:** What-if analysis is generally performed by a computer and involves complex statistical analysis of events and probabilities.
>
> **D:** This represents the expected monetary value of the risk event occurring.

Question 335: After completing your risk register and a quantitative assessment of the financial value of prioritized risks on your project, you have a dollar amount added to your project budget. What is this amount typically called?
The correct answer is D.

> **A:** A contingent response strategy is a type of risk response that is triggered by a predefined trigger or event.
>
> **B:** A management reserve is generally an amount held and controlled by management; projects that encounter completely unforeseeable risk events can apply to use some of it.
>
> **C:** A slush fund is a common term used by some organizations to describe an amount of money used for various unspecified purposes.
>
> **D:** A contingency reserve is budget included in the cost baseline that is allocated to identified risks that have been assessed quantitatively.

Question 336: Which of the following is not an example of a probability distribution?
The correct answer is B.

> **A, C, D:** Beta, Normal, and Triangular distributions are all used in quantitative risk analysis.

> **B:** Obtuse distribution is not a term referenced within the PMBOK® Guide.

Question 337: Your team is completing an exercise to determine which risks have the greatest potential impact on your project. They are assessing the extent to which the uncertainty of each element of the project affects the risk being examined when all other uncertain elements are held at static baseline values. What is this technique commonly known as?
The correct answer is C.

> **A:** A tornado diagram graphically represents risk areas of the project and the relative degree of uncertainty or sensitivity of each risk category.

> **B:** Expected monetary value analysis takes the probability and known numerical impact to determine a financial or time analysis of the risk.

> **C:** Sensitivity analysis is the technique to determine the relative impact of a particular risk on independent project variables. A tornado diagram can be used to show the results of the sensitivity analysis.

> **D:** Modeling and simulation of risk are generally completed by computers because there is statistical analysis that needs to be completed.

Question 338: You are currently performing risk analysis on a large and extremely complex project. Your project team decides that the most comprehensive way to approach the process of risk analysis is to examine all the possible outcomes using an iterative computer simulation process to model a range of variables taken from a probability distribution. What is this technique known as?
The correct answer is C.

> **A:** Sensitivity analysis is the technique used to determine the relative impact of a particular risk on independent project variables. A tornado diagram can be used to show the results of the sensitivity analysis.

> **B:** Expected monetary value analysis takes the probability and known numerical impact to determine a financial or time analysis of the risk.

C: Monte Carlo, or what-if, analysis examines a range of possible outcomes from different project variables to present a risk profile for the project.

D: Ishikawa analysis is the process of using a cause and effect, or fishbone, diagram to determine the root cause of risk events.

Question 339: You have documented and quantitatively assessed the risk to your project and the potential outcomes in a diagram to show the different outcomes of events should a particular probability occur, in order to determine the expected monetary value. What is this technique generally called?
The correct answer is B.

A: What-if scenario analysis uses computer simulations to look at all the potential risk pathways, probability, and impact throughout the project to get a likely probability of each risk path.

B: A decision tree analysis sets out in a diagram the various probability of outcomes and a value of each outcome so that an overall expected monetary value can be determined.

C: Ishikawa analysis is the process of using a cause and effect, or fishbone, diagram to determine the root cause of risk events.

D: A tornado diagram graphically represents risk areas of the project and the relative degree of uncertainty or sensitivity of each risk category.

Question 340: Your team has completed the process of assessing and documenting risks that may occur on your project. What is the next step to complete?
The correct answer is C.

A: Identifying risks is not the next process because it would have already been completed in order to get to this stage.

B: Control risks is not the next step becuase you first have to plan your risk responses.

C: After identifying your project risks, the next step is to plan a response to each one.

D: Execution of the project tasks is not related to whether you have completed the process of assessing and documenting risks that may occur on your project.

Question 341: A project manager is faced with making a large decision about a risk that her project team has identified. The risk involves the design of a car component. It has been found that the weld of the component where the load-bearing flange is located will corrode in a high salt environment. If this takes place, the component may fail and injure the driver and passenger. The project team decides that the design of the component should be modified by using corrosion-resistant materials. This will eliminate the risk from consideration. What is this risk response technique called?

The correct answer is C.

> **A:** Risk rejection is not a term referenced within the PMBOK® Guide and not one of the appropriate risk response strategies.

> **B:** Risk acceptance is allowing the risk to happen and dealing with it if it occurs.

> **C:** Risk avoidance is eliminating the risk from consideration by doing something that will eliminate it as a possibility.

> **D:** Risk transfer is transferring the risk to someone other than the project team, such as an insurance company or outside supplier.

Question 342: You are managing a project to build a large hydro dam for electrical power generation, which will be built over a known seismically active area. Your team decides to strengthen the core structure of the dam to better tolerate any earth movements that may occur. This is an example of what sort of risk response?
The correct answer is D.

> **A:** This is an example of risk mitigation; acceptance would be taking no action and accepting the consequences should the dam be struck by an earthquake.

> **B:** This is an example of risk mitigation; risk transfer is usually in the form of insurance.

> **C:** This is an example of risk mitigation; risk avoidance would mean building the hydro dam in a less seismically active area.

> **D:** Strengthening the dam shows that you are trying to mitigate the damage to the structure should an earthquake occur.

Question 343: You have decided to take out insurance on your project to cover your project financially if a risk occurs. This is an example of what sort of risk response?
The correct answer is A.

> **A:** This answer is correct because buying insurance is a process of transferring the impact of the risk to another party.

> **B:** Taking out insurance is an example of risk transference, not risk mitigation.

> **C:** Taking out insurance is not an example of a sharing risk response. Partnering with another organization to minimize the risk would be an example of sharing.

> **D:** Taking out insurance is not an example of avoidance. Deciding not to do the project would be an example of avoidance.

Question 344: All of the following are acceptable responses to positive risks except?
The correct answer is B.

> **A:** You can choose to accept positive risks as an acceptable risk response.
>
> **B:** Mitigation is a response to negative risks.
>
> **C:** You can choose to enhance the chances of positive risk occurring as an acceptable risk response.
>
> **D:** You can choose to exploit the strengths you have to increase the chances of a positive risk occurring as an acceptable risk response.

Question 345: You are about to tender for a large, multi-billion dollar infrastructure project, and your general manager has just announced a joint venture with another company to help with risk management. This is an example of what sort of risk response?
The correct answer is A.

> **A:** Sharing involves allocating some or all of the ownership of the risk to a third party.
>
> **B:** Avoidance is a strategy for a negative risk response, and the question outlines a positive risk.
>
> **C:** Mitigation is a strategy for a negative risk response, and the question outlines a positive risk.
>
> **D:** If you were to use an exploit strategy, it would, for example, be to appoint senior members of your team to the project.

Question 346: You and your project team have completed your risk register, including planned responses to identified risks. What is your next step?
The correct answer is A.

> **A:** Planned risk responses represent extra work to be done on the project and as such they must be included in the scope baseline for the project. The scope baseline includes the scope statement, the work breakdown structure, and work breakdown structure dictionary.
>
> **B:** Before beginning any other processes, the extra work required and the planned responses should be captured in the scope baseline, which includes the work breakdown structure. You cannot yet begin to control the risks.
>
> **C:** Before updating the risk register, you should ensure that the required work was included in the scope baseline.
>
> **D:** Before updating the sponsor, the planned responses should be captured in the scope baseline, which includes the work breakdown structure.

Question 347: You have completed the final steps to develop a complete risk register with identified risks, a priority assessment, a qualitative assessment of all risks, a quantitative assessment of the top priority risks, and you have also identified appropriate risk responses for each risk. Which of the following is not an expected output from completing this work?
The correct answer is D.

A: The specific project documents that will be updated will be the risk register to include your planned risk responses.

B: Once you have produced your plan risk responses, you may need to update several aspects of the project management plan to reflect the plan risk responses.

C: A specific part of the project management plan that may be updated as a result of the plan risk responses will be the cost management plan, especially if there are costs associated with your planned risk responses.

D: Contingent response strategies are techniques used in the Plan Risk Response process in the PMBOK® Guide, which is what the information contained in the question is indicating you have just completed.

Question 348: Your project has been underway for 9 months when a major problem occurs that is not included in the risk register. What is your BEST course of action?
The correct answer is C.

A: Given that the question outlines that this is a major problem, you will not have time to evaluate the risk in any manner.

B: Given that the question outlines that this is a major problem, you will not have time to evaluate the risk in any manner. If you were to do so, however, you would perform qualitative analysis.

C: In this case, the risk has occurred and has created an impact on the project, so there is no need to begin a formal evaluation process. Your risk response plan would identify that a workaround is the best option for unanticipated risks.

D: Given that this has been identified as a major problem, your best course of action in this instance is to create a workaround first and then contact your project sponsor.

Question 349: Despite your best efforts at anticipating and documenting all risk and uncertainty on your project, you have encountered a completely unforeseeable risk that will incur significant extra cost to your project. You decide to approach your project sponsor and ask for permission to get these extra funds from a pool of money that they control. What is this pool of money generally referred to as?

The correct answer is C.

> **A:** A slush fund is a generic term sometimes used by companies to refer to a pool of money used for various purposes, not all of which are risk-related.

> **B:** A contingency reserve is an amount added to a project budget to reflect the quantitative analysis of probability and the financial impact of identified risks.

> **C:** The management reserve is a pool of money controlled by project sponsors and senior management to be used for projects that encounter unforeseeable risks.

> **D:** The control account is a management control point where scope, budget, actual cost, and schedule are integrated and computed to an end value for performance measurement.

Question 350: The project you are working on is over halfway through, and you have begun to measure that price increases on the steel that you require for the project have gone 8% over your estimate for price increases over the timeframe of the project. As a result, you put in place a policy to procure all the remaining steel required for the project and pay for it to be stored in a warehouse instead of ordering the steel as you require it. This is an example of what?

The correct answer is A.

> **A:** In this instance, your contingent response strategy would have documented that should prices increase over the estimates, this would constitute a trigger to enact a particular contingent response strategy.

> **B:** This is not an example of risk mitigation; it is an example of a contingent response strategy being enacted in response to defined triggers.

> **C:** This is not an example of transference; it is an example of a contingent response strategy being enacted in response to defined triggers.

> **D:** This is not an example of exploiting; it is an example of a contingent response strategy being enacted in response to define triggers.

Question 351: You are using your risk management plan and your risk register to check if your assessment of risks is accurate, if there are any new risks, or if new information is available about existing risks. Which of the following inputs would not be of use to you to complete this work?
The correct answer is B.

> **A:** The project management plan is an input into the Control Risks process because it contains several subsidiary plans that will be useful in effectively monitoring and controlling risks.
>
> **B:** Quality control measurements are not an input into the Control Risk process in the PMBOK® Guide, so this is the correct answer.
>
> **C:** In order to effectively control risks, you need some sort of information about what is occurring on the project in order to determine if there is a variance between what you are planned in relation to risks and what is occurring.
>
> **D:** The risk register is an essential input into the Control Risks process because it outlines all the identified risks, their probability, and impact, plus the plan risk responses.

Question 352: You are conducting the process of implementing your risk response plans, tracking identified risks, monitoring residual risks, and identifying new risks. What is this PMBOK® Guide process called?
The correct answer is D.

> **A:** There is no process called Assess and Control Risks.
>
> **B:** Risk management is the broad term used for the Risk Management knowledge area.
>
> **C:** There is no process called Risk Assessment.
>
> **D:** The Control Risks process is where you continually track the identified risks and look out for new risks.

Question 353: During your regular monitoring of the risks identified on your project, you examine and document the effectiveness of risk responses in dealing with identified risks and their root causes. What technique are you using?
The correct answer is B.

> **A:** Ishikawa analysis uses fishbone, or cause and effect, diagrams to look at root causes of identified effects.
>
> **B:** Conducting a risk audit is a useful technique for ensuring that your planned risk responses are effective.
>
> **C:** Risk urgency assessment looks at the timeframe for the risk occurring, with those risks in the near future deemed to be more urgent than those that may occur further off.
>
> **D:** Trend analysis is used to document and determine any trends that may be developing in quality management.

Question 354: The project team members assigned responsibility for controlling risks on your project are doing a great job. Which of the following is not an expected output of the work they are completing?
The correct answer is D.

> **A:** Specific parts of the project management plan that will be updated as a result of carrying out the Control Risks process risks will be the risk management plan.

> **B:** Change requests are an output from the Control Risks process in the PMBOK® Guide.

> **C:** Organizational Process Assets updates are an output from the Control Risks process in the PMBOK® Guide.

> **D:** Work performance data is an input into, not an output from, the Control Risks process in the PMBOK® Guide, so this is the correct answer.

Project Procurement Management

Question 355: During the process of procurement management the organization you work for can be all of the following except?
The correct answer is C.

> **A:** You can be both a buyer and seller of products and services on your project.

> **B:** You can be the seller of services responding to some form of request.

> **C:** During procurement management processes you need to be aware that any question on the PMP® exam could indicate your company as either a buyer or a seller of products or services.

> **D:** You can be the buyer of goods and services from other providers as part of your procurement strategy on your project.

Question 356: As part of your commitment to advancing the profession of project management you are tutoring candidates wishing to sit the PMP® examination. The session you are about to give is focused on the Project Procurement Management knowledge area in the PMBOK® Guide. What is the generally accepted correct sequence of processes in the Project Procurement Management knowledge area?

The correct answer is A.

> **A:** The logical order of this knowledge area is to Plan, then Conduct, then Control, and finally Close Procurements. Remember, though that this knowledge area, like all the others, has a strong iterative component and there will be feedback loops throughout the processes.

> **B-D:** These answers are incorrect because the logical order of this knowledge area is to Plan, then Conduct, then Control, and finally Close Procurements. Remember, though, that this knowledge area, like all the others, has a strong iterative component and there will be feedback loops throughout the processes.

Question 357: You are carrying out the Contract Management and Change Control processes required to develop and administer contracts for you project. What is this PMBOK® Guide knowledge area called?
The correct answer is D.

> **A:** Plan Procurement Management is a specific process whereas the Project Procurement management knowledge area includes all the processes referred to in the question.

> **B:** Close Procurements is a specific process whereas the Project Procurement management knowledge area includes all the processes referred to in the question.

> **C:** Project integration management does not specifically address all of these processes.

> **D:** Plan Procurement Management is the knowledge area focused on the processes necessary to purchase or acquire products, services, or results from external sources.

Question 358: All of the following are examples of legally binding agreements except?
The correct answer is C.

> **A:** An agreement when used to mean a legal contract between two or more parties is a legally binding agreement.

> **B:** A subcontract is a legally binding agreement.

> **C:** Organizational Process Assets do not constitute a legally binding agreement. Depending on the industry, country, context, or project type, there are many types of legally binding documents in addition to the usual contracts.

> **D:** A purchase order given by a buyer to a seller is a legally binding agreement and promises to pay for goods or services rendered.

CHAPTER 2 ▓ ANSWERS

Question 359: You are just about to begin the process of procuring services from external providers and you think there may be a standard set of rules governing this process. Where would it be BEST to look for these rules?
The correct answer is B.

> **A:** Any lessons learned from a previous project may give you an insight into what went well and what did not go so well, but it will not contain the standard set of rules governing the processes in the organization.

> **B:** The Organizational Process Assets will describe the processes, templates, and other documents the organization uses in the procurement process.

> **C:** The PMBOK® Guide does not contain a standard set of rules or procuring services from external providers. The Organizational Process Assets would, though.

> **D:** Your organization's legal team will most likely directly access any Organizational Process Assets that the organization has.

Question 360: You have completed the work described in the contract as per the required specifications but the customer is complaining that the product is not what they wanted. What is your BEST course of action?
The correct answer is D.

> **A-C:** These answers are incorrect because the question clearly states that you have completed the contract work as per the contract specifications. You must enter the Close Procurements process. This process should have provision for any contractual disputes.

> **D:** The question clearly states that you have completed the contract work as per the contract specifications. You must enter the Close Procurements process. This process should have provision for any contractual disputes.

Question 361: Which of the following is not a term used to describe the buyer in a contract?
The correct answer is B.

> **A:** Your client is a good example of a buyer in a contract, and your organization would be the seller.

> **B:** The term entrepreneur is never used to describe the buyer in a contract. The term buyer is a very formal way of describing a variety of more usual descriptions. This is one of those situations where you may need to translate a formal PMBOK® Guide term into one you use more regularly.

C: Somebody requesting services from you is a good example of a buyer in a contract.

D: The prime contractor to a contract will go on to buy services and goods from other sellers, and as such they are buyer in a contract.

Question 362: Which of the following is not a term used to describe the seller in a contract?
The correct answer is C.

A: A service provider will sell goods or services to a buyer.

B: A vendor is simply another way of saying seller.

C: The term seller is a very formal way of describing a variety of more usual descriptions. This is one of those situations where you may need to translate a formal PMBOK® Guide term into one you use more regularly.

D: A contractor will provide goods and services to the buyer in contract, and as such they are a seller.

Question 363: You and your project team are completing the process of producing your procurement management plan and want to make sure that you have completed a robust process and used all possible and appropriate inputs. Which of the following is not an input into the work to plan procurement management on your project?
The correct answer is D.

A: Your requirements documentation will be a very valuable input into this process because it will outline any contractual or legal implications that need to be taken into consideration when making procurement decisions.

B: The activity resource requirements is a useful place for you to be able to determine whether there are particular resources you will have to procure from external providers.

C: The stakeholder register will provide useful information on individual stakeholders and their interest in the project, particularly as they relate to contractual decisions.

D: Make-or-buy decisions are an output of the Plan Procurement Management process. It is worth noting that with 11 inputs this process is the one with the most inputs.

Question 364: You are carrying out the procurement of services necessary for your project. After consulting with your Organizational Process Assets, specifically the procurement guidelines, which specify that you are to use the most commonly used contract type, you offer the seller what type of contract?

The correct answer is B.

> **A:** A time and materials form of contract is generally only used in small or emergency works and as such is not the most common form of procurement contract.
>
> **B:** The firm-fixed-price is the most common form of procurement contract.
>
> **C:** The Fixed-price-incentive-fee form of contract is a popular form of contract, but the most popular form of contract is the firm-fixed-price contract.
>
> **D:** The cost-plus-incentive-fee form of contract is a popular form of contract, but the most popular form of contract is the firm-fixed-price contract.

Question 365: You discover that there is a part of the project that contains some risk. Your strategy to deal with this risk is to subcontract the work to an outside supplier by using a firm-fixed-price contract. Which of the following must you do?

The correct answer is D.

> **A:** This answer is incorrect. Assigning one of your staff members does not address an issue that the suplier should be dealing with.
>
> **B:** This answer is incorrect. You should ensure that the supplier is aware of all potential risks before the contract is signed.
>
> **C:** This answer is incorrect. It is suggesting you engage in unethical behavior.
>
> **D:** In a fixed-price contract, the supplier is obligated to deliver the contracted-for item at a fixed price. The supplier is aware of the risk and will put an allowance for the risk in the contracted price. This often means that the project team will pay the supplier for the cost of the risk regardless of whether the risk occurs.

Question 366: You are the project manager for a project that is well underway. You are using a contractor that has agreed to a fixed-price contract that calls for a single, lump sum payment on completion of the contract. The contractor's project manager contacts you and informs you that cash flow problems are making it difficult for the contractor to pay employees and subcontractors. The contractor then asks you for a partial payment for work accomplished to date. What is your best course of action?

The correct answer is B.

> **A:** This may seem to be the technically correct thing to do, but it will cause major problems for your project and for the contractor. You would be better off making a provision to pay the contractor by negotiating a change to the contract.
>
> **B:** Although it is not to exactly to the letter of the contract, you are going to have much more trouble if the seller cannot make the payroll and cannot complete the contract because their employees will not work without pay. The best thing would be to change the contract in some way that is mutually beneficial. This is not really a procurement question but an ethical one, although there is considerable overlap.
>
> **C:** You may end up paying for the work, but you must first negotiate a change to the current contract to allow such payments to the contractor.
>
> **D:** You may end up paying for the work, but you must first negotiate a change to the current contract to allow such payments to the contractor.

Question 367: Your organization is providing services to another organization as part of a project. Which of the following contract types would your organization most prefer to engage in to carry out the work?

The correct answer is D.

> **A-C:** These answers are incorrect because as the seller (in this instance, you) would prefer a form of contract that is not fixed-price.
>
> **D:** The type of contract selected will reflect which party adopts the most risk for carrying out the work. The seller prefers one where the price is not fixed. In fact, you would probably prefer to work with a time and materials contract but it is not one of the options presented.

Question 368: Your project has begun with a planned series of iterations that will gradually define the scope of work required. You are negotiating with a potential supplier of services. What is the BEST form of contract to enter into?

The correct answer is C.

> **A:** Fixed-price-with-incentive-fee is best when the scope of work can be fully defined. Where the scope or work is not fully defined, a cost-reimbursable contract, such as cost-plus-fixed-fee, is the best for both seller and buyer because it allows for continued development of the scope.
>
> **B:** Time and materials is best for small work or emergency work. Where the scope or work is not fully defined, a cost-reimbursable contract, such as cost-plus-fixed-fee, is the best for both seller and buyer because it allows for continued development of the scope.

255

C: Where the scope or work is not fully defined, a cost-reimbursable contract, such as cost-plus-fixed-fee, is the best for both seller and buyer because it allows for continued development of the scope.

D: Any form of fixed-price contract is best in the scope of work can be fully defined. Where the scope or work is not fully defined, a cost-reimbursable contract, such as cost-plus-fixed-fee, is the best for both seller and buyer because it allows for continued development of the scope.

Question 369: During your project there has been an unforeseen amount of work that requires urgent and immediate attention from an external contractor to ensure it does not adversely affect the project. What sort of contract for services is BEST to use in this instance?
The correct answer is B.

A: Given that the situation in question is urgent and requires immediate attention, you do not have the time to go through the process of negotiating any form of fixed price contract; therefore a time and materials contract is best.

B: A time and materials contract is suitable when the work is urgent or when the scope of work is largely undefined.

C: Given that the situation in question is urgent and requires immediate attention, you do not have the time to go through the process of negotiating any form of cost reimbursable contract; therefore, a time and materials contract is best.

D: Given that the situation in question is urgent and requires immediate attention, you do not have the time to go through the process of negotiating any form of cost reimbursable contract; therefore, a time and materials contract is best.

Question 370: You are leading your team through the process of making procurement decisions and selecting the appropriate procurement documentation to use when procuring services from external contractors. Which of the following is not a form of procurement document?
The correct answer is A.

A: Request for fixed price contract is not a term referenced within the PMBOK® Guide.

B: A request for proposal is a form of procurement document that goes to potential sellers, outlining the work required and asking for a response from them.

C: A request for quotation is a form of procurement document that goes to potential sellers, asking for a quote for a prescribed scope of work.

D: A request for information is a formal procurement document. It goes to all potential sellers, requesting information about the seller, their capabilities, and the organization.

Question 371: Several procurement specialists on your team have completed the procurement management plan for your project. Which of the following is not an output you would expect from them?
The correct answer is D.

A: The source selection criteria, which outlines how you will select potential sellers, is an output from the Plan Procurement Management process.

B: The procurement statement of work, which describes the work to be completed as part of the contract, is an output of the Plan Procurement Management process.

C: The procurement management plan is the primary output from the Plan Procurement Management process.

D: The project scope statement is not an output from the Plan Procurement Management process. It is an output from the Define Scope process.

Question 372: You are the project manager on a large project to develop a new customer information database for your organization. You are currently assessing the merits of developing key components of the required software in-house by your own development team compared to getting an external contractor to complete the work. What technique are you using?
The correct answer is B.

A: Risk-related contract decisions would be completed as part of project risk management and not as part of make-or-buy analysis.

B: Make-or-buy analysis is exactly what it says it is: the decision to make something in house or buy it from outside of the organization.

C: Source selection criteria are other criteria you developed to help you choose which sellers will be invited to be part of the procurement process and how successful sellers will be selected.

D: Expert judgment is a tool or technique used to solicit information with people with experience in a particular area.

Question 373: You are letting your project team analyze responses received to some of your procurement documents and you are beginning the process of selecting the successful seller. Which of the following is not an example of selection criteria used to select sellers?
The correct answer is B.

> **A:** Technical capability would most certainly be one of the criteria by which you would judge potential sellers.

> **B:** Make-or-buy decisions are an output of the Plan Procurement Management process.

> **C:** Management approach would most certainly be one of the criteria by which you would judge potential sellers.

> **D:** The issue of proprietary rights and who owns the service or goods produced as a result of the contract would most certainly be one of the criteria by which you would judge potential sellers.

Question 374: You are currently obtaining seller responses to an RFP you issued and, after assessing the responses, you expect to select a seller and award a contract for delivery for services on your project. What process are you carrying out?
The correct answer is C.

> **A:** The Close Procurements process is focused on making sure that all contracts used in the project are successfully closed.

> **B:** The Plan Procurement Management process produces the procurement management plan and the procurement statement of work, which are then used to assist the Control Procurement process, which is the correct answer.

> **C:** The Conduct Procurement process is where you put into practice the process of acquiring external contractors outlined in your procurement management plan.

> **D:** The Control Procurements process is focused on checking whether the procurement management plan is working and if any changes are required.

Question 375: You are carrying out the process of obtaining seller responses, selecting a seller, and an awarding a contract. You wish to make sure that you complete the process thoroughly and use any and all inputs that may be useful to you. Which of the following is not an input into the Conduct Procurements process?
The correct answer is C.

> **A:** The procurement statement of work is an essential input because it describes the work to be done as part of contract.

> **B:** Source selection criteria are other criteria you developed to help you choose which sellers will be invited to be part of the procurement process and how successful sellers will be selected.

C: Resource calendars are an output from the Conduct Procurements process.

D: The project management plan, particularly the procurement management plan, will be an essential input to help you carry out the planned work in procurements.

Question 376: You have just finished preparation of an exhaustive RFP for your project and are about to send it out to potential service providers. Based on past acceptable performance, you decide to send the RFP to a small group of potential suppliers and not all of the suppliers who may be interested in providing a response. What technique are you using?
The correct answer is B.

A: A bidder conference is a real and virtual meeting of all sellers bidding to be part of the contract.

B: It is not uncommon for organizations to have a predetermined list of sellers who are qualified to offer services or products in a particular area. Inclusion on the list is usually dependent on prior experience or meeting defined criteria.

C: The procurement management plan is an output from the Plan Procurement Management process and it outlines how you will carry out your project procurement.

D: Proposal evaluation techniques assist you in evaluating responses from sellers.

Question 377: After soliciting responses from prospective sellers, you are in the process of considering each seller's response against a set of criteria in order to determine who will be the seller selected to provide the required services. The process is giving a greater weight to previous experience in this type of work than it is giving to the price submitted. What technique are you using?
The correct answer is B.

A: A weighted average calculation would be used in something like three-point estimating.

B: It is common to have a predetermined set of criteria to assess responses from sellers. The buying organization may decide to give greater or lesser weight to certain of these criteria depending on the circumstances.

C: Expert judgment is a tool or technique that is used to solicit information from people with experience in a particular area.

D: Procurement negotiations are carried out prior to signing the contract.

Question 378: You are carrying out a bidder conference that is attended by five potential sellers of services to your project. You have spent a considerable amount of time explaining the statement of work and answering questions from the sellers at the bidder conference. During a break in the afternoon, one of the sellers approaches you and asks a question relating to the statement of work. What is your BEST course of action?
The correct answer is D.

> **A:** What the seller has done is not an ethical mistep. As long as it is handled correctly, they do not need to be removed from the room or process.
>
> **B:** You should refuse to provide an answer to the seller right there, but you should make it clear that you will provide an answer to all sellers.
>
> **C:** You should not provide an answer to just that seller. Instead, you should provide an answer to all sellers.
>
> **D:** A bidding conference should be fair to all those involved in the process. In this instance, the seller is not doing anything unethical, and it is up to you to ensure that all sellers hear the question and answer.

Question 379: You are in the process of ensuring that the seller you have engaged to provide a product for your project is meeting the contractual requirements expected of them. What PMBOK® Guide process are you carrying out?
The correct answer is B.

> **A:** Conduct Procurements is the process of procuring goods and services from external sellers.
>
> **B:** The Control Procurements process is completed as part of the Monitoring and Controlling process group. Both parties in a contract will administer the contract to ensure the other party of completing the work as per the contract documentation.
>
> **C:** Close Procurements is the process of making sure that all contracts used on the project are closed.
>
> **D:** Plan Procurement Management is the process that produces the procurement management plan and the procurement statement of work.

Question 380: As part of your project you are looking to make sure that you complete the Control Procurements process properly in order to ensure that you are managing procurement relationships, monitoring contract performance, and making changes and corrections to contracts as appropriate. As part of this process, you want to make sure that you are using all the appropriate inputs. Which of the following processes does not provide an input into the work to control procurements?

The correct answer is A.

> **A:** The Control Procurements process requires a lot of information from other processes to ensure you are capable of judging whether or not the other party to a contract is fulfilling their obligations. Control Costs is not one of these processes.
>
> **B:** The Monitor and Control Project Work process provides work performance reports as an input into the control procurements process.
>
> **C:** The Perform Integrated Change Control process provides approved change requests as an input into the control procurements process.
>
> **D:** The Direct and Manage Project Work process provides work performance data as an input into the control procurements process.

Question 381: As part of your project you are looking to make sure that you complete the Control Procurements process properly in order to ensure that you are managing procurement relationships, monitoring contract performance, and making changes and corrections to contracts as appropriate. In order to do this process thoroughly, you have decided to review all the possible tools and techniques that you could use. All of the following are tools or techniques used in the Control Procurements process except?

The correct answer is C.

> **A:** Inspections and audits are a tool and technique used to ensure that both the processes outlined in the contract and the expected deliverable of the contract are being delivered as per the terms of contract.
>
> **B:** Performance reporting is a valuable tool to use during the Control Procurements process because it allows you to determine whether the terms of the contract are being met as planned.
>
> **C:** Work performance information is an input, not a tool or technique, into the Control Procurements process.
>
> **D:** Claims administration is a tool and technique for dealing with any disputes over the terms of contracts.

Question 382: You are the project manager on a large project that has been underway for five years. Your project has consistently reported a CPI of 1.2 and an SPI of 1.3. Delivery of the expected product of the project has been in accordance with the customer's expectations and you are beginning the process of closing the project. Your project team is confused about which process to complete first, the Close Procurements process or the Close Project process. What is your BEST advice to your project team?

261

The correct answer is C.

> **A:** You must first complete the Close Procurements process before completing the Close Project process because contract closure comes before project closure.

> **B:** The Close Project process and Close Procurements process are separate and distinct processes. You must first complete the Close Procurements process before completing the Close Project process.

> **C:** A contract is just one part of a project. As such, before you can close the project, you need to ensure that all contracts are closed.

> **D:** You must first complete the Close Procurements process before completing the Close Project process because contract closure comes before project closure.

Question 383: You and your project team are completing the work required by contract with a buyer when your general manager decides to suddenly terminate the contract due to factors that are outside of your control. What is your BEST course of action?

The correct answer is B.

> **A:** You may do this as part of closing your procurement but the best answer is to begin the Close Procurements process.

> **B:** This is a tricky question that you may have had difficulty answering. The question itself does not give a lot of information about why the general manager has decided to terminate the contract so we must assume it is for legitimate reasons, in which case the best answer is to begin the Close Procurements process.

> **C:** This may end up being part of your lessons learned process. The best answer is to begin the Close Procurements process.

> **D:** This is a tricky question that you may have had difficulty answering. The question itself does not give a lot of information about why the general manager has decided to terminate the contract so we must assume it is for legitimate reasons, in which case the best answer is to begin the Close Procurements process.

Question 384: As part of closing out all contracts used on a project, you want to make sure that you demonstrate to your team what is considered best practice in this area and have available to you all of the potential tools and techniques that could assist. Which of the following is not a tool or technique used in the Close Procurements process?

The correct answer is A.

> **A:** Bidder conferences are a tool from the Conduct Procurements process.

> **B:** Not all contracts end cleanly, and procurement negotiations and negotiated settlements are an effective tool or technique to use during this process.

C: A procurement audit is a structured review of the procurement management process from the beginning to the end to see whether it was followed, whether it was appropriate, and whether any improvements could be made.

D: A records management system is a tool and technique used in the Close Procurements process to manage contracts, procurement documentation, and records with archiving.

Question 385: You are .completing the Close Procurements process and are informing sellers that the contract has been completed. What is the BEST way to do this?
The correct answer is D.

A-C: These answers are not correct because contracts are a formal written form of communication. It is best that all communication about the contract be in the same formal written form.

D: A contract is a formal written document, and all correspondence about the contract should also be completed in a formal written format.

Question 386: You have entered into an agreement with a seller to provide the goods you require for your project. You have selected to use a fixed-price-incentive-fee form of contract with a target cost of $100,000, a target price of $120,000, a ceiling price of $140,000, with a sharing ratio of 80/20 to the buyer. What is your point of total assumption?
The correct answer is A.

A: To calculate the point of total assumption you need to use the following formula: ((ceiling price - target price) / buyer's share ratio)+target cost), which gives a point of total assumption of $125,000.

B-D: These answers are not correct because to calculate the point of total assumption you need to use the following formula: ((ceiling price - target price) / buyer's share ratio)+target cost), which gives a point of total assumption of $125,000.

Project Stakeholder Management

Question 387: You are putting together your stakeholder management plan and have identified the need to gather information about all of the different project stakeholders as soon as possible. This recognizes that the ability of stakeholders to influence the project is greatest at which point in the project?
The correct answer is C.

A: Stakeholders are able to influence the project during project execution but not as much as they can at the beginning of the project.

B: Toward the end of the project stakeholders have less influence because the deliverable is close to completion.

C: The higher levels of uncertainty at the beginning of project, reflecting the process of progressive elaboration, mean that stakeholders can have more influence during this time.

D: Stakeholder influence is greatest at the beginning of a project and slowly diminishes as the project progresses.

Question 388: You are compiling a register of all people, groups, and organizations that can potentially and actually be affected by the project. What is the collective term for this group?

The correct answer is D.

A: A sponsor is a specific type of stakeholder. Stakeholder is the best answer to this question.

B: A customer is a specific type of stakeholder. Stakeholder is the best, or most correct, answer to this question.

C: A team member is a specific type of stakeholder. Stakeholder is the best, or most correct, answer to this question.

D: A stakeholder is anyone or any organization who can affect or be affected by the project. It is important to identify all stakeholders on a project and manage or influence their expectations.

Question 389: During work to initiate your project you have begun to identify stakeholders and gather information about them to allow you to successfully manage their expectations. All of the following are stakeholder attributes you should analyze as part of this work to identify stakeholders except?

The correct answer is D.

A: As part of identifying stakeholders, you should identify and document their interest in the project.

B: As part of identifying stakeholders, you should also identify and document their expectations of the project so that you can effectively manage them.

C: As part of identifying stakeholders, you should identify and document their influence on the project.

D: It is doubtful that you would be able to document the personal conflict resolution style of stakeholders. Having a thorough stakeholder analysis completed early in the project is an effective aid into several processes. When analyzing stakeholders you should note their interests, expectations, importance, and influence.

Question 390: During work to initiate your project you have begun to identify stakeholders and gather information about them to allow you to successfully manage their expectations. Which of the following is not an input you would use to complete this work?
The correct answer is C.

> **A:** Procurement documents are used as an input into the Identify Stakeholders process because parties to the contract are key project stakeholders.

> **B:** The project charter is used as an input into the Identify Stakeholders process because it can provide information about internal and external parties related to the project.

> **C:** The stakeholder register is an output from the Identify Stakeholders process in the PMBOK® Guide, so this is the correct answer.

> **D:** Lessons learned, which are a part of Organizational Process Assets, are an important input into the Identify Stakeholders process in the PMBOK® Guide.

Question 391: With the help of your project team, you identify all potential project stakeholders and information about them. You then interview all the stakeholders you have identified in an effort to learn more about their interaction with your project and also to gain knowledge of any other stakeholders you may not be aware of. After completing this process, you then identify the potential impact or support each stakeholder could generate. Finally, you assess how the key stakeholders are likely to react in various situations so you can plan for this. What are you carrying out?
The correct answer is B.

> **A:** The stakeholder management strategy is not a term found in the PMBOK® Guide. Although it may be a commonly used term, it does not analyze stakeholder impact and interest in the project.

> **B:** You are completing the stakeholder analysis. You may choose to show the results in a diagram such as a power/interest grid, which shows the relative power and interest each stakeholder has in the project.

> **C:** This answer is incorrect because stakeholder register assimilation is not a term referenced within the PMBOK® Guide.

> **D:** Although this answer may sound correct, the best answer is stakeholder analysis.

Question 392: You are showing your team the relative interest and power each identified stakeholder has in your project. What is the BEST way to show this information?

The correct answer is D.

> **A:** The salience model maps the degree of power, urgency, and legitimacy of each stakeholder.

> **B:** A control chart is a tool used in the project quality management.

> **C:** A stakeholder register template is an organizational process asset for listing and documenting information about stakeholders.

> **D:** A power/interest grid plots the relative power and interest each identified stakeholder has in your project.

Question 393: You have just taken over a project that has been underway for 8 months. The project is performing well and is currently reporting a CPI of 1.2 and an EAC of $1.2 m. As part of your familiarization process, you want to understand who the stakeholders on the project are. Where would you find this information?

The correct answer is C.

> **A:** The stakeholder management strategy, if such a thing exists, would not document who the individual stakeholders are.

> **B:** Your Organizational Process Assets may include a blank stakeholder register. If you wish to get the information you are seeking in this question, the stakeholder register is the best answer.

> **C:** The stakeholder register contains all the information you know about all stakeholders on the project.

> **D:** A simple e-mail distribution list may be part of your communications plan but it would certainly not document all stakeholders on the project.

Question 394: You have just taken over a project that is nearing the end of its life cycle. Shortly after taking control of the project you note that a particular stakeholder is having a negative impact on the project. You decide that this presents an unacceptable risk to the project and look for a way to manage the stakeholder. Which document will you look for to help you do this?

The correct answer is A.

> **A:** A stakeholder analysis matrix lists the stakeholders, plus their potential impact and assessment, as well as potential strategies for dealing with any impact on the project.

> **B:** This answer is incorrect because the term is too vague. The correct term is stakeholder analysis matrix.

C: The stakeholder register documents each stakeholder and their interest in the project. It is not the best answer to this question because the stakeholder analysis matrix analyses the impact and interest each stakeholder has on the project.

D: This answer is incorrect because it is not a term referenced within the PMBOK® Guide.

Question 395: After considerable effort involving your project team members and experts with experience in communications, you have developed your project communications management plan. This can now be used as an input into which of the following PMBOK® Guide processes?
The correct answer is C.

A: The communications management plan is not used as an input into the Estimate Costs process.

B: The communications management plan is not used as an input into the Plan Quality Management process.

C: Communication with stakeholders represents a positive risk if done effectively and a negative risk if done poorly. As such, the communications management plan is an important input into the Manage Stakeholder Engagement process.

D: The communications management plan is not used as an input into the Close Project or Phase process.

Question 396: You are completing the process of communication and working with stakeholders to meet their needs and addressing issues as they occur. Which process are you completing?
The correct answer is C.

A: Stakeholder analysis is a tool and technique, not a process.

B: The Manage Communications process is focused on creating, collecting, distributing, and storing project information in accordance with the communications management plan.

C: Managing stakeholder engagement is one of the most important processes a project manager can focus on to contribute to project success.

D: The Control Communications process is focused on monitoring and controlling communications throughout the project.

Question 397: Your project is halfway through its expected duration and has a CPI of 1.3 and an SPI of 1.2. Your project sponsor has told you during a meeting that in her eyes the project is a failure because of the feedback she has been getting from important stakeholders on the project. You are surprised at this because the project is performing well financially and is ahead of schedule and you are sure the quality of the work you are completing is of a high standard and meets customer requirements. As the meeting closes your project sponsor asks what you intend to do about the situation. Your BEST response would be what?

The correct answer is A.

> **A:** The problem is that you are paying too much attention to the cost and time metrics and not paying enough attention to what it is that stakeholders consider to be a measure of success. By revisiting your communications management plan, especially the manage stakeholder process, you will increase the probability of project success.

> **B:** Quitting the project is not be what a professional project manager would do. The problem is that you are paying too much attention to the cost and time metrics and not paying enough attention to what it is that stakeholders consider to be a measure of success. By revisiting your communications management plan, especially the manage stakeholder process, you will increase the probability of project success.

> **C:** Saying nothing would be withdrawing from the problem, and this is not what a professional project manager would do. The problem is that you are paying too much attention to the cost and time metrics and not paying enough attention to what it is that stakeholders consider to be a measure of success. By revisiting your communications management plan, especially the manage stakeholder process, you will increase the probability of project success.

> **D:** This would not solve the issue. The problem is that you are paying too much attention to the cost and time metrics and not paying enough attention to what it is that stakeholders consider to be a measure of success. By revisiting your communications management plan, especially the manage stakeholder process, you will increase the probability of project success.

Question 398: What is your primary goal in managing and identifying stakeholder expectations?

The correct answer is C.

> **A, B, and D:** These answers are incorrect because with any of the activities undertaken in association with managing and identifying stakeholder expectations, your primary goal is to get stakeholders to support your project. Failing this, your goal should be to ensure that they do not oppose the project.

C: With any of the activities undertaken in association with managing and identifying stakeholder expectations, your primary goal is to get stakeholders to support your project. Failing this, your goal should be to ensure that they do not oppose the project.

Question 399: You and your project team are systematically gathering and analyzing quantitative and qualitative information to determine which stakeholder's interests should be taken into account throughout the project. You have identified the interests, expectations, and influence of individual stakeholders and related to them the purpose of the project. What tool or technique are you using?
The correct answer is D.

A: Meetings are an effective communications and information distribution tool, but they are not related to assessing attributes about individual stakeholders.

B: Expert judgment is a tool and technique used to solicit information from people with experience in a particular area.

C: There are several information gathering techniques, all of which are used to gather information you require on the project from subject matter experts and technicians.

D: The purpose of stakeholder analysis is to document information about individual stakeholders, their interest in the project, and their impact on the project, so that you are able to influence them if required.

Question 400: You are using a classification model for stakeholder analysis that describes classes of stakeholders based on their power, urgency, and legitimacy. What is the name of this particular model of stakeholder analysis?
The correct answer is D.

A: A Pareto chart is used primarily during quality management to determine which 20% of the issues are causing 80% of problems.

B: The power/interest grid is used to classify stakeholders based on the amount of power and interest they have on the project.

C: The influence/impact grid is used to classify stakeholders based on the amount of influence and impact they have on the project.

D: The salience model is used to describe classes of stakeholders based on their power, urgency, and legitimacy.

Question 401: As part of your analysis of stakeholder engagement, you have classified each stakeholder as either being unaware, resistant, neutral, supportive, or leading when it comes to the level of their engagement with the project. This is an example of what sort of technique?

The correct answer is C.

> **A:** This question outlines a situation in which you are using a specific form of analytical technique to carry out stakeholder analysis. The best answer is analytical techniques.

> **B:** This is not an example of information gathering techniques. There are several information gathering techniques, all of which are used to gather information from subject matter experts, technicians, and other stakeholders.

> **C:** Classifying stakeholders by the level of engagement (either unaware, resistant, neutral, or support) is an example of an analytical techniques used during the Plan Stakeholder Management process.

> **D:** Expert judgment as a tool and technique used to solicit information from people with experience in a particular area.

Question 402: As a senior project manager on a complex project with many stakeholders, you are consistently having to coordinate and harmonize stakeholders towards supporting the project and accomplishing the project objectives. In order to do this, you are using your skills to facilitate consensus, influence people, negotiate agreements, and modify organizational behavior to accept the project outcomes. These are examples of what?

The correct answer is D.

> **A:** This is not an example of information gathering techniques. There are several information gathering techniques, all of which are used to gather information from subject matter experts, technicians, and other stakeholders with information you require on the project.

> **B:** The best answer to this question is management skills, which are a specific subset of interpersonal skills that facilitate consensus toward project objectives, influence stakeholders to support the project, negotiate agreements to satisfy the project needs, and modify organizational behavior to accept project outcomes.

> **C:** This is not an example of communications methods. It is an example of management skills.

> **D:** This answer is correct because management skills include the ability to facilitate consensus toward project objectives, influence stakeholders to support the project, negotiate agreements to satisfy the project needs, and modify organizational behavior to accept project outcomes.

Question 403: You are managing a complex project with many stakeholders, each with their own interest in the project. You have begun the process of monitoring overall project stakeholder relationships and adjusting your stakeholder expectation management strategies and plans for engaging stakeholders to suit the changing project circumstances. Your goal is to increase the efficiency and effectiveness of stakeholder engagement activity. What process are you are engaged in?
The correct answer is B.

> **A:** Manage Stakeholder Engagement is the process of working with the stakeholder management plan and communicating when working with stakeholders to ensure their needs and objectives.

> **B:** Control Stakeholder Engagement is the process focused on monitoring overall project stakeholder relationships, engagement, and satisfaction, and of adjusting your stakeholder engagement strategies to ensure they remain effective.

> **C:** Control Communications is the process of checking, monitoring, and controlling your project communications against the communication management plan.

> **D:** Manage Communications is the process of preparing to create, collect, and distribute project information in accordance with the communications management plan.

Question 404: As a result of controlling stakeholder engagement on your project you are generating a number of Organizational Process Asset updates relating to monitoring overall project stakeholder relationships and their level of engagement and satisfaction with your project. Which of the following is not an Organizational Process Asset that would be updated as a result of this process?
The correct answer is A.

> **A:** The issue log is not an Organizational Process Asset; it is a project document. This question is asking about the types of Organizational Process Asset updates that may be done as a result of the Control Stakeholder Engagement process being carried out.

> **B:** This question is asking about the types of Organizational Process Asset updates that may be done as a result of the Control Stakeholder Engagement process being carried out. The specific Organizational Process Assets that may be updated as a result of carrying this process out are stakeholder notifications, project reports, project presentations, project records, feedback from stakeholders, and lessons learned documentation.

> **C:** This question is asking about the types of Organizational Process Asset updates that may be done as a result of the Control Stakeholder Engagement process being carried out. The specific Organizational Process Assets that may be updated as a result of carrying this process out are stakeholder notifications, project reports, project presentations, project records, feedback from stakeholders, and lessons learned documentation.

271

D: This question is asking about the types of Organizational Process Asset updates that may be done as a result of the Control Stakeholder Engagement process being carried out. The specific Organizational Process Assets that may be updated as a result of carrying this process out are stakeholder notifications, project reports, project presentations, project records, feedback from stakeholders, and lessons learned documentation.

Professional Ethics

Question 405: A colleague of yours, who was your mentor in your earlier career, still claims to have the PMP® credential but you know that it expired several years ago. What should you do FIRST?
The correct answer is B.

Complying with the professional code of ethics means reporting ethical, professional, or legal violations to the appropriate authority. In this case, the appropriate authority is the Project Management Institute.

Question 406: A project is nearing the end and is reporting a CPI of 1.01 and a SPI of 1.3. The project manager has been reassigned to another more urgent project, and you have been brought in to close the project. While reviewing the financial accounts for the project, you discover that the previous project manager made a large payment that was not approved in accordance with the policies of your company. What is the BEST thing you can do?
The correct answer is A.

A: Your best course of action is always to be up front and honest with information as soon as you become aware of it. In this instance, you should first inform the project sponsor.

B-D: These answers are not correct because your best course of action is always to be up front and honest with information as soon as you become aware of it. In this instance, you should first inform the project sponsor.

Question 407: The project administrator working for you on the project does not have the level of skills you assumed he had. What is your BEST course of action?
The correct answer is D.

A: You should not assign him lower-level tasks and bring in another more qualified person because you have an professional obligation to ensure people have the right amount of training to complete their job.

B: You cannot simply do nothing and assume that he will learn on the job. You have an professional obligation to ensure people have the right amount of training to complete their job.

C: You cannot simply assign the project administrator to another project. You have an professional obligation to ensure people have the right amount of training to complete their job.

D: You have an professional obligation to ensure people have the right amount of training to complete their job.

Question 408: You and your project administrator have been working on a detailed project progress report to present to high-level stakeholders. You leave it up to the project administrator to complete the report, and he e-mails it to you on the day of the meeting. You are having a busy day and don't get a chance to read the report, but as you walk into the meeting you notice some large errors in the financial reporting section of the report. What is your BEST course of action?
The correct answer is D.

A: As project manager, you are ultimately responsible for information presented to project stakeholders. Your best course of action is to reschedule the meeting to give you time to fix the errors.

B: It is important that you always present accurate information, so you should reschedule the meeting to give you time to fix the errors.

C: Although this answer seems like a noble thing to do, your first commitment is to provide accurate information, so you can't present the report. You should reschedule the meeting to give you time to fix the errors.

D: In this instance, you must not give wrong information to the stakeholders, so you must reschedule the meeting to give you time to fix the errors.

Question 409: You are completing a large infrastructure project in a foreign country. The government officials of the country are extremely grateful for the work you are doing and one of them sends a large cash payment to you to thank you and your team for the work they have done. What should you do?
The correct answer is C.

A, B, and D: These answers are incorrect because to accept payment would be unethical. Your only choice is to refuse the payment and let your project sponsor or manager know that it was offered.

C: To accept payment would be unethical. Your only choice is to refuse the payment and let your project sponsor or manager know that it was offered.

Question 410: You are currently preparing monthly status reports for your project and you are planning on reporting that the project has an SPI of 1.02 and a CPI of .83. Your project sponsor approaches you and says that she has been given a directive by the CEO of the company to report only positive figures or else he is afraid the shareholders in the company will demand changes to the organization. You are confident that the next month's status report will show a CPI greater than 1. What should you do?

The correct answer is A.

A: In order to be a professional and ethical project manager, you are required to show honesty at all levels of the profession and in all instances.

B: You cannot submit a report based on what you believe next month figures will be. In order to be a professional and ethical project manager, you are required to show honesty at all levels of the profession and in all instances.

C: Resigning from the project is an extreme action to take. You should first explain to your project sponsor the reasons why you believe the project reporting should always be honest. In order to be a professional and ethical project manager, you are required to show honesty at all levels of the profession and in all instances.

D: Your first step should be to explain to your project sponsor the reasons why you believe the project reporting should be honest.

Question 411: You are the project manager for a large project that has been completed on time and on budget. The customer and all of the stakeholders are very pleased with the results. As a direct result of the successful completion of the project, your project sponsor approves a bonus of $10,000 to you. There are twelve members on your project team. However, one of the people on the project team has been a very low contributor to the project; the other eleven have all been above standard. What should you do with the money?

The correct answer is B.

A: Given that there is some disparity between team members and their contribution to the project, the best way to address this issue would be to ask the team members how they would divide the money.

B: Probably the best thing to do in this situation would be to divide the money in the way determined by the team. This is an example of participative management and good leadership. It acknowledges that your efforts and successes were a result not just of your efforts, but that of your team's as well.

C: Probably the best thing to do in this situation would be to divide the money in the way determined by the team. This is an example of participative management and good leadership. It acknowledges that your efforts and successes were a result not just of your efforts, but that of your team's efforts too.

D: Given that there is some disparity between team members and their contribution to the project, the best way to address this issue would be asked to team members how to divide the money.

Question 412: You are the project manager for a large software implementation project that is nearing completion when you discover that one of your technicians has been taking shortcuts with the code being written and it is below the standard required in the technical specification. You and a senior team member review the code and form the opinion that it will probably not affect the functionality of the final software product. What is your NEXT course of action?

The correct answer is C.

A: It would be difficult to get a change request approved for a deliberate error in the project. Instead, you should record the discrepancy, inform the customer, and look for ways to ensure the project won't be affected.

B: Since you have formed the opinion that the error will probably not affect the functionality of the final software product, it would not make sense to stop the project and start again. You do need to record the discrepancy and inform the customer of the issue, however.

C: In this instance, the best solution is to record the issue and make an effort to remedy it to the satisfaction of all parties.

D: You cannot simply ignore the problem. In this instance, the best solution is to record the issue and make an effort to remedy it to the satisfaction of all parties.

Question 413: You are the project manager for a project that has high visibility, and your project sponsor wants you to prepare a presentation for her to present at a conference. Most of the material in the presentation will be facts that are the results of your project. Your sponsor intends to present the material under her own name, and your name will not appear. What is your BEST course of action?

The correct answer is B.

A: Intellectual property belongs to the author of the property. If you create a presentation based on your own work, you have a right to receive credit for it.

B: Intellectual property belongs to the author of the property. If you create a presentation based on your own work, you have a right to receive credit for it.

C: You should not present your own presentation because the invitation was extended to your project sponsor. The best course of action is to explain to your sponsor that intellectual property belongs to the author of the property. If you create a presentation based on your own work, you have the right to receive credit for it.

D: Meet with the project sponsor's manager and explain to the sponsor that the correct thing to do is to acknowledge all authors and contributions to the work.

Question 414: You are working in a foreign country delivering a reconstruction project after a large natural disaster. It is normal in this country for government officials to request bribes to assist with processing the consents you require. During a meeting with a government official, he mentions that if you pay a $500 bribe you can have the consent you require tomorrow. What is your BEST course of action?
The correct answer is B.

A: It doesn't matter how the money is paid; at no time can you pay a bribe. A bribe is an illegal payment regardless of accepted custom.

B: At no time can you pay a bribe. A bribe is an illegal payment regardless of accepted custom.

C: At no time can you pay a bribe. A bribe is an illegal payment regardless of accepted custom.

D: Reporting the official to his manager will probably do no good because bribery is probably ingrained with and culture.

Question 415: You are working on a project to construct a new water treatment plant and are waiting on consents required from the government before you can proceed with the work. During a meeting with a government employee to discuss the required consent, the employee mentions that the consent can be processed faster if you are willing to pay a processing fee. What is your BEST course of action?
The correct answer is C.

A: You should not walk out of the meeting and notify your project sponsor because the question does not say that this is a bribe. It clearly says that it is a processing fee, so you should assume that it is a legal form of fee to rush applications.

B: The question does not say that this is a bribe. It clearly says that it is a processing fee, so you should assume that it is a legal form of fee to rush applications.

C: The questions does not say that the fee is a bribe. As such, you can go ahead and pay it if your project has allowed for it. If not, you may wish to submit a change request to acquire the funds needed.

D: There is no need to hide the transaction because it is a legal fee that he is requesting in order to rush your application.

Question 416: You have just completed the selection of a preferred seller for an upcoming project and have scheduled a meeting in 2 days to finalize the contract when your manager informs you that due to current economic conditions the project will now probably not be going ahead but the definite answer will be provided by the CEO in 3 days. What is your BEST course of action?

The correct answer is B.

> **A:** You should inform the other party that the meeting have been postponed for at least three days. You must act ethically at all times, and clearly there is no way you can act in good faith if the meeting goes ahead.

> **B:** You should inform the other party at the meeting have been postponed for at least three days. You must act ethically at all times, and clearly there is no way you can act in good faith if the meeting goes ahead.

> **C:** You should inform the other party at the meeting have been postponed for at least three days. You must act ethically at all times, and clearly there is no way you can act in good faith if the meeting goes ahead.

> **D:** Cancelling the meeting and telling the other party why may cause a rift in the relationship if the project does go ahead. You should inform the other party at the meeting have been postponed for at least 3 days. You must act ethically at all times, and clearly there is no way you can act in good faith if the meeting goes ahead.

CHAPTER 3

■ ■ ■

Formulae to Remember

Communications (how many people in a communications network)

$$N = (n (n - 1)) / 2$$

Present value (PV)

$$PV = (FV / (1 + r)^n)$$

where

> FV = Future value in $

> r = Discount rate percentage expressed as a decimal number (i.e. 10% = 0.1)

> n = The time period (i.e. 5 years)

Net present value (NPV)

> NPV = Initial outlay + the sum of all subsequent present value calculations

Earned value management

> Planned value (PV) = Time % complete x BAC

> Earned value (EV) = PV x % complete

> Schedule variance (SV) = EV - PV

> Schedule performance index (SPI) = EV / PV

> Cost variance (CV) = EV - AC

> Cost performance index (CPI) = EV / AC

Estimate at completion (EAC) - 1 of 4 formulae

$$EAC = BAC / CPI$$
$$EAC = AC + ETC$$
$$EAC = AC + (BAC - EV)$$
$$EAC = AC + ((BAC - EV) / (CPI \times SPI))$$

Estimate to complete (ETC) = EAC - AC

Variance at completion (VAC) = BAC - EAC

To Complete Performance Index (TCPI)

TCPI = (BAC - EV) / (BAC - AC) if you are aiming for BAC

TCPI = (BAC - EV) / (EAC - AC) if you are aiming for EAC

Three-point estimating from PERT (Program Evaluation and Review Technique)
Three-point estimate = $(O + (M \times 4) + P) / 6$
where

O = Optimistic

M = Most likely (sometimes appears as an R for Realistic)

P = Pessimistic

Standard deviation = $(P - O) / 6$
Variance = $((P - O) / 6)^2$

Point of total assumption (PTA)
PTA = Target cost + ((ceiling price - target price) / buyers % share of cost overruns))

Index

© Sean Whitaker 2016
S. Whitaker, *PMP® Examination Practice Questions*, DOI 10.1007/978-1-4842-1883-9

Project time management (*cont.*)
    resource calendar, 34, 158
    resource leveling, 37, 165
    schedule compression, 38–39, 167–168
    schedule performance index (SPI), 40, 169–170
    slack, 41, 172
    standard deviation, 40, 170
    successor and predecessor activities, 32, 157
    work packages, 31, 154

▓ Q

Quality Control process, 30, 153

▓ R

Roles and responsibilities, PMO, 4–5, 112–113

▓ S, T, U

Sequential and overlapping project phases, 6, 114
Standardized terminology, project communications, 1, 107
Strategic consideration, 3, 111

▓ V, W, X, Y, Z

Validate Scope process, 29, 151

Get the eBook for only $5!

Why limit yourself?

Now you can take the weightless companion with you wherever you go and access your content on your PC, phone, tablet, or reader.

Since you've purchased this print book, we're happy to offer you the eBook in all 3 formats for just $5.

Convenient and fully searchable, the PDF version enables you to easily find and copy code—or perform examples by quickly toggling between instructions and applications. The MOBI format is ideal for your Kindle, while the ePUB can be utilized on a variety of mobile devices.

To learn more, go to www.apress.com/companion or contact support@apress.com.